W9-ASF-837

ISBN 0-8057-6912-9 $16.95

# Samuel Beckett

Nobel Prize-winning novelist and playwright Samuel Beckett has widely influenced the course of twentieth-century literature. The impact of his plays (*Waiting for Godot*, *Endgame*), novels (*Molloy*), and numerous short stories, fiction pieces, and poems have added the word *Beckettian* to the literary lexicon next to *Kafkaesque*. Beckett's work depicts the unrelenting plight of contemporary existence: living at the edge of an abyss, in an indifferent universe, trying simply to "go on" with daily life in the face of a recognition of futility. His ability to shape this modern experience into art has led the way for Sam Shepard, Harold Pinter, Edward Albee, and many other playwrights and novelists.

Linda Ben-Zvi's definitive study is based on rigorous scholarship, interviews and correspondence with Beckett himself, and unpublished material used with Beckett's special permission. This is the only discussion available of all Beckett's writings, and one of the few summaries of Beckett as a critic. Ben-Zvi offers fresh insights into both the familiar and the less well-known fictions and dramas. She makes Beckett accessible to every reader and demonstrates how sensitivity to the modern world prepares even a reader new to Beckett to appreciate his writing.

As Samuel Beckett enters his eighth decade, this timely book bridges the gap between the Beckett scholar and the first-time reader. Its introduction offers a clear, direct discussion of how one approaches a writer like Beckett. Subsequent chapters place the subject in dramatic context, relate his ideas to those of major philosophers, and discuss at length his experimentation with language and style. There is a complete summary

TEAS 423

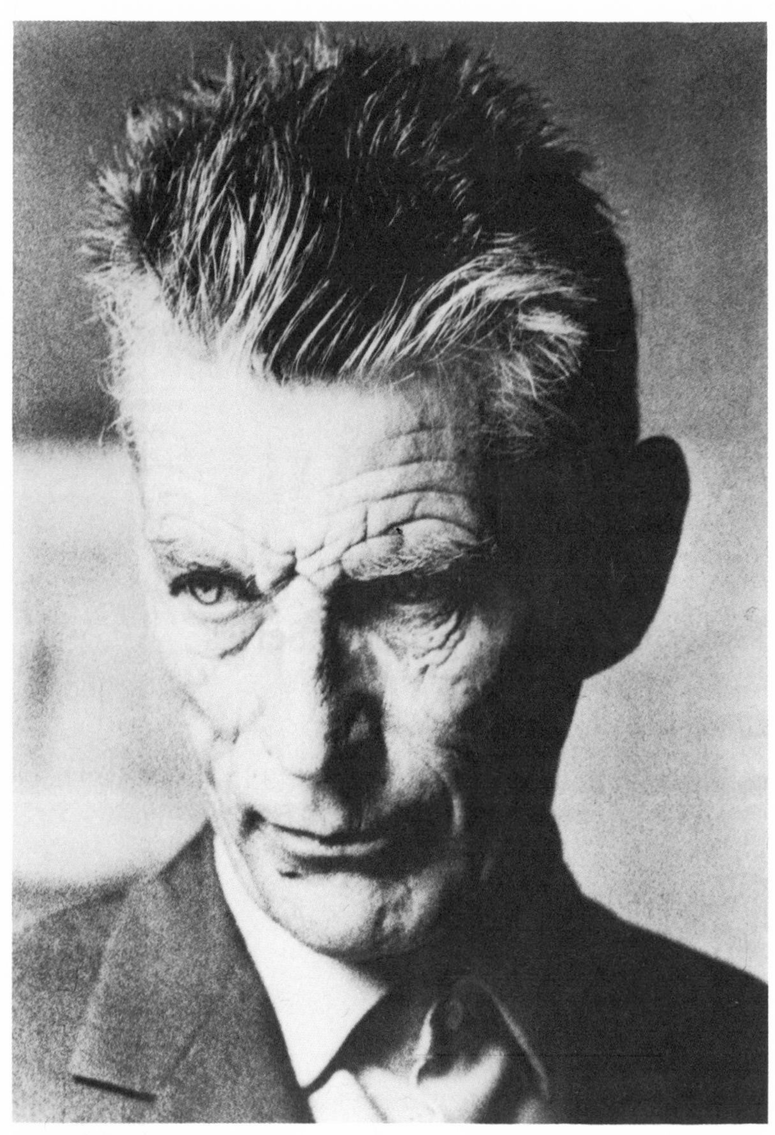

SAMUEL BECKETT
(1906- )
*Photograph by Guy Suignard*

# *Samuel Beckett*

By Linda Ben-Zvi

*Colorado State University*

Twayne Publishers

*A Division of G.K. Hall & Co.* • **Boston**

*Samuel Beckett*

Linda Ben-Zvi


Published by Twayne Publishers
A Division of G.K. Hall & Co.
70 Lincoln Street
Boston, Massachusetts 02111

Copyediting supervised by Lewis DeSimone
Book production by Marne B. Sultz
Book design by Barbara Anderson

Typeset in 11 pt. Garamond
by Modern Graphics, Inc., Weymouth, Massachusetts

Printed on permanent/durable acid-free paper
and bound in the United States of America

**Library of Congress Cataloging in Publication Data**

Ben-Zvi, Linda.
Samuel Beckett.

(Twayne's English authors series; TEAS 423)
Bibliography: p. 219
Includes index.
1. Beckett, Samuel, 1906– —Criticism and interpretation. I. Title. II. Series.
PR6003.E282Z573 1986 848'.91409 85–31828
ISBN 0–8057–6912–9

*For Ruby Cohn,*
*who led the way;*
*and Sam, Ori, and Arik,*
*who helped me follow*

# *Contents*

## *About the Author*

Linda Ben-Zvi is professor of English at Colorado State University. She has published articles on Samuel Beckett, James Joyce, modern drama, and language and literature in *PMLA*, *Comparative Literature Studies*, *Modern Drama*, the *Journal of Beckett Studies*, and other journals. Her bibliography "Philosophy as as Art Form" appeared in *Style*, vol. 16. She is presently completing a book on the American playwright Susan Glaspell.

# Preface

A critic studying the works of Samuel Beckett faces two immediate problems: how to include all the short stories, novels, poems, and plays of a writer who has published consistently over a fifty-five year period, and how to exclude those peripheral explorations, however interesting, that take the traveler too far from the primary texts. I struggled with the first problem, but was aided with the second. There simply was no room—if I wished to cover twenty-seven fiction works, thirty-three plays, collected poetry, and criticism—to employ the vast array of speculative tools that aid in Beckett studies.[1] Instead, I have concentrated on presenting the works themselves in necessarily abbreviated exegeses, and have connected them to general observations about the canon. The thesis of the book is that Beckett's writings offer a unique artistic whole, a continuum with each piece bearing traces of those that precede and each indicating the continuing battle Beckett has waged to create in the modern world.

The study is written for an English-speaking audience; therefore, only English versions of texts have been cited, though almost all the works exist in both English and French, translated by Beckett. To emphasize the notion of continuity, I have arranged the material in chronological order, dating from the first publication of a work, whether in English or French. In the bibliography dates of publication in both languages are listed.

Beckett's writings are particularly difficult to summarize; having done so, a critic still finds that the "it all" of the work eludes categorization. Therefore, the reader is asked to supplement discussions by direct trips to primary sources. "The danger is in the neatness of identifications," Beckett wrote in his first published critical essay. "Literary criticism is not book-keeping," he continued.[2] The warning and advice are well taken.

Linda Ben-Zvi

*Colorado State University*

# *Acknowledgments*

Portions of this study in altered form have appeared in the *Journal of Beckett Studies* and in *Modern Drama*. I thank the editors for permission to reprint. Unless otherwise stated, all quotations from Beckett's printed works come from Grove Press editions, and I thank them for permission to quote. Some of the research for this study was begun during an NEH Summer Seminar, directed by Ruby Cohn, and during an NEH College Teacher's Fellowship. I thank NEH for its support. I also thank Colorado State University for a Faculty Research grant and the College of Arts, Humanities, and Social Sciences for mini grants, which aided in the research for this manuscript. I am also indebted to my fellow Beckett critics for their friendship, support, and insights, which they have so generously shared. Finally, my thanks go to Samuel Beckett, who over the years has answered my queries, allowed me to quote unpublished material, and written the works that have made this study so rewarding.

# *Chronology*

1906 Samuel Barclay Beckett born in Foxrock, Dublin, on Good Friday, 13 April, the second son of William (Bill) Beckett, a building contractor, and Mary (May) Beckett, a former nurse.

1920 After attending Earlsfort House School in Dublin, sent to Portora Royal School in Northern Enniskillen, where he develops an interest in sports, plays on the cricket and rugby teams.

1923 Attends Trinity College (Dublin) as a day student, studying French and Italian.

1928 Spring term as French tutor at Campbell College, Belfast; in October begins two-year exchange fellowship at l'Ecole Normale Supérieure in Paris; through Thomas McGreevy, meets James Joyce and writers associated with *transition.*

1929 Publishes first mature fiction, "Assumption," and first criticism, "Dante...Bruno.Vico..Joyce," in June issue of *transition.*

1930 Wins £10 prize from Hours Press for poem on Descartes, entitled "Whoroscope," August; spends summer reading Proust in preparation for writing monograph; returns to Dublin in September to become Assistant in French at Trinity College.

1931 With Georges Pelorson, writes and acts in *Le Kid,* parody of Corneille's *Cid; Proust* published in March; poems printed in the *European Caravan* and *Dublin Magazine;* receives M.A. from Trinity College, December; leaves for Kassel, Germany, and resigns post from there.

1932 Six months in Kassel and Paris; returns to Dublin; begins *Dream of Fair to Middling Women,* which traces these journeys.

1933 Abandons *Dream* but salvages some material for collection of short stories, *More Pricks Than Kicks;* father dies in June, leaving Beckett a yearly annuity of £200, administered by his mother; moves to London to try journalism as a means of support.

1934 *More Pricks Than Kicks* published in May; "A Case in a Thousand" and reviews in August and Christmas issues of the *Bookman;* begins *Murphy.* Begins analysis under Dr. Wilfred Brion of Tavistock Clinic.

1935 *Echo's Bones,* a collection of thirteen poems, published in November.

1936 Completes *Murphy;* begins reading material for play on possible romance between Dr. Samuel Johnson and Mrs. Hester Thrale; travels to Germany in December.

1937 Distressed by signs of war, returns to Dublin in April; moves permanently to Paris last week of October, returning only for visits thereafter. *Murphy* accepted for publication by Routledge in December, after being rejected by forty-two publishers.

1938 7 January, is stabbed just above heart on Paris street; visited in hospital by pianist Suzanne Dumesnil, who later becomes his wife.

1939 Returns from visit to Dublin when war breaks out in Paris in September.

1940 Becomes part of an information-gathering resistance cell.

1942 Cell broken in August; Beckett and Suzanne escape through Vichy France to Roussillon, where they remain until end of war; Beckett begins *Watt* during this period.

1945 Receives croix de guerre and Médaille de la Résistance for war activities; returns to Dublin after Armistice in May. Reenters Paris in October.

1946 Begins his most productive period, writing in French; between July and December writes *Mercier et Camier* and the *nouvelles.*

1947 French version of *Murphy* published in May; *Eleuthéria* and *Molloy* completed.

1948 *Malone meurt (Malone Dies)* completed.

1949 *En attendant Godot (Waiting for Godot)* completed in January; *Three Dialogues* appears in *transition* in December.

1950 *L'Innommable (The Unnamable)* completed in January; returns home before mother's death in August; the trilogy *Molloy, Malone meurt,* and *L'Innommable* accepted for French publication by Éditions de Minuit in November.

1952 *En attendant Godot* published in October.

1953 5 January, world première of *En attendant Godot,* at Théâtre de Babylone, Paris, directed by Roger Blin; *Watt* published in August.

1954 *Waiting for Godot* published in New York; Beckett's brother Frank dies.

1955 *Molloy* translated into English and published in New York; *Nouvelles et Textes pour rien (Stories and Texts for Nothing)* published in Paris.

1956 First American production of *Waiting for Godot,* directed by Alan Schneider, in Miami Beach; under another director, opens later in New York to acclaim; *Malone Dies* published in New York; *Fin de partie (Endgame)* completed in June.

1957 *All that Fall* broadcast on BBC Third Program, 13 January; world première of *Fin de partie,* in French, at Royal Court Theatre in London; *All that Fall* published in London.

1958 First performance in English of *Endgame* at Cherry Lane Theatre, New York; *Krapp's Last Tape* in *Evergreen Review,* summer; world première of *Krapp's Last Tape,* at Royal Court Theatre, London, in October; *Endgame* and *The Unnamable* published in New York.

1959 *Embers* broadcast on BBC Third Program, 24 June. Receives honorary degree from Trinity College, Dublin; trilogy published in one volume in English, but never called trilogy.

1960 *Krapp's Last Tape* performed for first time in America, at Provincetown Playhouse, New York, in January.

1961 *Comment c'est (How It Is)* published in Paris; *Poems in English* published in London; world première of *Happy Days* at Cherry Lane Theatre in September, published in New York; shares the International Publishers' Prize with Jorge Luis Borges.

1962 *Words and Music* broadcast on BBC Third Program, 13 November.

1963 World première of *Play,* in German, at Ulm-Donau; *Cascando* broadcast in French on ORTF, 13 October.

1964 *Play* first performed in English, at Cherry Lane Theatre; *How It Is* published in New York. Travels to New York in July to assist on filming of *Film,* directed by Alan Schneider. *Cascando* broadcast in English on BBC Third program, 6 October.

1965 *Come and Go,* in German, performed at Schiller Theatre, Berlin. *Imagination Dead Imagine* published in London.

1966 Directs first production of his work *Va et vient (Come and Go)* in Paris, followed by a German television version of *Eh Joe; Eh Joe* broadcast on BBC television, 4 July.

1967 *Eh Joe and Other Writings* and *Stories and Texts for Nothing* published in New York; *Come and Go* and *No's Knife: Collected Shorter Prose 1947–1966* published in London. Directs *Endgame* in German at Schiller Theatre.

1968 *Watt* translated into French and published in Paris; *Come and Go* performed for first time in English at Peacock Theatre, Dublin; *Cascando and Other Short Dramatic Pieces,* published in New York.

1969 Awarded the Nobel Prize for Literature, 23 October; accepts the award but does not travel to Stockholm for presentation. Directs *Krapp's Last Tape* in German at Schiller Theatre.

1970 Directs *Krapp's Last Tape* in French and *Act Without Words I and II* at the Petit d'Orsay; *Lessness* published in London; *Collected Works* published in New York. Directs *Happy Days* in German at Schiller Theatre.

1972 *The Lost Ones* published in New York; world première of *Not I* at Lincoln Center, New York.

1973 *Not I, First Love, Breath and Other Shorts* published in London.

1974 *Mercier and Camier,* and *First Love and Other Shorts* published in New York.

1975 Directs *Waiting for Godot* in German at Schiller Theatre, and *Not I* in French at the Petit d'Orsay, Paris.

1976 *That Time* and *Footfalls* première during Beckett's 70th birthday celebration at Royal Court Theatre; *Fizzles* and *Ends and Odds* published in New York; American première of *That Time* and *Footfalls* at Arena Theatre, Washington, D.C. *All*

| | |
|---|---|
| | *Strange Away,* published in New York. *Radio II* broadcast on BBC Third Program 13 April. |
| 1977 | *Ghost Trio* and . . . *but the clouds* . . . broadcast on BBC television 17 April; *Collected Poems in English and French* published in London. |
| 1978 | *Poèmes suivi de mirlitonnades,* a collection of thirty-five poems written 1976–78, published in Paris; *Sounds* and *Still 3* published in *Essays in Criticism* in April. |
| 1979 | *A Piece of Monologue* printed in *Kenyon Review,* summer. |
| 1980 | World première of *A Piece of Monologue* at LaMama, New York; *Company* published in London. |
| 1981 | *Ill Seen Ill Said,* in *New Yorker* 5 October; world première of *Rockaby* at State University of New York at Buffalo, Samuel Beckett Festival; world première of *Ohio Impromptu* at Ohio State Beckett Symposium; both published in *Rockaby and Other Short Pieces* with *A Piece of Monologue.* |
| 1982 | World première of *Catastrophe* at Avignon Festival 21 July, written for Czech writer Vaclav Havel; *Ohio Impromptu, Catastrophe,* and *What Where* open at Harold Clurman Theatre, New York, published in New York. |
| 1983 | *Worstward Ho* published in New York. |
| 1984 | *Collected Shorter Plays of Samuel Beckett* published in London; Samuel Beckett Theatre on East 42 Street, New York, named and opens with production of *Endgame.* |

f all Beckett's works in both French and English. useful handbook for someone checking a pecific work, *Samuel Beckett* is also a general guide Beckett's development as a writer of fiction nd drama.

**The Author**

r. *Linda Ben-Zvi,* professor of English at Colorado tate University in Fort Collins, has published idely in the field of modern drama.

## *Chapter One*

# Illuminations through the Dark

An old man, unshaven, with disordered grey hair, sits alone in a room, caught in a circle of light from the bulb above his cluttered desk. At his elbow is a tape recorder into which he is about to offer, as he does every year, his observations about the preceding twelve months spent "on this old muckball" of an earth. He consults the few notes he has jotted on the back of an envelope, crumples it, broods, switches on the recorder, and begins: "Nothing to say, not a squeak. What's a year now? The sour cud and the hard stool." At first hearing, this line from Samuel Beckett's play *Krapp's Last Tape* offers little to arrest the attention of the audience that has been sharing the old man's recording ritual. The words *cud* and *stool* may puzzle, but not their intent: the depiction of bleakness. Yet the transparency of the line gives way when we realize that the man who has told us he has nothing to say has taken seventeen words to say it. Out of the "nothing" he has fashioned a statement, transformation, question, and two images concretizing the situation. Like Clov in Beckett's *Endgame,* who begins with the word "Finished," and then moves back from the finality of the statement with "it's finished, nearly finished, it must be nearly finished," gaining respite from closure by his linguistic manipulations, Krapp makes of "nothing" a "something" about which to speak.

The process is repeated over and over in Beckett's writing. Words are spoken when there is "Nothing to say"; actions are performed when, as Vladimir and Estragon recognize in Beckett's most famous play, *Waiting for Godot,* there is "Nothing to be done." These examples illustrate the two constant poles in Beckett's writing: awareness of nihility and the evasion of such awareness by the imposition of diversionary tactics—both verbal and physical—to leaven the knowledge.

In a career that has now spanned over fifty years and produced twenty-seven works of fiction, thirty-three plays, poetry, criticism, and translations, Beckett has consistently focused on a central battle of modern existence: the battle of people against the awareness of their own meaninglessness. Unlike characters in classical tragedies who take the stage certain of their power to control events, Beckett's people enter aware of their limitations. It takes Shakespeare's King Lear three acts to reach the conclusion that "Man is no more but such a poor, bare forked animal." Vladimir in *Waiting for Godot* begins with this knowledge and proceeds to find ways of living under the burden it imposes.

The position into which Beckett thrusts his characters is the position he assumes for himself as creator, no more able to know or do than his fictive representatives. "I think anyone nowadays who pays the slightest attention to his own experience finds it the experience of a non-knower, a non-can-er," he told an interviewer in 1956.[1] In his earliest prose, the unpublished novel *Dream of Fair to Middling Women,* begun in 1932, the young Beckett inveighed against those writers who attributed to themselves the powers to control and understand reality that they, in fact, did not possess. Their creations became the stilted literature exemplified for Beckett by the Balzac novel: "To read Balzac is to receive the impression of a chloroformed world. He is absolute master of his material, he can do what he likes with it, he can foresee and calculate its vicissitude, he can write the end of his book before he has finished the first paragraph."[2]

Against such authorial omniscience, Beckett argues for a position in keeping with the limited purview of man, a "fidelity to failure," he calls it. "To be an artist is to fail, as no other dare fail, that failure is his world and the shrink from it desertion, art and craft, good housekeeping, living," he told the French art critic Georges Duthuit in their conversations of 1949, published under the title "Three Dialogues."[3] Failure becomes the inevitable end for those who recognize the impossibility of ever controlling the materials of life or of ever piercing through the void that lies beyond the constructs of reality, Beckett holds. Yet, as his comments also indicate, he is fully aware of the human need to avoid such conclusions; the "shrink from it" becomes a necessary requisite of self-preservation. It is precisely this terrain between recognition and avoidance that Beckett explores.

To illustrate this dichotomous world, he has often cited two quotations as aids to critics seeking help with his writing: "Nothing is more real than nothing," by the Greek philosopher Democritus, and "Where you are worth nothing, there you should want nothing," by the Belgian Occasionalist Geulincx. The first quotation points to the nothingness that lies at the center of experience. It is the awareness that King Lear gains through the agency of his suffering. The second quotation alludes to the difficulty of reaching or sustaining such a view. Acceptance of the condition of nullity should be the clear response for those who admit the void as irremediable, but none of Beckett's all-too-human characters is able to follow such advice. "One is born of us, who having nothing will wish for nothing, except to be left the nothing he hath," Beckett writes in his novel *Mercier and Camier*. In Beckett's world, however, the annunciation of such a being is premature. Characters repeatedly show their adeptness at sidestepping despair—singing, joking, dancing, walking, adding, thinking, and above all, talking—to forestall the gloom they feel about the conditions of life they cannot control.

These diversions may only serve as a chain-linked fence of words and deeds to keep characters from straying too close to the void, but as such they provide temporary protection. That creation is even possible under such conditions and in such terrain is surprising, a fact the Nobel committee recognized when it awarded Beckett the prize for literature in 1969. The accompanying citation read: "For his writing which—in new forms for the novel and drama—in the destitution of modern man acquires its elevation." Elevation in Beckett's writing comes from the ingenuity of the human mind—Beckett's and his personae's—continually fashioning subterfuges as they live on the brink of the void, yet refusing to place their dwellings on more hospitable grounds where compact safe houses could be established, where traditional literature could be created.

## Reading Beckett

A writer who writes, as in "Three Dialogues," that "there is nothing to express, nothing with which to express, nothing from which to express, no power to express, no desire to express, together with the obligation to express" is a writer who cannot be approached in traditional ways by readers or critics. The first thing the reader of Beckett must do is to put aside predetermined expectations about literature. Since stories are never finished and can never be as long as the teller lives, the readers confronted with such chronicles must adjust themselves and their expectations to the conditions. First, it will be impossible to simply read *for* the story. There is no story or, to put it better, there are many stories, but each one will be interrupted in its course by a storyteller or writer who will intrude in the narrative, indicating that what appears is fiction, artifice, lies. Readers used to immersion in the fictional world may become annoyed at these intrusions and disruptions; they get in the way. But that is exactly their function. Beckett wishes to keep the impossibility of completion continually in the foreground. Should the storyteller be lulled by the power of his own story and believe in its veracity, then he would be lying, denying his own "fidelity to failure."

Gone, too, are those elements of character and place that are usually demarcated in literature and drama. Beckett peoples his world, but just barely. We are given very few distinguishing marks that allow for easy recognition and identification. The characters are mostly old, decrepit, and worn. They have been at it—whatever their particular *it* is—for a long time. Vladimir and Estragon have been together since the 90s, Hamm and Clov in their cell since something began "taking its course," Winnie and Willie incapacitated since the old days. Time takes its toll, blurring features and individual marks of character. Sex is sometimes difficult to determine. Molloy refers to himself and his mother as so old that they appear to be sexless. Even names become lost or forgotten or changed along the way. Vladimir is Didi, but he also answers to Mr. Albert.

Place is also not clearly defined. *Waiting for Godot* takes place on a road, but we are never told exactly where. The only mark of identification is a tree, but we are not sure what kind. Although some specific references to geographical location are given in most of the early works, these place names never seem to offer the fixity we would expect. Murphy lives in London's World's End and watches the men fly kites in Hyde Park, but it is more a Hyde Park of his imagination than a physical locale. More recent works shun even these distinguishing features. They tend to occur inside a "closed place": cylinders, rooms, or, in the novel *Company,* simply "in the dark." Whether light or dark, small or spacious, all these enclosures are variations of the same skullscape first explored by the Unnamable: "the inside of my distant skull where once I wandered, now am fixed."

Place is reduced to a metaphor, and time, too, becomes a blurred feature of the narrative since in the mind temporal laws have no sway. *Krapp's Last Tape,* for example, takes place on "a late evening in the future," and yet the evening focuses on events of times long since past. *Company* occurs in a timeless, present "now" although a good part of the novel relates to memories of "then." The present tense is most consistently employed in the writing; however, we must be wary of accepting the events and situations described as affixed to a specific moment of time. As Molloy explains, "I speak in the present tense, it is so easy to speak in the present tense, when speaking of the past." In the skull there is no fixity of time or anything else. All becomes blurred by the darkness within.

The stories spun in Beckett's writing are incomplete and so are the storytellers; for the same darkness that makes narrative verification impossible extends to the self: " . . . and even my sense of identity was wrapped in a namelessness often hard to penetrate," Molloy knows. Since the self exists in time, it becomes subject to the vagaries of memory; contiguity is derived only from the pictures of the past affixed to the moments of the present. At best, Beckett describes a fragmented vision of self emerging from the shadows of time: "the notion of an unqualified present—the mere 'I am' is an ideal notion," he writes in *Dream.*

Further complicating the quest for self, Beckett also indicates that at any given moment the self exists as two separate entities: an outer I, alive in the macrocosm, commingling with the physical world, and an inner me, unseen, unheard, alive only to the I. This microcosmic aspect of the self has no means of communication and is able to talk only through the I, constantly monitoring the physical external self, offering, as it were, a running commentary heard by the I alone. Its very existence causes the disjunction and schism that all Beckett figures experience. Because of this other self, characters are never able to use the singular pronoun; the other voice, alive in the head, disavows the limiting appellation: "did you ever say I to yourself in your life come on now . . . could you ever say I to yourself in your life," the inner voice in *That Time* asks. In particular works the focus may shift, sometimes on the external self, sometimes on the inner me. "It was he, I was inside," the speaker in *Fizzles* says. "My brother inside me, my old twin," the voice in *Radio II* claims. The question of pronoun juggling becomes more than a verbal game; it becomes a sign of the impossibility of ever uniting the parts of the self. Because of this disjunction, all of Beckett's people have the continual sense that they are being watched, if only by themselves. The motto that Beckett used for the working script of his film *Film* was Berkeley's *Esse est percipi,* "to be is to be perceived."

Finally, all that exists within the frame of the Beckett world, the confines of the skull, are words. Stories are the pasting together of lexical constructions—words, phrases, sentences, paragraphs—in the attempt to build a life. The same is true of the characters' search for a unified self. The self becomes an extension of the words that define it. Beckett's people know that they are in a hopeless predicament: for the stories can be finished only when the words stop, and the self can be known only in the silence that lies beyond language. The Unnamable speaks for all of them when he says, "I'm in words, made of words, others' words . . . I'm something quite different, a quite different thing, a wordless thing, in an empty place . . . where nothing stirs, nothing speaks." It is the "nothing" that Krapp referred to, the sign of the void, where all stories cease and all selves become one. Yet it is impossible to speak of what is unspeakable. The characters try to speak of nothing, but they always fail. The logorrhea in a Beckett work becomes a coda for the unsaid that it continually skirts but never reaches.

There may be "nothing but lifeless words" in a given text, but it is important to note that the words are not unimportant or lifeless. On the contrary, since what lies beyond them can never be known, the language takes on a new significance; it becomes all we know, an end in itself. And it must be approached in this manner. Beckett, in his first printed criticism, an apologia for James Joyce's *Finnegans Wake,* warned of the human tendency to read the story oblivious to the language that shapes it. The same warning must be heeded in approaching Beckett's work. How a line is written becomes as important as what it says. Beckett called his friend and mentor James Joyce a *Homo Logos*—a "word man." The title is appropriate for Beckett as well. Rhymes, plays on words, puns, inversions, verbal games are found throughout the writing, bringing humor to the bleakest situations. To overlook the play of the language is to miss the very inventiveness that is part of the brain's denial of its own limitations. It is also to overlook an important key to the literature since how a line is written becomes an indicator of what is meant. For example, in *Endgame* we don't need three forms of the verb "to finish" in order to understand what Clov says, but the repetitions do indicate the character's hesitation about finality; and the ordering of the forms—from the isolated "Finished" to the conditional and predicate forms—also points to Clov's careful stepping back from the thought of cessation and his grasping at language to militate against closure.

While made aware of the language in its own right, not as a transparent medium for the expression of ideas, we are also continually asked to witness the very act of composition, the piling up of word upon word, the careful selection and honing of form. For example, in the short play *Rockaby* ninety-six lines are altered to produce the 251 lines of the play. The repetitions reflect the back-and-forth motion of the rocker, but they also allow the audience to view the painstaking attempts of the mind to play with its few blocks of thought, coded in the few phrases it obsessively repeats.

The same self-conscious construction of language, calling attention to itself, is seen in the opening of *Ill Seen Ill Said,* the work that follows *Rockaby.* It begins "From where she lies she sees Venus rise. On. From where she lies when the skies are clear she sees Venus rise followed by the sun." The sentences offer a good example of the danger in reading for information alone. The astronomical observation is less important than the shift from sentence one, in its simple form, to sentence three, with its added clauses. The verbal expansion offers a linguistic equivalent to the classical Venus emerging from the sea. In this instance, however, she does not come forth full-formed, like her mythical parallel. We witness the pain of self-generation through the struggle to find words—the one way Beckett's people create themselves. We also hear the inner voice offering comment on the process through the prodding word "On."

Such complexities are inevitable in the skullscapes Beckett explores. Those who travel in this world should be prepared for the confusions they will encounter. Uncertainties will not be an indication of their own limitations as much as a sign of the limits of the world Beckett is attempting to portray.

## Living Beckett

"Birth was the death of him," the speaker says at the beginning of *A Piece of Monologue.* A biographical fact that may have shaped Beckett's belief in the inimical connection between birth and death is his date of birth. Samuel Barclay Beckett, the second son of William (Bill) and Mary (May) Beckett, was born in the family home, Cooldrinagh, in Foxrock, a suburb of Dublin, on Good Friday, 13 April 1906. Born on the day Christ died, and on Friday the thirteenth, Beckett in later years was able to find irony in the coincidence of events. The number thirteen appears or is used as a structuring device in several works, particularly in the biographical poems in *Echo's Bones;* and the image of man crucified—without accompanying resurrection—is a prevailing image, stated in *Watt,* implicit in other works.

The Beckett family was of French Huguenot extraction, and Beckett was raised a Protestant, though he has described his background as "practically a Quaker." Whatever the leaning, the influence of his early religious training was not significant beyond his early years. When asked to comment on his religious feeling, Beckett has responded: "Well, really there is none at all. I have no religious feeling. Once I had a religious emotion. It was at my first Communion. No more. My mother was deeply religious. So was my brother. He knelt down at his bed as long as he could kneel. My father had none. My family was Protestant but for me it was only irksome, and I let it go.[4] The one available picture of Beckett as a young child shows an angelic boy, kneeling on a pillow, hands clasped in prayer, looking down as his mother hovers over him. The beatific atmosphere of the scene, however, is contrived. Lady Beatrice Glenavy in her book *Today We Will Only Gossip,* which provides scenes of life in Foxrock during Beckett's youth, says that the picture was actually posed by her sister, who needed a scene to fit the caption "Bedtime" and elicited the help of her neighbors, the Becketts.[5]

From Glenavy's book we get the sense of the privilege and ease surrounding the lives of upper-class Protestants of the period. Bill Beckett was a quantity surveyor, a respected position; and his business successes allowed the family a large, formal, well-appointed house with servants to minister to daily needs. For Sam and his brother, Frank, four years his senior, there were tea parties in the summer, pony cart rides, and formal dinners, organized and presided over by May Beckett. When Beckett has been asked to describe his childhood, he has called it " . . . uneventful. You might say I had a happy childhood . . . although I had little talent for happiness.

My parents did everything that could make a child happy. But I was often lonely."[6]

If May was the dominant figure in the domestic sphere and seemed to enjoy running the home, Bill Beckett offered the boys a chance to share with him his own particular interests: swimming, hiking, and sports. Beckett's father took his sons, at a very young age, to the Forty Foot, a nearby swimming hole. The image of being forced to jump from a high cliff is one that has remained with Beckett, and the following scene in *Company* is only one of several in his writings that re-create the experience: "You stand at the tip of the high board. High above the sea. In it your father's upturned face. . . ." In the same novel there is also reference to the elder Beckett's love of hiking, another thing he imparted to the boys. When his father died in 1933, Beckett wrote to a friend: "What am I to do now but follow his trace over the fields and hedges."[7] Fifty years later, in *Company,* the image of the two walking side by side is still intact: " . . . your father's shade. In his old tramping rags. Finally on side by side from nought anew."

Images of a father figure—often shown walking hand in hand with another male—are suffused with affection, a feeling that seems to have sprung from Beckett's own relationship with his father. Images of the mother are ambiguous, denoting perhaps Beckett's relation to May Beckett. Deirdre Bair, in her biography of Beckett, paints her as a mother who wished to dominate her sons, particularly the younger one, who in appearance so resembled her. May appears to have been a woman of widely varying moods. Her neighbors remember her as warm and loving; one describes her as "the type of neighbor a girl kisses in public."[8] However, she also had periods of depression. In Beckett's autobiographical *Dream of Fair to Middling Women* he describes his mother's habit of wandering through the darkened house late at night, after everyone had retired, walking often until dawn. In the play *Footfalls* he makes this solitary pacing the central visual image. More than his father, it is the image of his mother that appears most consistently in his works. Beckett often uses variations of her name for his female characters: Meg, Mag, Milly, Mildred, and, in *Footfalls,* May. Molloy writes his story in his mother's room and goes into great detail describing his efforts to communicate with her by knocking on her skull. Krapp relives the moment of his mother's death, viewed from the park bench where he sat, below her hospital window. In *Company* the mother appears twice, and in both scenes she censures her son.

Although there seems to have been little intellectual interest on the part of either parent, both were intent on providing their sons with what they considered a proper education for boys of their station. Frank and Sam were sent to Miss Ida Elsner's Academy at age five, continued their education at Earlsfort House School in Dublin, and at age fourteen entered Portora Royal School in Northern Ireland, a prestigious institution for Protestant boys who intended to enroll at Trinity College (Dublin). Beckett's record while at Portora was undistinguished and indicates that sports and music were of far greater importance to him than academic subjects. He excelled at cricket, boxing, and swimming, and references to him in the school paper comment upon his physical abilities. He also continued to display an interest in music, which was first nurtured by enforced piano lessons as a child but has continued throughout Beckett's life. His teachers at Portora recorded that "he knew Gilbert and Sullivan by heart."

In October 1923, at the age of seventeen, Beckett entered Trinity College, an institution with a long tradition of writers among its alumni: Congreve, Farquhar, Swift, Goldsmith, Wilde, and Synge. His tutor, responsible for advising him on general academic matters, was the philosopher Arthur Aston Luce, whose interests in Descartes and Berkeley were later transferred to Beckett. For his field of concentration Beckett chose modern languages, an uncommon major at the time, but one that brought him under the influence of the French professor Thomas B. Rudmose-Brown. It was through Rudmose-Brown that Beckett seems to have finally turned to serious academic pursuits, so that by the time he received his B.A. degree, in the fall of 1927, he stood first in his class, and had won a prestigious fellowship that gave him an exchange lectureship at the French Ecole Normale Supérieure for the years 1928–30. Rudmose-Brown hoped that the young Beckett, who had already distinguished himself in philosophy and languages, would spend the time in Paris doing research in preparation for launching an academic career when he returned, one that might include taking his mentor's place. Certainly in 1928, when Beckett left for Paris to assume his post, his chances for such a future looked promising. He had a strong foundation in literature, had traveled twice to the Continent—in the summer of 1926 to the Loire Valley, and in the summer of

1927 to Florence—and he had taught a year, between his graduation and the beginning of his fellowship, at Campbell College in Belfast. Although Beckett called the teaching "grim," he seemed committed to returning to Trinity at the end of the appointment.

In the summer of 1928, before beginning at the Ecole Normale Supérieure, Beckett visited Germany, staying at the home of his aunt, Cissie Beckett Sinclair. Cissie Beckett was his father's sister, somewhat of an outcast in the family because of her bohemian ways and her marriage to a Jewish man against her family's wishes. Beckett had seen little of the Sinclairs while they lived nearby in Dublin, but on one of their visits from Germany, where they had moved, Beckett met his cousin Peggy Sinclair and became fascinated by her. Over the next several years he made frequent trips to Kassel, Germany, to stay with the Sinclairs and woo Peggy, until the affair cooled. She is a model for the Smeraldina Rima or Smerry in *Dream* and in *More Pricks Than Kicks.* The tragedy of her early death from tuberculosis is also referred to in *Krapp's Last Tape,* as is her love for the color green.

In October 1928 Beckett traveled from Germany to Paris to take up his teaching assignment. "Paris in the twenties was a good place for a young man to be," he has said.[9] It was the center of the literary experimentation and avant-garde movements of the time, a far cry from the provincialism of the Dublin he had known. Through his predecessor from Trinity College, Thomas McGreevy, whom he had come to replace, Beckett soon met many of the young men of letters, particularly those who had formed a coterie around the leading literary figure of Paris at the time, James Joyce. Beckett met Joyce his first month in Paris and soon became part of "Joyce's runabout men,"[10] doing errands and seeking out material for the nearly blind writer who was completing *Finnegans Wake.* It was Joyce who enlisted the aid of the twenty-three-year-old Beckett in writing one of the twelve apologia for the *Wake* that attempted to clarify certain difficulties that the novel had presented when serialized in *transition* magazine. Beckett's article, directed by Joyce, was entitled "Dante . . . Bruno . Vico . . Joyce," the dots indicating the centuries connecting the three Italians and their Irish descendant. Although published in a separate book, the essay also appeared in *transition,* in June 1929, along with Beckett's first published story, "Assumption." His year in Paris also brought him a prize and a separate publication. In June 1929 the Hours Press, run by Nancy Cunard and Richard Aldington, sponsored a contest for the best poem of under one hundred lines that had time as its subject. Beckett heard of the contest only twenty-four hours before the deadline for submissions. On three sheets of stationery taken from the Hotel Bristol he wrote the poem *Whoroscope,* based loosely on a biography of the life of René Descartes, whose works he had been reading for his academic research. So impressed were Cunard and Aldington with the quality of his entry that they immediately awarded it the prize of one thousand francs and the promise of publication.

This award was soon followed in the summer of 1930 by a contract from Aldington for Beckett to do an extended essay on the French writer Marcel Proust. Instead of traveling to Germany as he had planed, Beckett spent the entire summer in Paris, reading the sixteen volumes of Proust's works, twice. The result is a seventy-two-page study, which offers an excellent introduction to Proust. It also introduces themes that Beckett would later pursue.

The essay was not the project that Beckett had intended to complete during his stay in Paris, but it was an impressive beginning for the academic career upon which he embarked on his return to Dublin in October 1930. From the beginning of his lectureship at Trinity College in the Modern Languages department it was clear, at least to a friend who knew him then, that Beckett was not happy in the role of teacher. "Sam would stand for minutes staring through the window and then throw a perfectly constructed sentence to his crumb-picking avid audience," A. J. Leventhal remembers.[11] He gave lectures on de Musset, Balzac, Flaubert, Stendhal, Racine, and Bergson. During this time he also read Kant, Schopenhauer, and the Belgian Occasionalist philosopher Arnold Geulincx. Beckett has remarked that he could not bear the indignity of teaching others what he did not know himself. "I saw that in teaching I was talking of something I knew little about, to people who cared nothing about it. So I behaved very badly; I ran away to the Continent, and resigned from a distance."[12] It was during this spring holiday in Germany with the Sinclairs that Beckett sent his letter of resignation, shocking Rudmose-Brown and his family. Beckett has often repeated that when he left Trinity he "lost the best."

In 1932 when he resigned, Beckett may have had a clear idea of what he did not want to, or could not, do with his life, but he seems to have had very little idea of what he would do. After an unhappy, abortive stay in Germany, where it became clear that his relations with Peggy were leading nowhere, Beckett briefly returned to Paris, and once more met with Joyce. However, their friendship was strained because of the infatuation that Joyce's daughter, Lucia, had developed for the young Beckett. There has been much speculation about the relationship. Lucia, Joyce's younger child, had first met Beckett during his visits to the Joyce apartment in 1929 and 1930, and although he had made clear that he was visiting the father, not the daughter, Lucia believed that Beckett had a serious interest in her. In 1932 her feelings for him were once more aroused, and Beckett was forced to tell her that a relationship between them was not possible. During this time Lucia began showing signs of the severe mental disturbance that would lead to her eventual institutionalization. Therefore, connections with Joyce were difficult.

While still in Paris, Beckett did begin work on his first novel, *Dream of Fair to Middling Women.* It is set in Dublin, Paris, and Kassel and includes fictionalized portraits of his family, friends, and, most prominently, Peggy Sinclair. The protagonist is one Belacqua Shuah, a name derived from a character in Dante's *Purgatorio,* a Florentine lute-maker described as "more indolent than if sloth were his sister." Belacqua became the central character in the collection of short stories *More Pricks Than Kicks,* which Beckett wrote next, salvaging some of the characters and materials from the aborted *Dream.*

Beckett worked on the book on his return to Dublin in 1933. It was during his stay, in June, that his father suddenly died. With Frank going into the family business and looking after his mother's affairs, and with his mother evidently growing more irascible after the loss of her husband, Beckett decided that it was time to try seriously to establish himself as a writer. The London publishers Chatto and Windus accepted *More Pricks,* and Beckett began to receive assignments as a reviewer for several periodicals. So he decided to move to London in the hope of gaining more commissions. In his will, Beckett's father had left him money, but he could receive it only at the behest of his mother, and it was she who disapproved of his desire to be a writer and of his life abroad. But in late 1933 illnesses that had plagued Beckett through childhood—headaches, boils, and colds—reached such proportions that May Beckett was convinced that her son needed a change, if only temporarily. Deirdre Bair reports that Beckett had sought medical help while in Dublin, and had been advised by his friend Geoffrey Thompson that his problems might be connected to the stress of living at home and dealing with his mother. Thompson suggested analysis. Bair says that during much of Beckett's stay in London he was under the care of a psychiatrist named Wilfred Bion.

Beckett calls his time in London, from 1933 to 1935, "bad in every way—financially, psychologically."[13] He suffered from the English antipathy for the Irish. "They always know you're an Irishman. The porter in the hotel. His tone changes. The taximan says, 'Another sixpence, Pat.' They call you Pat."[14] The period, however, did provide material for Beckett's first completed novel, *Murphy*. It is set in the places around World's End, Chelsea, and Hyde Park where Beckett lived and walked during his time in London. It features a mental institution, called Magdalen Mental Mercy Seat in the book but very likely modeled on Bethlehem Royal Hospital, where Geoffrey Thompson, who had moved from Dublin, had worked and where Beckett had visited. *Murphy,* and subsequent Beckett works, may also have been influenced by lectures by the famous Swiss psychiatrist Carl Jung, which were given from September to October 1935 as part of the Tavistock Clinic series that Beckett attended in the company of Bion. Several of Jung's points about the development of the ego have parallels in Beckett's works and one incident, Jung's description of a young girl who had not fully developed an ego, who, Jung said, "had never been born entirely," finds a direct echo in Mrs. Rooney's speech in the radio play *All That Fall.*

During 1935 and 1936 Beckett continually traveled between London and Dublin. He had finished *Murphy* but was unable to get a publisher for it. This was to be the first of his long battles for publication. *Murphy* was rejected by forty-two publishers before Routledge accepted it in 1937. Such consistent rejection of his work caused Beckett to write to his American director Alan Schneider, after the fame that *Godot* brought him: "Success and failure on the public level never mattered much to me, in fact I feel much more at home with the latter, having breathed deep of its vivifying air all my writing life, up to the last couple of years."[15] So sure was he that publication of his works spelled disaster for any publisher brave enough to agree to handle the books, that when Jérôme Lindon, of the small French press, Éditions de Minuit, agreed in the early 1950s to publish the trilogy, Beckett was depressed lest the commitment destroy the company.

In 1936, with *Murphy* completed but still unpublished, Beckett set out once more for Germany, staying this time for six months, and traveling through most of the major cities. However, at this date signs of the impending war were already visible; and Beckett found that his time spent for the most part in the museums could not overshadow the growing threat of Nazism, which he witnessed personally and through his contact with Jewish intellectuals whom he met.

During his trip Beckett was preoccupied with getting a publisher for *Murphy.* He was also compiling material for a project that he had started before his departure: a play on the possible love between the eighteenth-century man of letters Dr. Samuel Johnson and his longtime friend and patron Mrs. Hester Thrale. The work was to focus on the four-year period, 1781–1785, between the death of Thrale's first husband and her marriage to the Italian musician Gabriel Piozzi. The play never got beyond a title—*Human Wishes* derived from Johnson's poem "The Vanity of Human Wishes"—and a brief scene. However, Beckett did fill three notebooks with research on the life of Johnson, his attitudes toward death and fame, and on biographical material concerning Mrs. Thrale. The extant scene, published for the first time in 1980,[16] shows many of the characteristics that Beckett used fifteen years later in *Waiting for Godot.* He returned from Germany in the spring of 1937 with Murphy unpublished and *Human Wishes* unfinished. He had left London permanently, so he moved back once more to Dublin, Cooldrinagh, and his mother. His letters to friends during the period reflect his feeling that there was little in life for him if he remained in his present situation: "I am quite convinced . . . that at this rate it is only a matter of a few years before a hideous crisis," he wrote to one. To another he said, "I am deteriorating now very rapidly."[17] Finally, in the fall, after Frank's marriage, the situation must have reached an impasse that made it possible for Beckett to do what he had tried to do for the past eight years—leave Ireland permanently. October 1937 found him once more in Paris. This time he remained. He was thirty-one years old and had a small body of published material behind him: the poem *Whoroscope,* a collection of poems written during a fiften-year period and published in a volume entitled *Echo's Bones,* a collection of short stories, several individual short stories, assorted criticism, and a completed novel that no one seemed to want.

The beginning of his life in Paris boded well for the future. *Murphy* finally was accepted, and Beckett was able to reestablish relations with the Joyce family. Then on 7 January 1938, an event occurred that seemed taken directly from an existential story by Camus. Beckett, on his way home from friends in the early morning hours, was suddenly attacked by a pimp who had accosted him requesting money. The man, whose name ironically was Prudent, quickly produced a knife and without a word stabbed Beckett in the pleura, just missing the heart. Later, when Beckett had recovered and was forced to face his attacker in a Paris court, he asked the man before the hearing why he had attacked him. "I don't know" was the only reply. It was during his stay in the hospital that Beckett was visited by a young pianist, Suzanne Deschevaux-Dumesnil, who shortly became his companion and later his wife.

Sometime after his release from the hospital Beckett and Suzanne moved into a small apartment at 6 rue des Favorites, in a working-class neighborhood of Paris. In this seventh-floor apartment Beckett lived for the next twenty-three years and wrote most of his major works. However, before he could settle down to serious composition after his convalescence, the war that he had seen fomenting in Germany finally spread to France. When war was declared in Europe in September 1939, Beckett was in Dublin visiting his family. He immediately made plans to return to Paris, although Ireland was a safe haven, never directly involved in the war. He explained later, "I preferred France in war to Ireland in peace."[18]

His resistance activities during the war, which he has termed "Boy Scout stuff," were far more significant than the modest Beckett admits. He was recruited into a small information-gathering cell with the code name *Gloria,* by his longtime friend Alfred Péron. It was Beckett's responsibility to collect, synthesize, and microfilm information about German movements. Of the original eighty members of the group, only thirty survived the war. It was for this resistance work that Beckett was awarded the French croix de guerre at the end of the war.

Aside from a four-month stay in Vichy, France, when the Germans first entered Paris, Beckett remained in the occupied city for two years. He did resistance work until 15 August 1942—Assumption Day—when he received an urgent telegram from Mme Péron informing him that the cell had been infiltrated and her husband captured, and that the Gestapo were about to arrest him. Within three hours of receiving it, Suzanne and Beckett had left their apartment, seeking refuge with friends in Paris, and eventually making their way through Vichy to the small village of Roussillon in the Vaucluse, where they remained for the rest of the war. Although Beckett occasionally aided some farmers in the area, he kept mostly to himself during this difficult period. It was "to get away from war and occupation" that he began to write *Watt* at this time.[19]

When the war ended, Beckett immediately went to Dublin to see his mother, who had been ill. He found her suffering from the onset of Parkinson's disease—which would eventually kill her in 1950—and living in a small house near Cooldrinagh, which she had earlier sold. Frank, grown "middle-aged," Beckett observed, was the father of two children, Caroline and Edward. The stay in Ireland was brief, for Beckett was anxious to return to Paris. In order to circumvent restrictions against aliens, he decided to volunteer to act as a storekeeper/interpreter for an Irish Red Cross unit that was sent to aid in the recovery of the destroyed city of Saint-Lô in Normandy. After four months in this position, he was finally able to return to Paris and continue his life and career. He was then almost forty years old.

"*Molloy* and the others came to me the day I became aware of my own folly," Beckett told a critic. "I realized that I knew nothing. I sat down in my mother's little house in Ireland and began to write *Molloy*."[20] Whether because of the enforced limitations on his writing during the war years, or because he had crossed the threshold of middle age, Beckett found the four years immediately following the war, from 1946 to 1950, the most fertile period of his professional life. In rapid succession he produced four novels, four stories, six poems, two plays, thirteen texts, and assorted criticism. It was also during this time that he began to write in French.

There has been much critical discussion surrounding Beckett's shift of languages. The critic Ruby Cohn, in her book *Back to Beckett,* lists seven separate answers Beckett has supplied over the years to those who have queried him on the reasons for the change. The responses all seem to point to what Professor Cohn describes as "a way to strip his language to the bare essentials of his vision."[21] As early as the composition of *Dream* in 1932 Beckett had begun to mention the possibility of writing in French: "Perhaps only the French can do it. Perhaps only the French language can give you the thing you want," Belacqua says. He also observed, "I don't know how to write a stinger in English, I always overdo it. In French I can write a fine stinger, but in English I overdo it." The conscious repetition within the quotation points to Beckett's awareness that his mother tongue had led him into verbal excesses in his earlier writing.

Although Beckett had begun to compose in French, he never stopped writing in English as well; in fact, he personally has translated each of his French works into English, re-creating each work in the process. His writings provide a rich source of material on the nature of translation, for he is perhaps the only writer to write simultaneously in two languages and to do his own translations. Several times he has also reversed the process; for instance, the play *Happy Days* was originally written in English and then translated into French. The same is true of the radio play *All that Fall,* the novel *Company,* and several other works.

Fame, which had eluded Beckett for so many years, came rather quickly when it finally arrived. With the production of *Waiting for Godot* in 1953, Beckett began to receive the attention that his earlier novels and fiction had not brought him. In 1959 he was honored by Trinity College; in 1961 he shared the prestigious International Publishers' Prize with the Argentine writer Jorge Luis Borges, and in 1969 he was awarded the Nobel Prize for Literature.

*Godot* also began Beckett's active involvement in theater. As consultant or director, he has now had a hand in staging all of his major plays, working in England, France, and Germany.[22] In America director Alan Schneider introduced Beckett's plays, usually with written assistance from the author. Not content merely to see the printed texts take shape on the stage, Beckett produced elaborate workbooks detailing every move and gesture of his characters, often changing lines and stage business as he rethought his entire play.

Although writing came more slowly after the initial spurt of activity following the war, due in part to the responsibilities accompanying his growing reputation and his commitments in the theater, Beckett continued to write both fiction and drama and to translate each work. A mark of his vigor and undiminished creativity is the outpouring of material in the years immediately preceding his seventy-fifth birthday: two novels, three plays, one television play. Since then, Beckett, now eighty, has written two plays for theater, two for television, and one novel.

Some may find it ironic that the writer who began his career by stating that there was "nothing to say" and that an artist must of necessity fail has been continuing the struggle for almost fifty-five years. "I can't go on," has always been balanced by "I must go on." And if in the intervening years he has come no closer to piercing the void, to bringing forth the essential truth of life—the nothingness at the center of experience—he has been able to outline the parameters of this world within, providing illuminations through the dark.

## *Chapter Two*

# Beckett as Critic

When Samuel Beckett arrived in Paris in the fall of 1928, he was a twenty-two-year-old graduate of Trinity College (Dublin), with a B.A. degree in modern languages and a fellowship to serve as exchange lecturer at the Ecole Normale Supérieure. When he returned to Dublin two years later, he was a published critic, poet, and short-story writer. Although Beckett has made little of his productivity during the period, the years provided an impressive basis for the career that would follow. In his first month in Paris his predecessor, Thomas McGreevy, introduced him to James Joyce and to many of the young men and women who surrounded and aided the nearly blind Irish writer in the composition of his encyclopedic work *Finnegans Wake.*

Most of the Joyce coterie were contributors to *transition,* the journal that carried Joyce's book in serial form, seventeen installments in eleven years, under the working title of "Work in Progress." *Transition* had been started in 1926 by Eugene Jolas in the hope of bringing European experiments with the new isms—dadaism, surrealism, irrationalism—to a yet uninitiated English-speaking audience. In editorials and manifestos Jolas continually demanded forms of language and art that would embody the burgeoning experiences of contemporary lfe. In one of the most famous of these tracts, "The Revolution of the Word," published in *transition* in the combined issues 16–17, he listed twelve declarations, all in large-face black letters, concerning the new literature he espoused. Among his points he stated:

"THE IMAGINATION IN SEARCH OF A FABULOUS WORLD IS AUTONOMOUS AND UNCONFINED"; "THE LITERARY CREATOR HAS THE RIGHT TO DISINTEGRATE THE PRIMAL MATTER OF WORDS IMPOSED ON HIM BY TEXTBOOKS AND DICTIONARIES"; "THE WRITER EXPRESSES. HE DOES NOT COMMUNICATE"; "THE PLAIN READER BE DAMNED."

In the same issue, under the heading "British Isles," were two selections—a short story entitled "Assumption," and a critical essay entitled "Dante . . . Bruno . Vico . . Joyce"—by a young, unknown Irishman named Samuel Beckett.

It is important to understand the milieu from which Beckett's writing sprung, particularly the influence of *transition* and its most famous contributor, Joyce. The echoes of both reverberate through Beckett's early works. Their emphasis on new forms of language, rejection of traditional modes of literature and art, advocacy of imagination over intellect, and absolute belief in the possibilities of creation played an enormous part in molding Beckett's attitudes, which he expresses in the following criticism. Therefore, before turning to the fiction and the drama, I consider the body of criticism Beckett has produced, much of it written in these early years before he had put the theory into practice.[1]The ideas offer helpful insights into Beckett's own work.

## "Dante . . . Bruno . Vico . . Joyce"

While Joyce's novel *Ulysses* had received an enthusiastic reception from the intellectual community fortunate enough to be able to buy copies of the book, banned in both England and America, the serialized *Finnegans Wake* was greeted with storms of protest and dismay, often by champions of the earlier experiment. In order, therefore, to aid his readers and to clarify ambiguous aspects, Joyce gathered twelve disciples from his group and parceled out various topics or explications he wished covered. The title of the collection, also supplied by Joyce, was *Our Exagmination Round his Factification for Incamination of Work in Progress*. Beckett's article was first in the collection, though probably last written, and his name on the cover, which showed the face of a clock, appeared at the designated place for one o'clock. Other contributors included Beckett's friend McGreevy, Joyce's friends Frank Budgen and Stuart Gilbert, and the American poet William Carlos Williams.

The Beckett essay was entitled "Dante . . . Bruno . Vico . . Joyce," a title Joyce gave him, the dots indicating time; as Beckett explained, "From Dante to Bruno is a jump of about three centuries, from Bruno to Vico about one, and from Vico to Joyce about two."[2] The intention of the title and the dots was to indicate the lineal descent from the three Italians to the Irishman Joyce, inheritor of their traditions and ideas.

When Beckett wrote his nineteen-page essay, he had already developed a love for Dante, which went back to his youth when, at the age of ten, he acquired a bust of the Florentine to place on his windowsill next to a smaller bust of Shakespeare that had arrived first.[3] The works of Vico and Bruno were probably unfamiliar to Beckett at the time of writing, although he had studied Italian in Dublin and was able to read them in the original when Joyce indicated the importance of the philosophers in the structuring of the *Wake*.

The essay, Beckett's first published writing, except for juvenilia, begins with a warning against the critical process itself: "The danger is in the neatness of identifications." It is a warning against the human desire for clarity and order that causes people to create false analogies and simplifications in order to make sense of events and literary works. The tendency and the inherent dangers are to be constant refrains in Beckett's criticism and fiction. Having issued the warning here, he immediately describes the present temptation that confronts him: to present the dualities of Vico's theories of philosophy and philology as they are usually presented, "like the contemplation of a carefully folded ham-sandwich." It is against such complacent identifications and easy solutions that Beckett stands "with my handful of abstractions" battling the temptation to "make a really tidy job of it." But such tidiness is to be avoided at all costs, Beckett declares. "Must we wring the neck of a certain system in order to stuff it into a contemporary pigeon-hole, or modify the dimensions of that pigeon-hole for the satisfaction of the analogy-mongers? Literary criticism is not book-keeping." It is ironic that the very first paragraph Beckett published speaks across the decades to the armies of Beckett critics—analogies in hand—who have attempted ot treat his works like "carefully folded ham-sandwiches." What Beckett recognized about Joyce's writing is equally true of all criticism: bookkeeping will not suffice for critical evaluation.

Having issued his basic warning more to his readers than to himself, Beckett begins the process of connecting Joyce to the writings of the three Italians. He then turns to the matter at hand: a vindication of the clarity of the *Wake*. The assault becomes unequivocal and arrogant: "Here is direct expression—pages and pages of it. And if you don't understand it, Ladies and Gentlemen, it is because you are too decadent to receive it." The tone is bravado, the voice of an ardent twenty-three-year-old, and Beckett has since repudiated its excesses. It also bears the mark of *transition,* chiding the "plain reader." What is significant about Beckett's argument is his contention that the readers of Joyce must put aside their usual habits of perusing story and plot; they can no longer skim for events, they must focus on the *how* as much as the *what*. The injunction will apply as well to readers of Beckett, as will Beckett's recognition: "Here form *is* content, content *is* form. You complain that this stuff is not written in English. It is not written at all. It is not to be read—or rather it is not only to be read. It is to be looked at and listened to. His writing is not *about* something; it is *that* something itself."

One further point should be noted. In a brief comment Beckett mentions that "Mr. Joyce has desophisticated language. And it is worth remarking that no language is so sophisticated as English. It is abstracted to death." This assessment of the dangers of English may help explain Beckett's later shift to French.

More than its vindication of Joyce, the essay is of interest to Beckett students because of its emphasis on the following points which will be found in Beckett's own work: (1) the recognition of the inherent connection between form and content; (2) the denial of the primacy of rational thought and abstract language in favor of the power of the imagination and the poetic language that informs it; (3) the rejection of the possibility of absolutes, paradisaical or otherwise, and the recognition that this is a world of purgatory, i.e., unrelieved perpetuity. Taking our cue from Beckett's own words, we must also pay attention to the way the essay is written, to its form. In the violent lashing together of styles, literary and colloquial, and the use of foreign and arcane words, we get some idea of Beckett's erudition and his tendency to draw from numerous sources. We also find a pattern that will become more prominent in later critical writings: the undercutting or deflating of a serious position, a kind of ironic self-negation.

## Proust

Like his essay on *Finnegans Wake,* Beckett's next critical study was also a commission. At the request of Richard Aldington who, with Nancy Cunard, had awarded Beckett first prize in the Hours

Press poetry contest for *Whoroscope,* Beckett was given the assignment of writing a critical essay on Marcel Proust for the Dolphin series of the English publishers Chatto and Windus. Beckett's friend McGreevy had written one on T. S. Eliot, and Beckett undertook to write a similar short study of Proust, in the summer of 1930. In preparation for the assignment, he reread the entire sixteen volumes of Proust's writing in what Beckett called the "abominable edition of the *Nouvelle Revue Française.*"[4]

Again, as in his former essay, Beckett begins with an essential point: "The Proustian equation is never simple. The unknown, choosing its weapons from a hoard of values, is also the unknowable." He discovers in Proust what he will find in those writers and artists he will champion over the succeeding generations: the recognition of the impossibility of ever piercing the center of human experience through any medium of expression. The void at the center of experience remains inviolate, unknown and unknowable. Beckett does attempt to give three reasons for the condition of impermeableness: time, memory, and habit. Time, he calls "that double-headed monster of damnation and salvation" that condemns characters to the condition of "victims and prisoners." Its effects are unavoidable. "There is no escape from yesterday because yesterday has deformed us or been deformed by us. The mood is of no importance. Deformation has taken place." People deform the days by altering the pictures of past actions which reside in the memories stored in the mind. They also are deformed by time because the self, the ongoing ego, is not in reality continuous but is constantly in flux, changing with the alternations of time.

Beckett strikes an important note here that will reverberate through his own writing: the recognition of the inconstancy of the self because of the vicissitudes of time. An individual may assume that the ego is fixed, but the assumption is only pretense perpetuated through agreements struck with the events of daily life, contracts providing a kind of blind belief in the reality of the self. Beckett calls these contracts habits. For Beckett habit is synonymous with the basic activities of daily life. "Breathing is habit. Life is habit. Or rather life is a succession of habits, since the individual is a succession of individuals." The habits of life provide safety; however, they preclude the possibility that people can change or alter in any way their self-induced fossilized positions. "Habit is the ballast that chains the dog to his vomit," Beckett says.

The world seems safe as long as individuals can perform their routine actions without thought or hesitation. It is only when new situations occur that the actual pretense of solidity and order slips and the true nature of human experience can be seen. Beckett calls these moments of slippage "the perilous zones in the life of the individual, dangerous, precarious, painful, mysterious and fertile, when for a moment the boredom of living is replaced by the suffering of being." He defines the ambiguous term "suffering of being" as "the free play of every faculty." It is not easily achieved; the old ego holds on fast to the protections afforded it by the habits of the past. "It disappears—with wailing and gnashing of teeth." Just as Beckett noted in his discussion of Joyce's work, individuals try hard to avoid the new, preferring to deal with the unusual or the unexpected as if it were a "neatly folded ham-sandwich," rendered familiar and unthreatening. Again, in *Proust,* Beckett indicates this natural tendency of human nature: "to avert the disaster, to create the new habit that will empty the mystery of its threat—and also of its beauty." The individual who experiences "the mystery" is made aware of the precariousness of his own sense of self and of his own mortality, two recognitions to be avoided at all costs.

Beckett then turns to memory, the third element that works against the struggle to grapple with the unknown. It is in this section of the essay that Beckett is most directly concerned with exegesis of Proustian texts, and his comments are substantiated by numerous examples. It was Proust who distinguished between two types of memory: one which the individual could consciously dredge up from the past, and one not prey to volition, which had a will of its own and could be triggered only through a reenactment of an event or sensory stimulus from the past. This memory, unlike the first, was not kept in readiness and so did not have the blemishes and smudges that continual handling causes. It sprang up unimpaired, clear as the event it encapsulated. Proust called this memory involuntary, which Beckett says "revealed what the mock reality of experience never can and never will reveal—the real." The term *real* is one Beckett does not use often but in the case of Proust he indicates that the images brought forth from their storage in the unconscious are as close to a total reduplication of experience as humans can achieve. Such clarity of vision is rarely experienced by Beckett characters; they suffer instead with memories that constantly alter and shift in time and almost obliterate the present by their force, yet are never fixed or clear.

Having explained the limits under which characters and writer must function and having given specific reasons for the impossibility of ever representing reality or plumbing the unknown, Beckett completes his essay by briefly touching on several points about the nature of the creative act itself. These comments offer some insights into the ways that Beckett, at least in 1930, viewed the role of the artist. First he denies once more the possibility of communication: "the attempt to communicate where no communication is possible is merely a simian vulgarity, or horribly comic, like the madness that holds a conversation with the furniture." The word *comic* used to describe the situation of one who tries to do what can't be done is important; the attempts at sharing ideas will in Beckett's later works take on just such comic and horrible proportions. What is true for characters is true for the artist himself. Beckett here paints the isolation that the creator experiences along with his creations: "For the artist who does not deal in surfaces, the rejection of friendship is not only reasonable, but a necessity. . . . The artistic tendency is not expansive, but a contraction. And art is the apotheosis of solitude." Whether Beckett is thinking about his own growing independence from Joyce or about the impending necessity of returning to the society of Dublin is not certain; but the necessity for solitude is clear. Beckett then states more directly than in any of his criticism the dilemma facing anyone who wishes to create in the contemporary world: "There is no communication because there are no vehicles of communication." Given this unalterable situation, Beckett sets the parameters of artistic possibility. "The only fertile research is excavatory, immersive, a contraction of the spirit, a descent. The artist is active, but negatively, shrinking from the nullity of extracircumferential phenomena, drawn in to the core of the eddy." The section ends with the elegiac pronouncement: "We are alone. We cannot know and we cannot be known." Fifty years later, in his novel *Company,* Beckett will utter the same final pronouncement about the human condition: "Alone."

*Proust* carries further several of the points first raised in "Dante": (1) the inseparability of form and content—"the one is a concretion of the other, the revelation of a world"; (2) the dichotomy between realistic and imaginative thought and language, what he calls in this essay Proust's impressionism; (3) the recognition of the absence of all absolutes. However, in *Proust* Beckett specifies that this loss of fixity extends to the very notion of self and the possible tools of any artistic expression. There seems no area of experience that does not fall under this heading.

## Critical Reviews, 1933–1938

The two preceding essays were written during Beckett's first stay in Paris, from 1928 to 1930. When he left Trinity College he decided to pursue the fledgling career he had embarked upon with the publication of the early essays. Between the time Beckett left Dublin for London, in 1933, and the time he settled permanently in Paris, at the end of 1937, he received commissions from such periodicals and newspapers as the *Bookman,* the *Spectator,* the *Dublin Magazine,* the *Irish Times,* and the *Criterion* to write critical reviews. Although these short essays are devoted to particular books and writers, they do provide important insights into Beckett's attitudes about art and literature during this period.

The first thing that can be noted about these reviews as a group is the uniqueness of their style. They are eclectic, flashy, and often quite witty in their dispensation of opinion and their play with words. For instance, in the 1934 Christmas edition of the *Bookman* Beckett wrote a review entitled "Ex Cathezra," on the book *Make It New,* a collection of essays by Ezra Pound. Describing one section of the book, Beckett comments, "The essay on the French poets is full of acumen and persimmon." The essay concludes with the following evaluation of the book as a whole: "It is no disparagement of Mr. Pound to observe that Sidney's 'verse no cause to poetry' has not been ousted but merely made to move up a little in the bed, by the 'blocks of verbal manifestation.' *Raum für alle.* . . ." The flippancy and erudition, juxtaposed in such an outrageous fashion, stand in clear distinction to other reviews in the issue, with titles such as "The Romance of Engineering," and "Alice in Orchestra Land." The review immediately preceding Beckett's is entitled "All About Art"—a title that Beckett would no doubt have found amusing—and it concludes summarily, "This book [John Dewey's *Art as Experience*] can be safely commended to all who take a keen delight in metaphysics."

Beckett employs the same style and voice in a review of the poems of the German poet Rilke, in the *Criterion,* July 1934. He faults the poet for " . . . the breathless petulance of so much of his verse (he cannot hold his emotion)." His final assessment of the poet is that "he has the fidgets, a disorder which may very well give rise, as it did with Rilke on occasion, to poetry of a high order. But why call the fidgets God, Ego, Orpheus, and the rest? This is a childishness to which German writers seem specially prone."

On a book concerning a poet closer to Beckett's taste—Dante—the critic complains about the writer's judgment of the Florentine: "the initial confusion distributes itself over the book. Analysis of what a man is not may conduce to an understanding of what he is, but only on condition that the distinction is observed." Beckett faults the writer, Giovanni Papini, for judging Dante for what he is not. In the conclusion of the review Beckett also comments on the writer's tendency to shower Dante with love. "But who wants to love Dante? We want to READ Dante—for example, his imperishable reference [Paolo-Francesca episode] to the incompatibility of the two operations."

A variation of the idea expressed in the Dante review begins a review entitled "The Essential and the Incidental," devoted to an evaluation of *Windfalls,* a collection of the writings of fellow Irishman Sean O'Casey. Beckett observes, "What is arguable of a period—that its bad is the best gloss on its good—is equally so of its representatives taken singly." He does not say here that the danger lies in keeping the two discrete; the idea, however, is implied. Beckett first points out what he believes are O'Casey's "incidentals" or weak areas, namely his fiction. He then turns to his plays, the "essentials" of O'Casey's canon. His comments on what he finds remarkable about O'Casey's achievements in the theater presage some of the elements Beckett will employ when he, too, turns to this medium. "Mr. O'Casey is a master of knockabout in this very serious and honourable sense—that he discerns the principle of disintegration in even the most complacent solidities, and activates it to their explosion. This is the energy of his theatre, the triumph of the principle of knockabout in situation . . . mind and world come asunder in irreparable dissociation."

Beckett's most substantial reviews of the period are those devoted to poetry. In an article entitled "Recent Irish Poetry," which appeared in the *Bookman* in 1934, he returns to the themes he had introduced in *Proust,* particularly the need to acknowledge the impossibility of representation of experience through the medium of art and human perception. He divides the current generation of poets into two categories. The "antiquarians," who continue in the same, traditional avenues, he dismisses. Beckett is interested in the second group of poets who "evince awareness of the new thing that has happened, or the old thing that has happened again, namely the breakdown of the object, whether current, historical, mythical or spook . . . [the] rupture of the lines of communication." Such writers, disparaged by William Butler Yeats as "fish that lie gasping on the shore," are the poets Beckett believes offer the possibility of a renewed Irish revival.

A poet Beckett admires is his friend Thomas McGreevy. In a review entitled "Humanistic Quietism" published in the *Dublin Magazine* July-September 1934, discussing McGreevy's poems, Beckett offers his most direct comments about what he considers to be the nature of poetry. He begins with the assertion, "All poetry, as discriminated from the various paradigms of prosody, is prayer. A poem is poetry and not Meistergesang, Vaudeville, Fragrant Minute, or any of the other collects for the day, in so far as the reader feels it to have been the only way out of the tongue-tied profanity."

An even longer essay, written four years later, when Beckett was living in Paris, is devoted to the works of Denis Devlin. Again, Beckett draws his guns against "the antiquarians"—here called "the monacodologists"—who rely on rationalism and the intellect and deny the power of the senses and imagination as the source of poetry. After offering examples from Devlin's poems that challenge "the country of Bentham," Beckett coyly suggests, "The time is perhaps not altogether too green for the vile suggestion that art has nothing to do with clarity, does not dabble in the clear and does not make clear, any more than the light of day (or night) makes the subsolar, lunar and stellar excrement." The notion of art seeking as its end not order or clarity but a depiction of the chaos is a theme that will run through much of the following criticism and will be central to Beckett's own works. He calls the struggle to grapple with the void "the extraordinary evocation of the unsaid by the said," and indicates that the only possible way to talk about the unknown is to talk of it through indirection. This idea will help explain why so much of Beckett's writing is devoted to conversations about shoes, the weather, mathematics: all those thing that are "other" and yet point, indirectly, to the central theme underlying all exchanges—recognition of the void.

Another essay of this period, Beckett's review of Jack B. Yeats's *The Amaranthers,* is entitled "An Imaginative Work!" and again there is the call for an art that escapes the carping of the rationalists, particularly the critics against whom Beckett first warned in his "Dante" essay. In this review he says of such "pigeon-holers," "The chartered recountants take the thing to pieces and put it together again. They enjoy it. The artist takes it to pieces and makes a new thing, new things. He must." The review ends with Yeats's call for imagination over controlled thought. It is this "imaginative work," with its exclamation point, that Beckett admires and is championing, work that does not provide answers or explanations, but rather underlines the impossibility of doing so.

"An Imaginative Work!" was published in *Dublin Magazine* in 1936; in 1937 Beckett wrote one of his most important critical statements, one never intended for publication. Perhaps because of that fact he is more direct in his statement of the type of writing he foresees and that he wishes to create himself. The document is a letter to a German acquaintance, Axel Kaun, written from Dublin in July 1937 three months after Beckett returned from a six-month trip to Germany and three months before he would leave permanently for Paris.

Beckett begins by refusing Kaun's request to translate into English some poems by the German poet Ringelnatz, offering the opinion that they aren't worth the effort. He then takes the occasion to talk of his own problems with writing during the period: "It is indeed becoming more and more difficult, even senseless, for me to write an official English. And more and more my own language appears to me like a veil that must be torn apart in order to get at the things (or perhaps the Nothingness) behind it. Grammar and Style. To me they seem to have become as irrelevant as a Victorian bathing suit or the imperturbability of a true gentleman. A mask."

Beckett states his hope that there will soon be a time when, instead of the writer attempting to write in the best language, language will be "efficiently used where it is being most efficiently misused." He continues, "As we cannot eliminate language all at once, we should at least leave nothing undone that might contribute to its falling into disrepute." Such assaults on language should be attempted "To bore one hole after another into it, until what lurks behind it—be it something or nothing—begins to seep through; I cannot imagine a higher goal for a writer today."

Beckett already notes the dissolution of traditional forms of painting and music and asks why a similar assault cannot be waged against writing. "Is there any reason why that terrible materiality of the word surface should not be capable of being dissolved, like for example the sound surface, torn by enormous pauses, of Beethoven's seventh Symphony, so that through whole pages we can perceive nothing but a path of sounds suspended in giddy heights, linking unfathomable abysses of silence?"

The problem now, Beckett says, is to find a method "by which we can represent this mocking attitude towards the word, through words." Although Joyce's *Finnegans Wake* is often cited as just such an experiment, Beckett denies that the *Wake* has this effect. "There it seems, rather, to be a matter of an apotheosis of the word. Unless perhaps Ascension to Heaven and Descent to Hell are somehow one and the same." It is important to note here that Beckett seems to be stating that the dancing of words which he cited as the central characteristic of the *Wake* in his earlier apologia is not to be confused with the tendency he now recognizes as crucial: the dissolution of words with words. It is as if Beckett were distancing himself from the writing of Joyce by clearly indicating that his journey will not be upward and outward, ascension, but downward and inward, a descent: not an expansion but a contraction.

The sentiments about capturing silence repeat what Beckett through his persona Belacqua stated in *Dream*: "The experience of my reader shall be between the phrases, in the silence, communicated by the intervals not the terms of the statement. . . . His experience shall be the menace, the miracle, the memory, of an unspeakable trajectory."

## Beckett on Art

Beckett has written critical articles about several artists, among them his friend Jack B. Yeats, brother of the poet William B. Yeats; the brothers Bram and Geer van Velde; Henri Hayden; and Avigdor Arikha.[5] The critical study that most directly relates to Beckett's own writing, however, is his "Three Dialogues with Georges Duthuit," first published in Duthuit's *Transition 49,* the magazine he published after the demise of Jolas's original publication. The essay is written in dialogue form, implying that it is a transcription of an actual conversation, but in fact Beckett wrote the entire discussion—Duthuit's comments and all—at the behest of the art critic and editor who had engaged in some preliminary conversations on the subject and had entreated Beckett to put them on paper.

In the essay Beckett takes the role of what his bibliographers Federman and Fletcher call "the intellectual clown." The exchanges concern three nonrepresentational artists: Pierre Tal Coat, Andre Masson, and Bram van Velde. Of the first, Beckett remarks, "Total object, complete with missing parts, instead of partial object. Question of degree." By indicating that the artist can fill in his canvas and totally represent his experience, Tal Coat distorts the limits of the form, which Beckett insists must be indicated by omissions and incompletion. He dismisses the works as "fundamentally those of previous painting straining to enlarge the statement of a compromise." These works, Beckett argues, have "never stirred from the field of the possible, however much they may have enlarged it." When he is asked by Duthuit, "What other plane can there be for the Maker?" Beckett admits that logically there is none. However, he still offers his hope for "an art turning from it in disgust, weary of its puny exploits, weary of pretending to be able, of being able, of doing a little better the same old thing, of going a little further along a dreary road." Beckett explains what art should offer, in a quotation often cited by his critics: "The expression that there is nothing to express, nothing with which to express, nothing from which to express, no power to express, no desire to express, together with the obligation to express."

Masson, the artist whom they turn to next, Beckett also dismisses because, while he describes the void, he does so from the outside "rather than in its clutch." Since Masson consciously wishes to plumb the void, Beckett believes that he will fail. It is only when the conversation turns to van Velde that Beckett sees the possibilities of the type of art he has described. "Yes I think he is the first to accept a certain situation and to consent to a certain act. . . . The situation is that of him who is helpless, cannot act, in the event cannot paint, since he is obligated to paint. The act is of him who, helpless, unable to act, acts, in the event paints, since he is obliged to paint." When Duthuit asks why the artist works under such an obligation, Beckett can provide no answer; he can only reply that the artist is helpless "Because there is nothing to paint and nothing to paint with." Van Velde, unlike the other two painters, is not afraid of leaving "the domain of the feasible," and of embracing the impotence of his form and of his vision; he does not turn tail "before the ultimate penury" of his medium. The stance that van Velde manifests is one that Beckett takes for his own; therefore, what he says about the painter in this essay is significant for those who would also understand Beckett's works. "Three Dialogues" provides the most direct description of the art of failure that Beckett has given us.

The body of Beckett's criticism, since it covers such a large stretch of time—from 1928 through 1966—cannot be taken as a whole; it continually evolves, as the selections indicate. In his comments in "Dante" Beckett writes that it is possible to find a way to overcome the limits of the verbal by doing what Joyce does, making "the words dance." In *Proust* he states that no vehicles of communication are possible and that the void does not allow for articulation. Finally, in "McGreevy on Yeats" he acknowledges that the "issueless predicament of existence" may be indicated not by direction but by indirection, the unsaid indicated by the said. What has remained unchanged in all these works is Beckett's adherence to an art of imagination and to the compulsion of creation despite the terrible limits such art must acknowledge and embody.

# *Chapter Three*
# Early Works

Samuel Beckett's apprenticeship was anomalous; it was both uncommonly brief and curiously long. Three years after abandoning his first novel, *Dream of Fair to Middling Women*—an erratic and rambling exercise—he was able to produce *Murphy,* a structured and coherent novel that stands among his most successful works; yet it took him over twenty years to gain a readership and following. When success finally did arrive, it arrived quickly. *Waiting for Godot* opened on 5 January 1953 and brought Beckett almost immediate attention by the literary world. Sixteen years later, a brief period to establish an international reputation, he was awarded the Nobel Prize for Literature. A reviewer for the first production of *Godot* noted, "Theatre-lovers rarely have the pleasure of discovering a new author worthy of the name."[1] When the words were written, the "new author" was already forty-seven, had been writing in several genres for a quarter of a century, and had produced sixteen short fictions, eight novels, two plays, and numerous poems and critical texts.

The following works from Beckett's first decade as an artist indicate two things: how quickly he was able to hone his talents and create significant fiction and poetry, and how early he had already developed an aesthetic—in theory if not in practice—governing the kind of writing he wished to create. All the major themes of the Beckett oeuvre are present in some form as early as 1935. To fully appreciate how they flourish and develop in Beckett's writing, it is important to trace their emergence in this early period of creation.

## Fiction

**"Assumption."** "Assumption," Beckett' first printed fiction, appeared in *transition,* vols. 16–17, along with "Dante . . . Bruno . Vico . . Joyce."[2] The three-and-a-half-page story sketches two conflicts facing his artist/hero: in society attempting "to gain himself a hearing," and alone, a self-imposed exile in a room, warring against "that wild rebellious surge that inspired violently toward realization in sound." Both public and private struggles are fought on the ground between speech and silence, the parameters of which are indicated in the first line of the story: "He could have shouted and could not." The speaker's ability to utter is held in check by "the involuntary inhibition" he imposes against the voice within—called "his prisoner," "the enemy," that which "tore at his throat." At first the character is seen among people, creating a ruse to win their attention. A man "who shrinks from argument," he attempts "whispering the turmoil down," a subtly manipulated effect. In the second and longer part of the story, it becomes clear that "the whispering" is more than an aesthetic pose; it is a life-preserving device leveled against the inner voice "that must destroy him."

In many ways, the nameless, nebulous figure in "Assumption" is the Beckettian Ur-character, a shadow man, presented without physical description or background, placed in an unclear situation, suffering from an ill-defined problem: a speaker that seeks a voice, and a voice that seeks an outlet from "that fleshlocked sea of silence." What the inner voice is we do not know; why it is feared we are not sure. Beckett depicts only the preoccupation of the character with the struggle and his awareness that "the very severity of his restrictions"—what he punningly calls the damning of the stream—makes the inevitable "flood," when it comes, more destructive. The character says he "knew the day would come when it could no longer de denied."

In the story it is Woman, capitalized, unnamed, eyes "green flecked," wearing "a hat of faded green felt" who arrives within the artist's sanctum, "carelessly," turning on the light, loosening the man's control, and providing a release that is described in sexual and religious terms: "Until at last, for the first time, he was unconditioned by the Satanic dimensional Trinity, he was released, acheived [*sic*] the blue flower, Vega, GOD . . ." With release comes the feared sound that can no longer be denied. The breaking of the inhibition leveled against the inner voice is achieved at a price, however. The last line reads, "They found her caressing his wild, dead hair."

Although the work is brief, the imagery more arcane, and the theme more allusive than in later fiction, "Assumption" portrays the central skirmish Beckett figures repeatedly will fight: an external I holding at bay an imprisoned, objective me whose constant inner buzzing threatens destruction; a schismatic self doing combat over the final possession of the singular, voiced pronoun *I*.

***Dream of Fair to Middling Women.*** In "Assumption" the character's struggles are undermined by the interruptive force of a woman. Against her the man is helpless; he can do no more than "sketch a tired gesture of acceptation." Three years later another Beckett persona sketches the same gesture, this time against onslaughts by multiple women. The work, *Dream of Fair to Middling Women,* was begun in the spring of 1932 after Beckett left Dublin and traveled to Germany, temporarily settled in Paris where the writing took place, and returned once more to Dublin. The book, a kind of bildungsroman—a youth's search for adventure and maturity—follows its hero Belacqua Shuah on an identical path.

The odd name Beckett gives his first persona is a grafting of Italian and Hebrew. Belacqua (beautiful water) is taken from Dante's *Purgatorio,* where, in canto 4, the pilgrim comes upon the Florentine lutemaker, condemned in death to Antepurgatory for his sin in life: sloth. Repeating the words of Aristotle *"Sedendo et quiescendo anima efficitur prudens,"* (Sitting quietly, the soul acquires wisdom), Belacqua accepts his punishment, to do in death what he has sought to do in life—nothing. It is an apt name for Beckett's slothful hero. The character's last name, Shuah, is derived from two biblical sources: Shuah, the grandfather of Onan (Gen. 38:2), and, spelled differently in Hebrew, Shuach, the son of Abraham and Ketura (Gen. 25:2). Besides offering the narcissistic and masturbatory associations of onanism, the name also provides other indications of Belacqua's personality. "Shuah" means to card, hackle, or be abrasive; to be discouraged and in despair; and—when in the latter spelling—to bow down, bend, or sink. All these definitions fit Belacqua, who is both acerbic and beleagured.

The title of the novel is also a blend, parodying the praise of good women offered by Chaucer in "The Legend of Good Women" (text G) and by Tennyson in "Dream of Fair Women." It takes its epigraph from the former: "A thousand sythes have I herd men telle / That ther is joye in heven, and peyne in helle; / But-" Beckett does not complete the line from the "Legend" prologue. In the original the "but" leads to Chaucer's recognition that both heaven and hell must finally be taken on faith since "for by assay there may no man it preve." It is in a world limited on both sides by man's verifiable powers that Beckett sets up his fiction. He also shifts from the conclusion of Tennyson's poem, which in the original states: "Because all, words tho' cull'd with choicest art / Failing to give the bitter of the sweet / Wither beneath the palate, and the heart / Faints, faded by its heat." In Beckett's story "the bitter of the sweet" is amply displayed, and if the heart wanes, it covers its failure by the feint of irony and sarcasm.

The novel begins when Belacqua takes leave of his home in Dublin because "he thought it would be nice to be slavered and slabbered on elsewhere for a change." He travels to Vienna to meet his love, the Smeraldina Rima (the little Emerald), so named for her penchant for green, a possible allusion to the young woman in "Assumption," and both most likely derived from Beckett's cousin Peggy Sinclair. Sex for the slothful hero "was a bloody business." Belacqua courts Smerry—his affectionate name for his hostess—until "She raped him. Then everything went kaputt." Bel quickly retreats from her amatory advances, no longer able to keep their relations "pewer and above bawd."

Part 2 finds him in Paris, seeking some distance between himself and the physically impetuous girl. However, from afar, she seems more desirable—and less threatening—than the even more voracious Syra-Cusa. Therefore, when called back to Vienna to spend the New Year's holiday, Belacqua accepts, despite a physical indisposition. The visit once more proves disastrous, and after a calamitous New Year's Eve party, the couple part, with Belacqua seeking refuge in Dublin. In Part 3, the longest section of the novel, he falls under the spell of yet another woman, the cerebral, ethereal Alba (White). The work ends with a long description of their courtship, the Dublin environs where they spend their time, the intellectual community of which Bel is a reluctant member, and a satirical sketch of a literary soirée, which draws together the many figures introduced in the section. The last image is of Belacqua slowly walking the streets of Dublin in a wet, early morning after leaving the Alba, whom he has seen home from the party.

The novel breaks off at this point, on page 214. Only two excerpts have been printed: an eight-page fragment, "Sedendo et Quiesciendo (*sic*)," in *transition* 21, describing Belacqua's journey to Vienna for the New Year, and a thirteen-line prose selection, "Text," from the same section.[3] Both illustrate the Joycean influence: arcane language, neologisms, foreign terms, puns, and circumlocutions. Unfortunately, both selections give a distorted picture of the whole.

They are among the most difficult, least accessible parts of the entire work, and they omit what is the most interesting aspect of "Dream," the running commentary of the narrator, who constantly interjects himself between the fiction and the reader, offering theories on the nature of writing, the difficulty of character depiction, and the relation between fiction and life.

The first Beckettian narrator is more than an intrusive storyteller, however; he becomes almost a character in his own right. He is not to be confused with the author Samuel Beckett, to whom he alludes twice in the work. The device of a foregrounded figure, a storyteller describing him, and an ever-more-distant author who creates them all is one technique Beckett will employ repeatedly. In later works the persona becomes fused with the narrator/writer, and both appear as parts of an ever-more-elusive creator of them all. "We (consensus, here and hereafter, of me)," Belacqua says.

The same plurality is applied within the work and within individual characters. Of Belacqua, the narrator observes, "At his simplest he was trine. Just think of that. A trine man! Centripetal, centrifugal and . . . not." The "not" becomes the most difficult form to describe. How to capture such a figure is the dilemma of the narrator who compares literary characters to a musical composition, what he calls the Chinese *liŭ-liū,* a sound embodying numerous notes simultaneously. Human beings are not so easily represented, the narrator realizes.

Beckett introduces the problem that will plague all his writer/protagonists, as it plagues the artist himself: how to write a fiction that approximates life, if life cannot be simply reduced to neat categorial causes and effects. If "the reality of the individual . . . is an incoherent reality and must be expressed incoherently," as Belacqua says, then the form such a literature must take is one that points not to unity as in a Balzac novel but to the incoherence that resides at its center.

Beckett intends that his novel will reflect this incoherence. It has constant stops and starts, interruptions by the narrator, shifts in characters, introduction of figures that seem to appear from nowhere and disappear for no reason. In *Dream* Beckett repeats the goal he presented in the letter to Axel Kaun, and will rephrase in "Three Dialogues": to say the unsayable. At this point in Beckett's writing, however, he still has difficulty filling the interstices in such a way that they point to the silence that lies behind them. Instead, he employs his narrator as a kind of instructor, pointer in hand, who says such things as, "The only unity in the story is, please God, an involuntary unity"; or "the fact of the matter is we don't know where we are in the story," or after a particularly long digression (the one appearing in "Sedendo and Quiesciendo" [*sic*]), "Perhaps the pen ran away, don't for a moment imagine that Belacqua is down the drain."

Fragmentation in the structure of the novel is mirrored by the fragmentation in the unity of the character, alive in his "trineness." Like the man in "Assumption" and like the numerous Beckett characters who follow, Belacqua suffers "from being born a son of Adam and cursed with an insubordinate mind." And when, like other Beckett avatars, he seeks refuge in his room "at home to nobody," he is exemplifying the wish of them all: to escape the body, to have literally *no body*. In a "tunnel" or "umbra" where thoughts cease and voices hush is where Belacqua tries to exist. In one scene we see him on his bed, pressing his body down into the mattress, trying to achieve this state, but Belacqua in the very act of seeking it is aware that such a condition is difficult to obtain, impossible to maintain. Total immersion in the dark, he finds, is finally impossible. Away from the glare of others, alone in a room, the character still must contend with the self-scrutiny that never ceases, the inner voice against which he must constantly battle.

***More Pricks Than Kicks.*** *Dream of Fair to Middling Women* was never published, but from the aborted fiction Beckett salvaged two stories: "The Smeraldina's Billet Doux," and "A Wet Night," a slightly revised version of the Dublin Christmas party story that ended the original novel. He also transferred his protagonist, Belacqua Shuah, to the center of the series of ten stories that form a loose narrative about the youth, maturity, and death of the character.

The title of the collection, *More Pricks Than Kicks,* is taken from Acts 9:5 where the voice of Jesus speaks to Saul of Tarsus, who later becomes the disciple Paul: "I am Jesus whom thou persecutest; it is hard for thee to kick against the pricks." The title implies the difficulty of recalcitrance against pain, of kicking or fighting against adversity, or pricks; a sexual pun playing on the words pleasure and phallus; and a reference to the original source of the Belacqua persona, Dante's *Divine Comedy*. The first of the ten stories in the collection, "Dante and the Lobster," begins: "It was morning and Belacqua was stuck in the first of the canti of the moon," a reference to canto 2 of the *Paradiso,* in which Dante is being instructed about the nature of heavenly bodies by his guide and inspiration Beatrice. In response to his incorrect assumptions about the causes of the spots on the moon, Beatrice explains to Dante: "If the judgment of mortals err where the key of sense fails to unlock, surely the shafts of wonder should not *prick* thee henceforth, since even following after the senses thou seest that reason's wings are short"[4] (italics mine). Like the Chaucer epigraph in "Dream," the words indicate the limits of human apprehension, the "prick" felt in the absence of surety and divine wisdom.

"Dante and the Lobster"—which along with the ninth story, "Yellow," is the most thoroughly developed and sustained in the collection—sets the theme for what follows: the difficulty of apprehending divine mercy while bearing the all too familiar burden of human suffering. Belacqua is first seen wrestling with the *Paradiso,* in a section that contains an image of Cain whose marks, Belacqua says, indicate not only his outcast state but "the first stigma of God's pity, that an outcast might not die quickly." Without a Beatrice to guide his deliberations, Belacqua is lost and puts aside exercises of the mind in favor of the demands of the stomach. What follows is his elaborate daily ritual for preparing his lunch. Yet suffering and pariahs follow him. He cuts his bread over a newspaper carrying the face of McCabe, a murderer whose plea for clemency has been rejected and who is to hang that day. The details of the preparation of the bread and cheese are colored with the language of violence and death: the bread is sawed through, the remaining "stump" put "back into prison"; its "spongy," "alive" white is soon converted into a black char that burns "that fat white look off its face." The cheese that will be placed between the waiting toast is "cadaverous" sweating with "A faint fragrance of corruption."

Having eaten his lunch—a host touched with the tang of death as well as gorgonzola—the hero turns to the remainder of the day's activities: picking up a lobster for his aunt's dinner and taking an Italian lesson. During his lesson Belacqua returns to thoughts of Dante and asks his teacher about a phrase containing a pun that has bothered him: *"qui vive la pietà quando è ben morta"* (Here pity / piety lives when it is dead). "Why not piety and pity both, even down below?" he thinks. As if to answer the question, Beckett provides an edifying culmination to the story through the fate of the lobster. When his aunt opens the package that Belacqua has been carrying all afternoon, and has even saved at one pont from the attack of a cat, he is horrified to see the creature move. "But it's not dead . . . you can't boil it like that," he protests. Finally he is quieted with the thought that "it's a quick death, God help us all." The story ends with the narrator's brief coda: "It is not."

"Dante and the Lobster" provides the theme for the stories that follow: the "lingering dissolution" and the gradual crawl toward the inevitable pot. As the story makes clear, there will be no Beatrice to offer commentary or divine enlightenment on the journey. Instead, Beckett provides his hero with a collection of decidedly earthbound Dublin women, who may climb hills with Belacqua but never lead him to paradise. In the second story, "Fingal," Winnie shares an afternoon's outing to the Hill of Feltrim, from whose rise they see the Portrane Lunatic Asylum. "My heart's right there," Belacqua says, before depositing her at its gates and making a hasty retreat to Dublin on a comandeered bicycle. In story five, "Love and Lethe," Ruby Tough accompanies Belacqua to the top of another hill, where they intend to carry out a suicide pact, leaving a death note, written on the back of an old license plate, that says, "TEMPORARILY SANE." In "A Wet Night," the fourth tale, the climb is strictly social and the woman is Alba Perdue, taken from *Dream*.

The most direct allusion to the lack of guide in modern Dublin occurs in story three, "Ding Dong," in which Belacqua, sitting in a pub, is accosted by an unnamed woman selling "Seats in heaven, tuppence a piece, four fer a tanner." The narrator comments on her celestial attributes: A "white voice," "her face . . . so full of light." Yet instead of illuminating anything for the hapless hero, all she can do in response to his queries is whirl her arms and say, "Heaven goes round . . . and round and round and round and round and round." Belacqua is left to whisper "Amen . . . into his dead porter."

Belacqua's aborted suicide attempt in "Love and Lethe" ends, instead, in an act of love. Placed precisely in the middle of the collection of stories, the tale signals a shift for him. As if imbibing of the sacred river of the title—reputed to offer forgetfulness and forgiveness for those returning to the world of the living—Belacqua leaves the hills, returns to the flat lands and marriage with three women: Lucy in "Walking Out," Thelma bboggs in "What a Misfortune," and the Smeraldina, transferred from *Dream,* somewhere before the concluding story "Draff," where she is presented as his surviving widow. In keeping with the offhand narrative of the stories, we are told that she became his wife after the death of Thelma who "perished of sunset and honeymoon that time in Connemara." Again, as in *Dream,* it seems the hero's fate is to be surrounded by women. In the ninth tale, "Yellow," where Belacqua is in the hospital for a routine operation, they proliferate in such numbers that he seems to succumb as much from their smothering as from the mistaken administration of the anesthesia that takes his life.

While women are present in each tale, it is the figure of Belacqua who holds the collection together. He is more accepting of them than in the earlier work—marrying three and outliving two—but no less caustic in his opinions: "They were all the same when it came to the pinch—clods." He also bears the same general characteristics noted in the earlier "Dream" and ascribed to later Beckett heroes: poor skin, spavined gait, weak eyes, "feet in ruins," and grotesque interior. He has a love for bicycles, is "sinfully indolent," and desires "to lie on his back in the dark." He attempts travel hoping "he could give the Furies the slip by merely setting himself in motion"; however, travel only leads to despair and "a long face."

*More Pricks Than Kicks* sprang from *Dream* but there are important differences. Gone is the elaborate language of the former work. For example, in the Christmas party scene, Beckett originally wrote: "But the wind had fallen, as it so often does with us after midnight, a negligence on the part of Aeolus alluded to in the most bitter terms by mariners of yore, as can be read in any of the old sea journals that constitute so important a fund of our civic records." The same description in "A Wet Night" is pruned to: "But the wind had dropped, as it so often does in Dublin when all the respectable men and women whom it delights to annoy have gone to bed."

Beckett also continues systematically to omit what in traditional literature is the basic fodder of fiction—births, love, marriage, deaths, murder—replacing the subjects with exhaustive descriptions of events that are never the events the reader expects. While Beckett minutely describes the activities of a dog in "Walking Out," he barely mentions the accident that causes his fiancée Lucy to become an invalid. Deaths are reported in an offhand fashion, the preparation of a meal in mock heroic detail. The result is humor and the creation of a world askew, where facts do not lead to understanding, causes produce no discernible effects, accidents not plans prevail, and the only undisputed lesson to be learned is "the world goes round and round and round and round . . ." Belacqua stays stuck in the first of the canti in the moon. No metamorphosis from a Saul to a Paul, rather a "boomerang" out and back returning to the recognition of the human constant: "Where were we ever?" "Where we were as we were." No change, or if any, only a gradual deterioration, is a constant theme. How then is one to act in the face of such a bleak prognosis? In the story "Yellow" Beckett provides an answer. Belacqua, awaiting his operation,debates between the two attitudes appropriate to his condition: "Was it to be laughter or tears? It came to the same thing in the end, but which was it to be *now*?" Belacqua fixes on the former for "weeping in this charnel house would be misconstrued." In *More Pricks Than Kicks*—and the bulk of the Beckett canon—laughter prevails; it doesn't alter but it prevails, as the characters prevail through its meliorative effect. "So his course was clear. He would arm his mind with laughter, laughter is not quite the word but it will have to serve," Belacqua thinks. Though not quite the word, the laugh, sometimes bitter sometimes forced, is the reverberating sound that bounces off the wall of the "charnel houses" where Beckett's writing is set.

**"A Case in a Thousand."** In the last story of *More Pricks Than Kicks,* the narrator in reminiscence of T.S. Eliot observes that "the bang is better than the whimper, it is easier to do." Yet the collection of stories offers no such explosion; it peters out in "draff." The technique is not gratuitous; it follows Beckett's intention to write a literature without culmination, where "the only kind of unity . . . is thank God an involuntary unity." In such a fiction any "BANGS"—like Lucy's accident or Bel's demise—take place offstage, and are relayed in the most offhand manner. Beckett carries this technique even further in the brief story "A Case in a Thousand," which he published in the *Bookman,* August 1934.[5] The story is simple. A young man, much like Belacqua in "Yellow," has been admitted to the hospital for an operation on the glands of his neck. The surgeon, a Dr. Bok, consults a young doctor named Nye, who "belonged to the sad men." When Nye meets the boy's mother—a constant visitor at her son's bedside—he discovers that she is his old nanny. "You were always in a great hurry to grow up so's you could marry me" she remembers, and the narrator explains that she "did not disclose the trauma at the root of this attachment."

As the boy's life slips, the doctor, who must decide on the advisability of a second operation, lies on the bed beside his patient, in a trance, while the mother sits averting her eyes. The operation is performed, the boy dies, yet the mother continues her vigil outside the hospital waiting to see the doctor. In the climactic scene the doctor approaches the woman and says, "There's something I've been wanting to ask you," and she replies, "I wonder would that be the same thing I've been wanting to tell you ever since that time you stretched out on his bed." Rather than apprise the reader of the question or the answer, the narrator says, "Thereupon she related a matter connected with his earliest years, so trivial and intimate that it need not be enlarged on here. . . ." The reader is left to share the vantage point of the doctors and nurses who have been gazing out a window on the scene from some remove, left to speculate without surety.

In this story Beckett refines two fictional devices. First, he pares down his style from the earlier works, omitting all literary allusions and elaborate description. Second, he calls direct attention to the fact that the reader's expectations of, and thirst for, details will not be satisfied, any more than those of the attending doctors and nurses who become a chorus conjecturing on the possible relationship between the old nanny and the young doctor. Only oblique references to the possible trauma are given: a recurrent mention of peppermint creams, a Wasserman's test Nye is about to perform on an old schoolfellow. The movement of the woman's walk and the configuration of the handle of her umbrella are described in exact detail, while the precise connection between the two people is never stated. It may be Beckett's way of calling attention to the impossibility of fixing in language experiences of the past that do not readily offer themselves up for fictional representation. While this slight story adds little to the Beckett canon, it does anticipate the spareness and method of indirection implicit in the important work to follow—*Murphy*.

***Murphy.*** Aside from "A Case in a Thousand," the other fiction that comes from Beckett's two-year stay in London, from December 1933 to December 1935, is *Murphy,* his first published novel. It bears the clear marks of the locale in which it was written: areas around World's End, where Beckett took rooms; the Round Pond in Hyde Park, where he observed kite flyers similar to Mr. Kelly and habitués like Miss Dew, who would come to feed the grazing sheep; Oxford Street, down which he could have ridden, as Murphy did, with closed eyes enjoying the new six-wheeled buses; a bench halfway between Battersea and Albert Bridges, where he might have been approached by prostitutes such as Celia, who often conducted business there; and the Bethlehem Royal Hospital in nearby Beckenham—the model for the fictional Magdalen Mental Mercyseat—where he did visit his Dublin friend Dr. Geoffrey Thompson, a psychiatric resident.

The novel is Beckett's most geographically precise work; whenever an event takes place, the reader is usually provided with exact details about streets, buildings, nearest intersections, and even underground stops. If city topography is the warp on which the story is woven, equally exact temporal details provide the woof. Although he does not give them in chronological order, Beckett intersperses his narrative with dates and times, particularly those occurring during the forty-four days from Thursday, 12 September to Saturday, 26 October 1935, when the events in the thirteen chapters of the novel occur. Not content with these elements of punctilious verisimilitude, he goes even further and charts the celestial map that marks the progress of the story, providing astrological signs and moon phases.

Yet all this welter of information, that requires a kind of mental juggling to sort and remember, does not illuminate the story Beckett tells. Facts seem chosen randomly; they do not explain anything. For example, at the beginning of chapter 2, Celia is introduced through a list of twenty items concerning her physical appearance, from height to calf and knee size. Next to two items—age and instep—Beckett writes "unimportant." Why calf size should be significant and instep irrelevant is never explained; why age is dismissed and the measurements of upper arm provided is left to speculation. "The facts—let us have facts, plenty of facts," the narrator in *Dream* requested. In *Murphy* there is no paucity of details, but they provide obstacles to be sidestepped, irrelevancies to be hurdled. They indicate how easily facts suffice for truth in life, how complacently seekers collect data hoping that they will provide answers to the dilemma of living. Like Belacqua, who "may be described but not circumscribed," Murphy, Watt, and the characters that spring from their shadows are easily described but never circumscribed, and they in turn find the world in which they live inexplicable despite "facts, plenty of facts."

The narrative, too, undermines traditional form: it begins in medias res and skirts back and forth among three different but interrelated plots. The foremost concerns the central character, Murphy, no first name given, lately of Dublin, with "no profession or trade," "a strict non-reader," called by others "a seedy solipsist," calling himself "a chronic emeritus," whose favorite color is yellow, the color of the bow tie that adorns his otherwise drab, "æruginous coloured suit." He had been studying in Cork under a Mr. Neary in hope of correcting an "irrational" heart, that alternates between wild palpitations and near surcease. In February he meets Miss Counihan who "for an Irish girl . . . was exceptionally anthropoid," and almost immediately is off to London, "the Mecca of every young aspirant to fiscal distinction," to gain for the lady—the lady says—"a habitation meet for her." In June Murphy, now more "suspirant" than "aspirant," standing transfixed between the star chart in his hands and the heavenly field it describes, is spotted by Celia, a prostitute, who quickly makes Murphy her own, living with him first in a small mews in West Brompton and later, when that is condemned, in a room on Brewery Road. All goes well except for one irritant: Murphy's refusal to work. The small amount he receives from padding the rent bill, paid by "his Dutch uncle" Mr. Quigley, is sufficient for his meager needs but not enough to support two without Celia taking up her old trade, something she is loathe to do. After much haranguing, Murphy agrees to seek employment in what he calls "the bigger world" where "*Quid pro quo* was cried as wares and the light never waned the same way twice," but only after he is provided with a star chart that gives him some direction and hints of the dangers he may encounter. After several weeks of half-hearted searching, he comes upon an acquaintance from Ireland, "the pot poet" Augustus Ticklepenny, lately employed as orderly at the Magdalen Mental Mercyseat, in a job he abhors. Murphy is quickly convinced to take Ticklepenny's position and leaves Celia to take up residence.

"Here was the race of people he had long since despaired of finding," Murphy thinks when he meets the patients, inhabitants of "the little world," the microcosmic world of the mind which he desires to enter. In the presence of such people he feels "respect and unworthiness." Murphy is particularly drawn to Mr. Endon, a certified psychotic, totally cut off from the society around him. The two men often play chess, and one particular game, played on the first night of Murphy's night duty in the wards, is given in exact detail. It is after this game that Murphy returns to his garret room and because of a failure to light the radiator, which dispenses gas to the unventilated room, dies of combustion caused by the candle near his bed. According to his wishes, conveyed in a letter, he is cremated; however, his ashes, instead of being flushed down the toilet in the Abbey Theatre in Dublin, as he desired, are accidentally scattered on the floor of a nearby pub. The end of Murphy.

The second plot involves four people whose "medians . . . or whatever the hell they are, meet in Murphy." They are the teacher Neary, who in Murphy's absence courts and tries to win Miss Counihan; the much desired Miss Counihan, who will not give in to Neary's proposals until she has found her missing suitor; Mr. Cooper, employed by Neary to ferret out information in London about the absent Murphy; and Needle Wylie, a former pupil of Neary, who also desires Miss Counihan and the financial support a liaison with her should bring. All travel singly and in groups from Cork to Dublin to London, ever after the elusive Murphy. They eventually track him to his room, find Celia there, Murphy gone, about to be extinguished by unextinguished gas. Their trails end in the mortuary of the Magdalen Mental Mercyseat where they go to identify the body.

The third plot focuses on Celia, who lives with and loves Murphy; her aged kite-flying uncle, Mr. Kelly, whom she visits and often pushes to Hyde Park; and the landlady Miss Carridge, who befriends her in Murphy's absence. There is one other character whose life touches Celia, an unseen figure referred to as "the old boy" whose footfalls Murphy and Celia hear in the room above theirs. He commits suicide on the day Murphy gets his job, and Celia moves into his room when Murphy leaves. Celia, too, travels to the mortuary and makes the only positive identification of Murphy's body, citing a birthmark on his buttocks. It is with her that the story ends when, in chapter 13, she once more returns to her trade and to her position as wheeler of her uncle.

While the details of the novel seem simple enough to follow—a humorous detective tale with characters in hot pursuit of an elusive hero—the focus of the story is elsewhere. Beckett is primarily concerned with the mind of his character, "the little world" into which Murphy desires to escape. In chapter 6 Beckett interrupts the progress of the narrative to offer a description of this skullscape, a self-enclosed entity, with little contact to the outer world. It is divided into three zones: light, drawn from the material world; half-light, an antepurgatory of sloth to which he tries to escape; and a dark zone, "a mote in the dark of absolute freedom." When the book opens, Murphy is found in his favorite position: sitting naked in a rocking chair, bound by scarves, attempting through the regular back-and-forth motion, to leave his physical body behind and become "free in the mind," in that second zone of dream which Belacqua, too, attempted to enter, face pressed downward on his bed, in a perpetual umbra of grey. This state, achieved rarely, seems to suffice for Murphy until he enters the Magdalen Mental Mercyseat, and meets Mr. Endon who seems to offer the end Murphy seeks, a total immersion in a world of nothingness, the true black. While among the patients, Murphy remembers the words of the Belgian philosopher Geulincx, "Where you are worth nothing, there you should want nothing." It is to achieve a state of nothingness beyond wants and desires that Murphy seeks to enter the world of the insane.

At the beginning of chapter 9, when Murphy starts his work, Beckett offers another epigraph, this time from the French novelist Malraux, "Il est difficile à celui qui vit hors du monde de ne pas rechercher les siens." (It is difficult for one who lives outside of the world not to seek his own kind.) For Murphy, his own kind are the psychotics whom he presumes "one and all to be having a glorious time," or would be if it were not for the intrusions of the psychiatrists determined to bring them back alive to the big world of reality. For Murphy, the insane possess an enviable "self-immersed indifference to the contingencies of the contingent world. . . ." He agrees with Neary's assessment earlier in the book that insanity is "the next best thing to never having been born," a state much desired by Beckett personae.

If success is measured by total indifference to the outer world, then Mr. Endon, "a schizophrenic of the most amiable variety," is supreme master. A tiny man, with an immense head, dressed in a scarlet dressing gown, with rings on his fingers, he stands as a model to Murphy, "as Narcissus to his fountain." But like the mythical figure, Murphy is destroyed by the image that he sees, a reflection of the self he would possess—and cannot. In the detailed chess game that forms the climax of the novel Murphy can only follow the moves of the totally self-immersed Endon, who takes no notice of the positions of his opponent. After all the chess men have been returned to their places, none taken, none victorious, Murphy looks deep into the unseeing eyes of his double and realizes that no contact can be made; Murphy can never will himself to be Endon. "The last Mr. Murphy saw of Mr. Endon was Mr. Murphy unseen by Mr. Endon. This was also the last Murphy saw of Murphy." Thus, Beckett ends the calamitous chess game that foreshadows Murphy's demise. Having looked into the face of total indifference and self-absorption, Murphy realizes his own inability to obliterate the outer world, short of death. Earlier, when Murphy had insisted that Ticklepenny provide gas for his garret domicile at the hospital, he mused on the etymological connections between gas and chaos. "Could it turn a neurotic into a psychotic. No. Only God could do that." Murphy dies of gas, the neurotic unable to become psychotic. Whether by accident or by suicide as his death note implies, Murphy's death marks his failure to enter that "little world of the mind."

The above description of Murphy's journey to such an awareness sounds bleak. In fact, Murphy's quest for the grail of oblivion is humorous, even more than Belacqua's lethargic thrusts in a similar direction. The humor comes from several sources. First Beckett creates a number of grotesque characters who circle the hero. There is Mr. Cooper, whose "only visible human characteristic was a morbid craving for alcoholic depressant; Miss Rosie Dew, "single woman, by appointment to Lord Gall of Wormwood," who suffers from Duck's disease, "a distressing pathological condition in which the thighs are suppressed and the buttocks spring directly from behind the knees"; and Miss Carridge, the landlady, a woman of few words, and strong body odor.

Another source of humor in the book is Beckett's pointed satirical thrusts at societal foibles and practices, particularly those of the Irish. In *Dream* Beckett had already introduced a character that becomes a stock figure in his fiction—the law enforcement man. Whether a policeman, a guard on a wharf, or protector of statues in the General Post Office, the figure is invariably stupid, bullish, and prone to sadism—usually at the expense of the hero. In *Murphy* he is specifically Irish. The narrator remarks, "the skill is really extraordinary with which analphabetes, especially those of Irish education, circumvent their dread of verbal commitments."

More scathing is Beckett's scorn for doctors, particularly psychiatrists, prompted perhaps by the fact that during the writing of the novel Beckett was a reluctant analysand. He makes his hospital attendants grotesque caricatures or ludicrous dupes and makes the patients seem alive in a far more pleasant and ordered world. The debate between the mortician and doctor over who will pronounce Murphy dead shows the inanity of medical hierarchies; and the sadism of the brothers Clinch points to cruelty masked as treatment.

A less apparent humorous device is Beckett's fragmentation of the narrative, where the reader is left scrambling among details trying to tie various threads of the multiple narrative together. For instance, at the end of chapter 5, when Murphy is offered his job, he returns home to tell Celia the news, and finds her spread-eagled on the bed. The chapter concludes with the one-sentence paragraph, "A shocking thing had happened." Before we are told what the shocking thing is, Beckett breaks in with his chapter on Murphy's mind and a following chapter on the Dublin cohorts. It is not until twenty-six pages later that we learn that the shocking occurrence was the suicide of "the old boy." Raising traditional expectations in fiction, employing the standard devices that further the narrative, and then ironically sabotaging them, allows Beckett to comment on standard fiction and to provide a situation in which the involved readers are forced to laugh at themselves for their insatiable need to know and for the sensationalist traps into which they so willingly fall.

"All the puppets in this book whinge sooner or later, except Murphy, who is not a puppet," the narrator says in one of his brief comments. The assortment of grotesques described above are puppets, designed for humor and contrast with Murphy. One character, however, emerges as something more than a foil. Celia is one of Beckett's most vivid female figures, a woman given dimensionality and nobility not afforded other Beckett women in the early fiction. While Murphy is an intellectual, Celia is an accessible everyperson, her reactions to Murphy and the world are those with which a reader can quickly identify. For example, after listening to Murphy describing the freedom he seeks, the narrator says that Celia "felt as she felt so often with Murphy, splattered with words that went dead as soon a they sounded; each word obliterated before it had time to make sense, by the word that came next; so that in the end she did not know what had been said. It was like difficult music heard for the first time." Celia's struggles to understand and her failures at decoding the words she hears are the struggles of one who remains in the larger world, but recognizes all too well its limitations. Unlike the other characters in the book, blindly complacent, Celia makes the attempt, albeit unsuccessful, to leave the physical world, employing the rocking chair Murphy temporarily leaves behind. At the end of the book, however, she returns to the world of quid pro quo and its most representative profession: prostitution. Yet as she slowly wheels her uncle away from the park, in the last image of the book and one of Beckett's most poignant passages, she is presented as a youthful Mother Courage in subdued Beckett tones.

That the book ends with Celia and not Murphy is in keeping with *More Pricks* that ends with Belacqua's widow. Murphy's ashes lie on the barrom floor, finally the Nothing that they could not be in life, and it is Celia, who must continue, as all do in the macrocosm, toiling along "the narrow path." The beauty of this end undercuts the harsh humor of what leads to it. Again in Beckett we find the laugh stopped by the tear, as the tear is halted by the ever-present chortle, the grotesque complementing the tragic.

## Drama

In 1935, while Beckett was still living in London and working on *Murphy,* he visited Litchfield, the birthplace of the eighteenth-century writer Samuel Johnson. The following year, once more back in Dublin and struggling with the completion of his novel, Beckett turned to a new project, a play that he called "the Johnson fantasy."[6] Just why the life of the Great Cham should have interested the young Beckett in 1936 is difficult to determine, and Beckett offers no explanation. There are certain parallels. The name Samuel Johnson, like Samuel Beckett and his first persona Belacqua Shuah, has thirteen letters, the birth number Beckett often wove into his works. Both Sams left home and traveled to London at the age of twenty-eight, still unsure of the course their lives would take. Both suffered from skin disorders, night fevers, and forms of melancholy, something that plagued Johnson throughout his career, and Beckett during this period. While Johnson is usually described as convivial, Boswell reports that he often lapsed into impenetrable silences among people, particularly loquacious ones—a habit Beckett shared. Beckett records this tendency in his copious notes on Johnson, along with another anecdote that may have reminded him of his own associations with Joyce—the ritual of Johnson and his fellow writer Cowper sitting, like ghosts, without conversation for long periods.

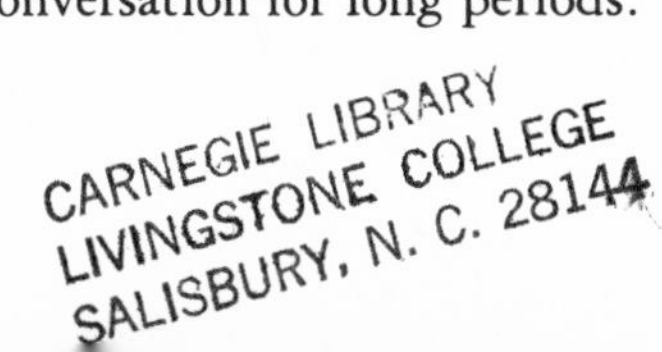

Both Johnson and Beckett also shared some interests: swimming, long walks, dogs, and a great fondness for arithmetic which Johnson, like so many future Beckett characters, believed a solace when he was depressed. Both men also were preoccupied with the world of the mind. "Will anybody's mind bear this eternal microscope that you place upon your own," Beckett notes as Mrs. Thrale's comment to her friend Johnson.[7] Both men also denied the possibility of happiness; Dr. Johnson did not like anyone who said he was happy or who said anyone was, Beckett recorded in his notes. For Johnson, as for Beckett, the vacuity of life was a favorite topic. Beckett writes the following words of a commentator on Johnson: "Such things as other philosophers attribute to various and contradictory causes, appeared to him uniform enough: all was done to fill up the time, upon his principle."[8] In 1936, twelve years before writing *Waiting for Godot,* Beckett held a similar view about the purposeless activities of life. Beckett shared another of Johnson's beliefs. More than anything else, it was probably Johnson's isolation and loneliness, feelings Beckett understood, that drew the young Irishman to the English literary giant. Beckett wrote to a friend: "there can hardly have been many so completely at sea in their solitude as he was or so horribly aware of it. Read the *Prayers and Meditations* if you don't believe me. . . ."[9]

Given the above, we might assume that Beckett's plan was to draw a sketch of the facets of the Johnson personality—perhaps a variation on chapter 6 of *Murphy*. What Beckett did fix on was not Johnson the man, nor even Johnson the mind, but Johnson in love. Beckett developed the theory that Samuel Johnson was in love with Mrs. Hester Thrale, who with her husband had befriended him and opened her home at Streatham for his use for sixteen years. It was Beckett's intention to concentrate on the four years that separated the death of Henry Thrale on 4 April, 1781, and the death of Johnson on 13 December, 1784. With Thrale gone, Beckett assumed that Johnson had hopes of marrying the widow. However, they were soon dashed when she, in April 1783, exactly two years after her husband's death, announced her intention to marry her children's Italian music teacher, Gabriel Piozzi, and move to Italy. After trying to dissuade her from an act Johnson wrote would be ignominious, he broke all ties with her, and died two years later, not seeing her again.

"It seems now quite certain that he was rather absurdly in love with her all the fifteen years he was at Streatham," Beckett wrote in April 1937 on his return from a six-month trip to Germany during which time he had been reading all available primary and secondary works on Johnson and those surrounding him.[10] The research eventually filled three notebooks: the first, purchased in Munich, contains ninety-three pages of closely written, single-spaced material from primary and secondary sources; the next two, purchased on his return to Dublin, have quotations from primary sources and—in the half-filled notebook 3—two possible scenarios to organize the material.

Beckett begins his first notebook by making a chronological list of the main events occurring to Johnson and Thrale in the four crucial years. Later in the notes he conjectures on the last meeting between the two, on 5 April, 1798 and indicates that he is not adverse to fictionalizing what cannot be proved: "*What happened at interview impossible to say* (I shall say it)."[11] In notebooks 2 and 3 Beckett copies down physical traits of Johnson that bear striking resemblances to characters that Beckett will invent in subsequent works. For instance, there is a description of Johnson's mouth "almost constantly opening and shutting as if he were chewing" (*Not I*); his counting his steps as he walked, and his body moving in a perpetual St. Vitus' Dance (Lucky's dance in *Godot*); Johnson's horror of repeated birthdays (*Krapp's Last Tape*); a notation about Johnson describing someone who "panted on to 90" (which Beckett underlines in blue pencil to indicate importance and which he alludes to in *Footfalls*); and Johnson's contention that "arithmetic cured depression" (*Molloy* and *Company*). Beckett, indicating his own fascination with the workings of the body, goes as far as to describe Johnson's autopsy, ending with the information "The cranium was not opened"—a fact Beckett with his preoccupations on the elusive mysteries of the skull must have found striking.

In notebook 2 Beckett begins to collect information about the five members of the Johnson household at Bolt Court, whom Mrs. Thrale called the "Nest of People" and Walter Bate, Johnson's biographer, described as the destitute and infirm that Johnson, ever good-hearted, had sheltered in his home. This odd assortment living in what Johnson liked to call his "Seraglio" was not a compatible group. In a note to Mrs. Thrale he describes his household: "Williams hates everybody. Levett hates Desmoulins and does not love

Williams. Desmoulins hates them both. Poll loves none of them." To flesh out these relationships, Beckett collects extensive material about the group. Eighteen pages are devoted to the blind Mrs. Anna Williams, a devoted friend and official hostess for the widowed Johnson. Eight and a half pages are given to Robert Levett, the kindly, unlicensed doctor who resided for twenty years under Johnson's roof. Beckett quotes a source that says that Johnson cared for Levett because few others did. Next to "His concern for the down and outer," Beckett writes in blue, "Balls. He was a symptom of J's anxiety." Beckett has four pages each on the free black servant Frank Barber who, with his wife, periodically worked in the Johnson home, and Elizabeth Desmoulins, a widow and friend of Johnson's late wife Tettie. Only one page is devoted to the somewhat mysterious Miss Polly Carmichael, a woman Johnson found on the street, destitute and ill, and whom Bate says was almost certainly a prostitute.[12]

It is with Williams, Desmoulins, and Carmichael that Beckett fashions what was to be the first scene of his four-act play entitled *Human Wishes,* the title a variation on Johnson's famous poem "The Vanity of Human Wishes." The date is Wednesday, 4 April 1781. (On the next week of that year the date would fall on a Friday, Beckett's birthday.) The women are anxiously awaiting the return of Johnson from the Thrale home, although Johnson's name is never directly mentioned, nor is Thrale or the subject of his imminent death. Instead, the conversation focuses on books, knitting, the cat, those things that the women do while waiting.

Mrs. Desmoulins begins with "He is late," and after a period of silence, continues, "God grant all is well," the two lines she will repeat later in the scene. Still receiving no response, she continues after another silence with, "Puss puss puss puss puss." The five repetitions parallel the five syllables in the line before, indicating Beckett's attempt, even at this early date of dramatic composition, to create a formal pattern of syllable numbers in order to provide an internal coherence to his dialogue and scenes. Another familiar Beckett device is apparent in the scene: wordplay. When Mrs. Williams says she is dying of a "pituitous defluxion"—a phrase Beckett recorded in one of his notebooks—Mrs. Carmichael notes her "colloquial powers." There is also much talk about proper language "of a gentlewoman," Mrs. Williams stating that she would not "abase myself to your syntax." In one extended section the trio dissect a sentence on the topic of mirth, reordering its parts, ironically creating mirth while presumably extracting all mirth from it, until Mrs. Williams fashions it into a rhymed verse which she demands be copied down. It is not.

Into this group enters Levett, inebriated. Unlike the others, he is silent, emitting only a loud belch as he crosses the stage. The others continue their talk that skirts continually on death, the ostensible subject on the minds of them all. Mrs. Williams talks of her own early demise; she then moves to the deaths of famous writers, and the scene concludes with Miss Carmichael reciting a passage on death from the book she is reading, attributed incorrectly by Mrs. Williams to Brown instead of Taylor.

In the poem "Cascando," written in the same year, Beckett says, "is it not better abort than be barren." Even though *Human Wishes* is aborted, it remains a nascent version of what will surface twelve years later when Beckett writes his first produced play, *Waiting for Godot.* First, there are the inane conversations that lead nowhere. Next, there are long silences that point to a subtext that is never articulated in the dialogue. In the ten-page fragment the stage directions indicate thirty-four silences. Third, there is the self-reflexive attention given to language and to the play form. Fourth, Beckett skillfully alludes to the central subject—death—through the use of quotations, current events, and allusions to reinforce the subject. Fifth, Beckett describes the relationship between the sighted and the blind, used in *Godot, Endgame,* and *Theatre 1.* Finally, he takes a potentially dreary, sombre scene and infuses it with humor. The vituperative banter among the women is lively, the images sharp.

Beckett was unable to transfer the voluminous facts of Johnson's life into a drama. There were the details, and there was the life, and in 1936 the two did not mesh into a dramatic, coherent form.

## Poetry

Throughout much of his career Samuel Beckett has written poetry.[13] His first separately published work was the ninety-eight-line poem *Whoroscope,* which he entered in a contest conducted by the Hours Press in the summer of 1930, and for which he received first prize, £10, and publication. During his travels in London, Paris, and Germany in the 1930s, Beckett continued to write poetry, publishing works in *Dublin Magazine* and *transition*, and collecting thirteen in a book entitled *Echo's Bones and other Precipitates*, published in 1935. These poems were written in English; but when Beckett moved permanently to Paris in 1937, he began almost immediately to compose in French. Twelve poems written from 1937 to 1939 appeared together in *Les Temps Modernes*, November 1946. Six poems from the postwar years 1946–48 were first printed in *Transition Forty-Eight*, June 1948, and in *Cahiers des Saisons*, October 1955. After a period of twenty-four years Beckett began in 1972 to publish poetry again, producing five poems from 1972 to 1976, all in English. In 1978 he published a collection of poems in French, *Poèmes suivi de mirlitonnades*. Along with these original compostions, he has translated poems of Paul Eluard, Arthur Rimbaud, Guillaume Apollinaire, and Sébastien Chamfort. Beckett also has two poems that appear in the addenda to the novel *Watt*, and poems in *Words and Music*.

While these poems written over a forty-six-year period present a considerable body of material, they have rarely received the critical attention given the fiction and drama. The most complete study of Beckett's poetry is Lawrence Harvey, *Samuel Beckett: Poet and Critic*. Harvey provides detailed discussions of texts; for example, his commentary on *Whoroscope* runs to thirty-five pages. He clarifies elusive references, gives biographical information about the compositions, and relates the poetry to Beckett's other writings and to the central ideas embodied in the canon; for, however, eliptical and esoteric, the poetry still explores the same relationships between life and art, the self and the world he pursues in other genres. In his 1934 critical essay, "Recent Irish Poetry," Beckett speaks of an ideal poetry: "The poem of poems would embrace the sense of confinement, the get away, the vicissitudes of the road, the wan bliss on the rim." Beckett's poetry covers this difficult terrain.

***Whoroscope.*** *Whoroscope*, like *Human Wishes*, was based on Beckett's extensive research on the life of a central figure, in this case René Descartes, the Seigneur du Perron, about whom he had done research during his stay at the Ecole Normale Supérieure. Since the subject of the contest was time, Beckett's borrowings from the Adrian Baillet biography of Descartes concentrated on the philosopher's peculiar peccadilloes about temporal matters: his failure to have his horoscope cast so that no one could predict his death, and his penchant for omelettes made of eggs hatched from eight to ten days. He also interspersed throughout names of friends and associates of Descartes, allusions the uninitiated reader misses. While admiring the vigor and wit of the language, Nancy Cunard and Richard Aldington requested that Beckett provide explanatory footnotes, much in the manner of those written by T. S. Eliot at the end of *The Waste Land.* Beckett wrote three general and seventeen specific references to lines, which help clarify some points. Still unanswered, however, are the central questions: why eggs and horoscopes, and what do they tell us about the philosopher Descartes? Beckett may once more be showing that the habits of daily life are often the central facts on which we focus, yet when gathered up and examined they offer little insight about the person. Eggs also point to fecundity and the physical process of maturation which lead inevitably to deterioration, a process to which all mankind—even philosophers—are subject. While Descartes posited the notion of a thinking, rational mind, this mind is irrevocably affixed to a physically decaying body, thus Beckett's emphasis on putrefaction in the poem: "sweet millèd sweat of my burning liver!"—"grey flayed epidermis and scarlet tonsils!"—"Stagnant murky blood."

Perhaps the most striking features of the poem are the lively language and blend of esoteric and colloquial elements. For example, he has Descartes reminisce: "Them were the days I sat in the hot-cupboard throwing / Jesuits out of the skylight." One doesn't have to know about Descartes' predilection for work in enclosed places to respond to the imagery and tone of the lines. Vivid effects are created as well by Beckett's use of dialogue, particularly a series of questions and answers, much like the exchanges that he will employ in his drama. The poem begins: "What's that? / An egg? / By the brothers Boot it stinks fresh. / Give it to Gillot." Immediately the reader is thrown into the world of the poem, without any notion of who is speaking or whether the questioner is perhaps answering his own queries. Beckett uses the same device in his 1976 poem "Something There."

***Echo's Bones* and poems of the 1930s.** In 1935 thirteen of Beckett's poems—only one of which, "Alba," had been published separately—appeared under the title *Echo's Bones and Other Precipitates.* The title refers to the mythological nymph, condemned by Hera to utter only the last word said to her, never to initiate speech, even to her love Narcissus, until—grieving for her loss of voice and volition—she fades leaving only bones as the residue or precipitate of thwarted speech and loveless life. Many of Beckett's poems reflect the same sense of despair, inability, frustration, and loss. If, in *Murphy,* Mr. Endon is the desired Narcissus figure, *Echo* repesents the poet's inability to articulate this love of the nothing.

Beckett experiments with several traditional poetic forms, taken from medieval Provençal troubadour songs. There are two *enuegs* or complaints; three *aubades* or dawn songs, and three *serenas* or evening songs. Beckett also creates a new form which he calls "sanies," derived from a word that means "blood tinged discharges from ulcers and infected wounds." The term describes the other poem as well, with their recurrent images of decay and deterioration, with little relief gained from love, nature, dawn, or night.

The poems, like *Murphy,* written during the same period, are crowded with specific geographical details that marked Beckett's own travels through Dublin, London, Germany, and Paris: Portobello Nursing Home and Parnell Bridge, in "Enueg I"; the American Bar in Rue Mouffetard in "Sanies II"; and the British Museum and Regent's Park in "Serena I." Yet, as in *Murphy,* the real landscape of the poems is the skull. The first poem in the collection, "The Vulture," lays the parameters of the world to be explored: "dragging his hunger through the sky / of my skull shell of sky and earth." The present participle form of the first word *dragging* indicates that the speaker is both moving and carrying—actions to be repeated throughout the poetry. "Keep on the move" is the last line of "Serena III." In "Enueg I" the speaker, tired of his love's "red sputum," leaves the hospital where she is confined and meanders around Dublin, encountering repeated pictures of exile: a child who cannot enter a building, verminous hens "perishing . . . against the closed door of a shed"; "a small malevolent goat, exiled on the road."

Unlike the fiction of the period, there is very little humor in these poems. Democritus, the laughing philospher invoked by Belacqua in "Yellow," is described in "Enueg I" as "scuttling along between a crutch and a stick, / his stump caught up horribly, like a claw." In the same poem, one of the bleakest and most violent in the collection, Beckett writes, "in my skull the wind going fetid." "Fetid" describes much of the scenery: the flower is the rafflesia, parasitic and malodorous; water "the livid canal," and nature "great mushy toadstool, / green-black."

Women, sometimes rejuvenators in Beckett's early fiction, have very little power to offset these stark images of pain, isolation, and suffering. In "Enueg I" the woman is dying; in "Alba," while she is equated with Beatrice, she brings with her—as she does in "Dante and the Lobster"—a branded moon, sign of Judas, and entrapment. After she has gone, the poet says he is left "only I and then the sheet / and bulk dead." When the cyclist sees his love in "Sanies I," all he says to her is "get along with you." Lovers, described in "Serena I," are "quarried," furtively seeking shelter in a hostile London.

There are recurrent allusions to day and night, light and dark, in the poems, yet no reconciliation between the contraries occurs. "This clonic earth" is the single line, placed alone, that begins "Serena II." In this collection, stasis is never achieved. Like Murphy, who sought a median ground for a heart given to extremes, the various speakers are buffeted by dichotomies that cannot be balanced. Contraries condemned to move in tandem—and on the move continually—are presented in the last poem in the group, "Echo's Bones," where Beckett describes "the gantelope of sense and nonsense run / taken by the maggots for what they are." Sense and nonsense are the general binaries subsuming the others—all attacked by the inevitable maggots of decay. For Beckett, in these poems, the concern is for mankind adrift in such a fragmented world. Playing on the Latin phrase "Of the dead only speak good" his concern in "Enueg II" is those who are about to die. And rather than good, he commits himself to speak about the "nothing" that shapes their lives.

Three other poems written in the 1930s were not collected in *Echo's Bones*. "Home Olga" is an acrostic of ten lines built on the first letters in the name James Joyce, whom the poem honors on the 28th anniversary of Bloom's Day in 1932. "Gnome," written two years later, is a more personal poem, describing poignantly in its four brief lines Beckett's struggles during the period: leaving his academic career for the exile and wandering that, even in 1934 when the poem was written, had still not come to a fruitful end. "Cascando," written in 1936, also illustrates this sense of lost opportunities and future uncertainties, but instead of the gnomic pattern of the former work, with its residual overtones of the learning not quite left behind, Beckett creates an almost lyrical mood in the evocation of love, the need for it, and the awareness of the impossibility of finding it. It is Beckett's most beautiful poem, a litany for a love he would have and cannot. In part 2 he writes: "saying again there is a last / even of last times / last times of begging / last times of loving / of knowing not knowing pretending / a last even of last times of saying / if you do not love me I shall not be loved / if I do not love you I shall not love." The repetitions enforce the habitual quality of a love that should offer freedom, but instead creates longing for what it fails to provide. The lover has not yet reached the "last time" when the redemption provided by love is finally forsaken, but his words indicate that he has reached the point where to be done with love—to be beyond its call and its pain—is the only hope that remains. Connected with the difficulty of finding love is the difficulty of finding language to express it—twin problems for the poet. Words, too, suffer from the deadening effects of habitual forms: "the churn of stale words in the heart again / love love love thud of the old plunger / pestling the unalterable / whey of words." The word *love,* used three times, denotes not heightened emotion but blunted routine. Joined to "stale," "thud," and "old," love becomes what the pun on "whey" denotes: residue, a pale extract in an ongoing process.

**Poems in French, 1937–39; 1947–49.** The first of the twelve poems written between 1937 and 1939, when Beckett had turned thirty, has a theme similar to that expressed in "Cascando": the experience of love that does not bring the hoped-for release from the world of the macrocosm. Once more, the formal repetitions of words, like "with each," and the careful, repetitive substitution of "the absence of love," for "it" give a sense of routine and inevitability, of unrelieved hopelessness about which the speaker does not even have the strength or passion to do any more than state: "they come / different and the same / with each it is different and the same / with each the absence of love is different / with each the absence of love is the same." Gone in this collection are the violent images, the anger, and the chafing that marked the earlier poems. The mood is sombre; a sense of ennui permeates. In "à elle l'acte calme" there is the inability to love; in "être là sans mâchoires sans dents," the inability of a gaping, toothless mouth to speak; in "Rue de Vaugirard," travel leads nowhere; and in "Arènes de Lutèce," the dual elements of the self fail to merge.

One of the starkest statements of the pull between the mental abode and the physical is presented in "Dieppe," which, along with the first poem, "they come," Beckett translated into English. In the four-line poem the setting is a beach where the speaker slowly walks, torn between the pull of the sea and the lights of the city behind him. It is only with regret and physical effort, indicated by the pause between "turning" and "then" that he rejects the former, and the death it brings, and reluctantly returns to the life of the latter: "again the last ebb / the dead shingle / the turning then the steps / towards the lights of old." The movement toward the light is not seen as a victory; darkness or death would be a resolution of the old struggles, now to be fought once more.

Another body of water, this time the river Vire, which in French means "to wind," offers the central image to another four-line poem, "Saint-Lô," written in 1946 while Beckett served as assistant in a hospital in the war-torn town. The river, running through a town about to be restored, is contrasted to the mind of the man "and the old mind ghost-forsaken / sink into its havoc." The plural form of "sink" indicates the duality of the mind, here both "the little world" and the "big world" one at least in their reflected "havoc," mind-made and man-made.

Several of the poems from the 1947–49 group deal with survival; yet there is no joy in the continuation of life, only hope for the eventual peace that death will bring. While "Mort de A.D." depicts the painful death of a friend, others speak yearningly for such a release. In "my way is in the sand flowing" Beckett once more uses a solitary walker, this time progressing along the length of a strand that is shrouded in mist and fog. As he walks, the circumscribed area of sight moves with him; the areas behind and in front are black. Caught, thus, in a continuous present, without clear past or future, the speaker desires to pierce the veil of shadow ahead, for it is in the "receding mist" that he says his peace lies. Yet he knows that his "treading" onward brings him no closer "to its beginning to its end."

Caught between land and sea, past and present, the mind and the world, the speaker in "what would I do without this world" presents the dilemma in one of the strongest poems in the Beckett canon. Organized like a sonnet, despite its fifteen lines, the poem begins with a nine-line question of how one can live in "this world faceless incurious / where to be lasts but an instant. . . ." In the sestet the speaker recognizes that exile to the world of the mind isolates him from needed companionship. Instead of retreating, he seeks a fellow traveler: "peering out of my deadlight looking for another / wandering like me eddying far from all the living." The poem is a preamble to the 1980 play *Rockaby.*

**Poems in English, 1974–76.** In 1974, after a break of twenty-five years, Beckett began to publish poetry again. *Collected Poems* offers four works: "dread nay" and "something there," written in 1974, and "Roundelay" and "thither" in 1976. "Neither," also written in 1976, appears in the *Journal of Beckett Studies,* Spring 1979. The poems provide a vivid contrast to those of the preceding periods. Gone are the elaborate puns, the literary and personal references. They are stripped of all accoutrements: less "draff" or precipitates than clean, polished bones, finely worn to the simple purity of thought.

The language is spare, almost all words of one and two syllables, often repeated with only slight variations. For example, in "thither," of its thirty-one words, all but three are repeated; and only three have two or more syllables; the rest are one-syllable. In the poem the complex notions of spatial and temporal spheres, so intricately plotted in *Echo's Bones,* are reduced to "then there / then there." It would seem that the poet can reduce no further. In "Roundelay," a poem of thirteen lines, four are repeated, and the middle five vary only slightly. "Unbidden stay" and "unbidden go," with a brief moment of silence and cessation of movement between: thus Beckett offers an image of life, perfectly balanced by the lines and repetitions of the words, a stark view of the coming and going he presents in more elaborate form in his fiction and drama. The sibilant voiceless *s* that is repeated in sixteen of the forty-four words infuses the poem with the sigh of continued struggle, a struggle beyond words, battling the compulsion of the voiced bilabial stopped *b* in "unbidden" and the lateral voiced *l* in "long."

A poem of similar brevity and beauty is "Something There." In it the speaker talks of the eye, in the singular, that opens, peering out at the world outside the self, an inner eye of the perceiver attempting to pierce what lies outside, in the macrocosm. Rather than concentrate on "what the ostrich sees in the ground," as Murphy attempted, the speaker acknowledges a world without albeit "not life / necessarily," and attempts unsuccessfully to focus upon it. The poem was written in 1974 and bears directly upon the play, *A Piece of Monologue,* written five years later, which also has the central figure attempt to light a "globe" in order to see through the darkness to a world beyond the limits of self-enclosed consciousness and memory.

The similarity of imagery and language between the poem and the play indicates a direction in which Beckett's writing has gone in the 1970s and 1980s. More and more, as the poetry gains a simplicity of form and language, the drama and the prose follow suit, so that it becomes increasingly difficult to categorize Beckett's writing using traditional genre demarcations. If we compare the following excerpts from the play *Rockaby* (1980) and the prose *Worstward Ho* (1983), it is impossible to tell, out of context, the genre in which the lines appear: "all eyes / all sides / high and low / for another / another living soul / one other living soul" *(Rockaby).* "On. Say on. Be said on. Somehow on. Till nohow on. Said nohow on" *(Worstword Ho).*

In one of Beckett's earlier poems, "Casket of Pralinen for a Daughter of a Dissipated Mandarin," written in 1938, the poet in an unaccustomed slip of the swaggering mask, steps forward and says: "Oh I am ashamed / of all clumsy artistry / I am ashamed of presuming / to arrange words / of everything but the ingenuous fibres / that suffer honestly." After this avowal he again takes up his cynical pose, and adds, attempting to undercut the words just written: "Oh yes I think that was perhaps just a very little / inclined to be rather too self-conscious." The poems of the 1970s, coming almost forty years later, achieve the desired honesty without the need to deflect the sentiment. They are precipitates of the highest order, a culmination of a long, arduous—and noteworthy—process.

# *Chapter Four*
# Solitary Wanderers

## Watt

Roussillon, a small village in the Vaucluse section of France, was Beckett's domicile from August 1942 to April 1945. There he and his wife, Suzanne, fled after the Germans discovered their resistance cell in Paris; and there Beckett, in an attempt to dispel the routine of life without work and, seemingly, without future, wrote his third novel, *Watt*. The little world and the big world—the purposeless routine of the author and the insane horrors of the war—meet in its pages in the character of its persona Watt, another of Beckett's sad men, this time no longer young. Like Beckett at the time of composition, Watt is almost middle-aged—ten years older than Murphy—but he still bears recognizable features of the earlier model. He is "probably a university man," has an odd gait, "a funambulistic stagger," disproportionate feet, yet is an "inveterate walker," usually found "on the street," and with "no fixed address." He is adorned in an odd assortment of hand-me-down clothes, that become standard attire in Beckett's world: a greatcoat from his father that falls almost to his feet, a block pepper-colored hat from his grandfather, but unlike Murphy, no tie or collar. His grotesque exterior causes people to stare: he has a "big red nose," "scant red hair," "poor healing skin," and an odd smile that never comes singly—"In this it resembled the fart," the narrator observes. Truthful, gentle, an imbiber only of milk, he is a man continually beset by strangers, so used to attack that he carries a special cloth to wipe the bloody blows, a Christ-like figure who would "turn the other cheek . . . if he had the energy." He is also an experienced traveler; and it is with Watt's travel that the book is concerned: his going to, staying at, and leaving the employ of a Mr. Knott, a mysterious man for whom he works as a servant—one in a series of servants—first on the ground floor, and then, after a time, on the first floor.

*Murphy* chronicles a young man's quest for escape into the world of the mind, and *Watt* charts an older man's quest for the meaning of the nullity that lies at the heart of the little world. And while Murphy is placed outside the Edenic/Endonic world, entering it only temporarily through the means of his scarves and rocking chair, Watt resides for a time under the roof of Knott, or naught, attempting, through close observation, to pierce his secrets.

But just as gas will not a psychotic make, habitation within the house of Knott will not offer up the secrets of "what the ostrich sees in the sand." Beckett's Watt is too much the modern man, a rationalist, committed to facts, order, and logic. "For to explain is to exorcise," for Watt, and he is constantly battling to control the phenomena he encounters, to shape them into some form he can examine, then verbalize and, thus, having conquered, forget. The results of his struggle for understanding are deadening, a torture for Watt and for the reader who follows page after page of calibrations, calculations, and repetitions that constitute thinking for this postlapsarian man: twelve possibilities about why Knott never complained about his food; four rejected solutions to the question of how to bring together the food remains and the dog assigned to finish them; a table of objections to each rejected solution; nineteen pages on the solution that was finally adopted, the methods of providing a ready dog in service and a ready family of retainers, the Lynches, to accompany the dog; a complete genealogical description of the family; three pages on the movement of Mr. Knott within his room and the placement of the furniture there; four pages deciphering the meaning of the one visit during Watt's residency, the "fugitive penetration" of the piano tuners Gall; ten pages on who pressed the bell that sounded in Erskine's room, and whether he even has a bell (He has. It is broken); and two pages on the intended meaning of the picture Watt finds there, a circle with a segment missing and a blue dot seemingly in search of the opening. These calculations involving Watt directly are supplemented by a long section in Part 3, some twenty-seven pages, in which the new servant Arthur tells of an Ernest Louit, his dissertation on *The Mathematical Intuitions of the Visicelts,* his specimen of same, Mr. Nackybal, and the committee that looks at both and at each other.

These endless attempts at explanation that make up a fourth of *Watt* are ironic, a biting satire of the modern rationalist computing endlessly, endlessly, endlessly. They are also funny, the befuddled thinker entwining himself in filaments of nonsense, squirming to understand, while becoming ever more tightly caught, in what Lucky in *Waiting for Godot* calls the dance of the Net, a grotesque visualization of the limits and entrapment of ratiocination.

The book is divided into four sections of uneven length and an addendum where a footnote indicates that "The following precious and illuminating material should be carefully studied. Only fatigue and disgust prevented its incorporation." This note, one of nine that appear in the text, points to the hand of a narrator, a figure who remains hidden like the elusive Knott himself, leaving only such calling cards as question marks, footnotes, pauses, and occasional comments explaining particular lacunae. For example, early in Part 7, when someone denigrates Watt, the narrator says, "He made use . . . of an expression that we shall not record," an example of narrative fastidiousness Beckett also employed in *Dream.* In Part 2 the narrative "we" gives way to "I" and the reader is informed of the limitations under which the narrator is working: "For all that I know on the subject of Mr. Knott, and of all that touched Mr. Knott, and on the subject of Watt, and of all that touched Watt, came from Watt, and from Watt alone." It is not until the beginning of Part 3, twenty-five pages later, that it becomes clear who the "I" is and the conditions of transferences of information: Watt is a patient in an asylum, occupying a pavilion with a private garden, and the transcriber, a man named Sam, is a fellow patient in an adjacent pavilion. During walks in their respective gardens Watt has told him of Mr. Knott; but Sam explains that the story may be distorted since Watt, at the time, was incapable of normal discourse, and shifted the order of words, syntax, and sometimes letters, forcing Sam continually to learn the new forms of communication. Also, Watt did not tell his story in chronological order but rather in the sequence two, one, four, and three. Therefore, if we are to believe Sam, the story we read in the pages of the novel called *Watt* is a story that a madman dictates to another madman in a garbled language and a broken chronology, "ill told, ill heard." To further fragment the situation of both the plot and the narrative form that shapes it, the disclosure takes place not at the beginning or end of the book, but in the middle—at the beginning of Part 3—after which the narrator returns to the house of Knott and the chronological sequence, now no longer a sequence and no longer chronological.

Yet the elusive source of the narrative is still not fully revealed; for while Watt can relate the events to which he is a party, he has no way of knowing about those activities in the prologue: Mr. Hackett, out for an evening stroll, meeting his friends the Nixons, and their conversation prior to the arrival, at the tram stop, of the traveling Watt. Beckett seems to be purposely creating doubt about the source and veracity of the fiction, offering Sam as a bogus—or partial—narrator, still not the central voice of the fictive world of the novel. Such doubt parallels the uncertainty Watt experiences within the walls of Knott's establishment; the narrative becomes the concomitant to the quest toward Knott, its circumlocutions an echo of the false starts and dead ends that Watt endures. In the novel Beckett makes a direct link between the hero's search for the meaning of the nothingness he experiences and the writer's search for a means to tell his story, for a grounding in a world of continual slippage.

While seeker and writer are not fused, Beckett indicates that they struggle under the same limitations: misleading and insufficient language, sketchy facts, and faulty senses. "For in truth the same things happen to us all," Arsene tells Watt, and, to make the point, Beckett begins his novel with Mr. Hackett, who has no direct connection with Watt or the events in Mr. Knott's house, but whose circumstances indicate that he, too, is beset by the limits of rational verification. Out for a walk in the "failing light" that bathes the entire story, Hackett comes upon his familiar bench and finds it occupied. Expelled, he must decide what to do about the situation. He is not helped by the language he uses to frame his choices. "Yes, it was not vacant," he thinks, the negative eroding the initial certainty, the apposition creating a stasis between yes and no. If words are no help, neither are his senses. When he first sees a form thrown from the tram, he is not sure if it is a man, a woman, or an object. What he sees is not certain, yet he burns with curiosity and wonder, the same curiosity that will not let Watt rest until he has investigated all phenomena.

Like Watt, Hackett tries to base his observations on facts. He immediately questions Nixon about Watt and learns that Nixon once lent him six shillings, nine pence, and that Watt has offered to repay four shillings and four pence. "That will leave two and three," Hackett calculates. While the error in subtraction is small, it is one in a series of miscalculations throughout the book, unimportant unless characters attempt to base conclusions upon them.[1] For example, after listing the number of Lynch family members that have served Mr. Knott, a footnote states, "The figures given here are incorrect. The consequent calculations are therefore doubly erroneous." Mathematics as a basis for investigation is, therefore, proven faulty.

Arsene, in his welcoming monologue to Watt, makes a similar observation about all facts. He tells of Mr. Ash who, one windy evening on Westminster bridge, went to considerable trouble to extract his watch (a half-hunter next seen in the possession of Pozzo in *Godot)* and tell the hour: "Seventeen minutes past five exactly, as God is my witness." Nearby Big Ben struck six. "This in my opinion is the type of all information whatsoever, be it voluntary or solicited," Arsene concludes.

These limits of language, fact, and sense are brought together by Beckett in the description of Watt's first act in Knott's house. While waiting for someone to appear, perhaps the someone who has mysteriously opened the kitchen door and allowed him to enter, Watt amuses himself by playing a game: covering the nearby lamp with his hat, so that the coals in the grate, which he had assumed grey and dead, redden in the created dark. The game is important because it indicates that what appears in the sensate world as a condition—dead coals—may through manipulation or shifts in perception be altered. How then is one to measure the phenomenal world or talk about what is measured? While Watt plays his game, he thinks that the coals "redden, greyen." If there were logic in the linguistic contructs, the word greyen should be as accepted as the word redden. It is not. The example provides yet another indication of the difficulties the seeker must surmount when describing the physical world with a limited language. He must also surmount inattention. Watt is so embroiled in his game that he does not hear Arsene enter: "Here then was something again that Watt would never know, for want of paying due attention to what was going on about him," the narrator says.

Watt's awareness of his inability to know anything with certainty comes to him during his period of tenure in the Knott establishment. The visit of the father and son piano tuners, the Galls, provides the catalyst for this awareness: "Galling" confusion and doubt. Watt tries to reconstruct the details after the pair leave; yet he cannot, for, as Beckett said of such attempts in *Proust,* "Deformation has taken place." Beckett has already indicated that words, facts, and even senses are faulty at best; therefore, the quest for total surety is doomed to fail. Watt, after much manipulation, is able, he says, to make "a pillow of old words, for a head," but in the process he must also admit a fissure between words and things. The world for Watt becomes unnamed, paradise lost through the unnaming, the reverse of the Adamic power of affixing word and object, or what Arsene, who experiences a similar awareness, calls "the laurel into Daphne." So bereft is Watt of the traditional assumptions of logical investigation of reality, that he can no longer find surety in even the most mundane thing, a pot, for instance.

The experience is the central one in the book, the loss of certainty in the physical world and in the language that describes it. Watt confronts Knott, the nothingness that lies at the heart of experience, but rather than accept it unquestioningly, even be comforted by it, he finds the situation unbearable.

Arsene, his predecessor, describes a similar experience of slippage by employing a ladder image. "What was changed was existence off the ladder." Hackett, too, describes a fall off a ladder. The imagery is borrowed from twentieth-century philosophers Fritz Mauthner and Ludwig Wittgenstein who employed it to describe a similar situation: the struggle to climb beyond the limits of language and the impossibility of ever doing so because of the need to frame insights in the very language one is refuting. Like Mauthner and Wittgenstein in his later writing, Beckett offers in *Watt* the position of the skeptical nominalist about the possibility of asserting anything with surety, even the sense of self or physical world, because of human inability to reconstruct the past and because of entrapment by language.[2] Watt's world becomes "unspeakable" and "unknowable"; of the "unutterable and ineffable," Arsene says, "any attempt to utter or eff it is doomed to fail, doomed, doomed to fail."

A novel that embodies such a nominalist position might be expected to be a dark study, morose or forbidding. *Watt* is not. Once more in Beckett's fiction, we find an array of characters who lighten the landscape: Hunch Hackett who in doubt strikes his stick on the pavement; the Nixons who tell of the birth of their first son; Lady McCann who heaves a stone at Watt in the opening section, and appears again at the close of the book; Mr. Spiro who shares the train compartment with Watt and describes his writing for a Catholic journal, "We keep our tonsure above water"; the gardener Mr. Graves who has sexual problems; Arsene, who regrets everything; the embedded fictional character Nackybal who does square roots in his head; and the hierarchy of workers at the train station, the transportation equivalent to the physician pecking order at the Magdalen Mental Mercyseat in *Murphy.* Humor is also provided by the exaggerated efforts at logic that quickly decline into nonsense. The laughter thus produced is the third of the three types of laughs Arsene describes, not the bitter, the hollow, but the mirthless: the laugh that laughs at unhappiness. It is the unhappiness of Watt and by extension all seekers after reason in an unreasonable world, whose trail, Beckett seems to be saying in 1944, leads to verbal dislocation in a madhouse.

Like *Murphy,* and *Mercier and Camier* that follows, *Watt* ends in a lyrical passage rather than in a laugh or a grimace, with the character alone, looking up at the heaven, a quietus after the pain of the quest. At the end of Part 4 the concluding image is of Mr. Gorman "looking straight before him, at nothing in particular, though the sky falling to the hills, and the hills falling to plain, made as pretty a picture, in the early morning light, as a man could hope to meet with, in a day's march." Its hackneyed language and images of descent are offset by the beauty and ascendancy of the description that concludes Part 3, the actual chronological end of the story, where Sam has his last view of Watt: " . . . he picked himself up and unmurmuring went on, towards his habitation, until I saw him no more, but only the aspens. And from the hidden pavilions . . . the issuing smokes by the wind were blown, now far apart but now together, mingling to vanish." Mr. Gorman stares at nothing and is not vexed, Watt seeks out the nothing, falls, gets up, and continues.

And yet, even here, the end is not the end, for Beckett adds addenda, thirty-five items—phrases, songs, quotations, poems—that are not included in the text of the novel: draff, again, or the detritus of the story told, but never completely told. Perhaps the true end of the work lies in the series of five questions, formed into a poem, that appears in the section, questions without answers: "who may tell the tale / of the old man? / weigh absence in a scale?

/ mete want with a span? / the sum assess / of the world's woes? / nothingness / in words enclose?"

## *Mercier and Camier*

In 1946 Beckett returned to his Paris apartment on rue des Favorites and continued the writing career he had interrupted six years before. The next four years he produced the core upon which his reputation still rests: four *nouvelles* or short fictions, one short novel, a trilogy of novels, two plays—one of which was *Waiting for Godot*—and several critical texts and poetry. It was as if the flood-gates held in check during the war years had opened, and Beckett at forty was finally free to write the literature he had described a decade before.

*Mercier and Camier* (its original title *Le Voyage de Mercier et Camier autour du Pot dans les Bosquets de Bondy* translates to The Voyage of Mercier and Camier Detouring Through the Grove of Thieves) has an important place in the Beckett canon. It is the first extended fiction that he wrote in French; "The End" preceded it by several months, but it is far shorter. It is also the first to employ two heroes, what Beckett in *The Unnamable* refers to as "the pseudo-couple." Murphy and Watt were solitary travelers; Mercier and Camier walk, albeit awkwardly, in tandem. It is also the last fiction for a time that Beckett wrote entirely in the third person. The *nouvelles* and the trilogy that follow employ a single presence spinning the story of his life. It is also one of the few works that Beckett has allowed to be published after consigning it to his "trunk pieces" for a number of years. Although written in French in 1946, it was not published until 1970, and not translated until 1974.

It is divided into eight chapters, with four summaries—key words, or phrases appearing in pairs after every two chapters. The narrator is present in the first line of the story—"The Journey of Mercier and Camier is one I can tell, if I will, for I was with them all the time"—but immediately assumes the traditional third-person omniscient position, content to describe scenery, make comments on the characters, and offer long asides, often filtered through the consciousness of Mercier and hard to distinguish in places from that character's soliloquies. Mercier he describes as "a big bony hank with a beard . . . hardly able to stand, wicked expression"; Camier as "Small and fat . . . red face, scant hair, four chins, protruding paunch, bandy legs, beady pig eyes." Camier is by profession a detective whose card says, "soul of discretion." The only biographical data provided for Mercier are a wife who "lives on" and children.

Like Watt, the pair are travelers, and the novel follows the meandering course on which they embark "driven by a need now clear and now obscure." The only objects they take are a sack (contents unsure), an umbrella (periodically unable to open), a raincoat (unfit to keep the rain out), and a bicycle, pulled by Mercier at the handlebars, and pushed by Camier at the seat. All four objects are lost, forgotten, or discarded along the way. As they walk, they talk in short and abrupt statements, and when they stop—as they repeatedly do—it is to assess their situation, and ask each other questions such as "Did what they were looking for exist?" or "What were they looking for?" They conclude "Only one thing mattered: depart."

Easier said than done for Beckett characters. Their beginning is fraught with confusion. They have arranged to meet at a specified place and time; but Mercier arrives first, and proceeds to take a short walk until his companion appears. In what amounts to a vaudeville routine, each misses the other, Beckett providing a timetable plotting these arrivals and departures, a mock train schedule, reminiscent of the lists of *Watt.* The voyage, therefore, begins in a fog of doubt that never entirely lifts.

It also begins in rain, a common climatic condition in Beckett's country, here Ireland despite the use of some French names. Against the weather, the pair seek shelter in a pagoda, situated in a small park, whose only predominant feature, a shining copper beech, was planted several centuries earlier by an obscure field marshall "struck dead by a cannon-ball, faithful to the last to the same hopeless cause." The narrator makes this remark, one of several comments on the insanity of warfare. When a park ranger appears—"the first of a long line of maleficent beings"—he too is described in terms of his war experience. Although an officer in uniform rankles Beckett characters, the passion here is tempered, for as Mercier remarks on hearing his "clatter of decorations," "Let us show him a little kindness . . . he's a hero of the great war. Here we were, high and dry, masturbating full pelt without fear of interruption, while he was crawling in the Flanders mud, shitting in his puttees."

The first day of their journey ends with the pair in their original position, until the insistent prodding of the ranger forces them into "the slippery streets" where "the crowd pressed on as towards some unquestioned goal." Equally unclear—but not unquestioned—is the goal of Mercier and Camier. At every opportunity they stop and reflect; at bars—"it is in bars that the Merciers of this world, and the Camiers, find it least tedious to await the dark"—or in the home of a woman known only as Helen, whose only distinguishing features beside her willingness to house and comfort the two, are her cockatoo and her rug—things both men swear they will never forget, but do.

At the beginning of Part 3 the pair are finally on a slow train heading south. They share the compartment with a Mr. Madden, a nascent monologist, model for Beckett's later storytellers, who harangues them with the story of his life, begun in medias res. To escape him, they detrain and enter an inn seeking food and lodging from the manager they mistakenly call Mr. Gall, the name of the piano tuner from *Watt.* Also present at the bar in the inn is a parson named Graves, another *Watt* holdover. A third gentleman, Mr. Conaire, appears, looking for Camier with whom he says he has an appointment. While the travelers sleep, the innkeeper, whose name is actually Gast, "treated his guests" to a brief monologue, a section of the ongoing story of *his* life, to a much less captive audience than Hamm finds when he unravels his ongoing tale in *Endgame.*

The next morning, in a field outside the town, Mercier and Camier assess their situation, find their sack and umbrella gone, and decide to return once more to town and Helen, Camier first declaring to Conaire that he has ceased to function as detective and will not look for the man's dog, the case for which he was to be hired. In the city, they are separated, and do not meet again until Part 6, in yet another bar, where they discuss their fruitless journey and the difficulties they have endured. On leaving, they walk in search of a brothel, encounter a policeman, whom they beat to death. In the last two parts they spend a night in a ruin; again, as in the first chapter, mistakenly think each has left; and separate. They meet after what appears to be a long interval of time, Camier now aged, Mercier more hobbled, brought together through the offices of a man named Watt, whom they call Daddy, and who tells the inevitable officer that prods them on their way, he is charged with "promenading these gentlemen, weather permitting." Watt is greatly changed from his novel: more blasphemous, shouting "Bugger life" and "Up Quin," the original name of Knott in Beckett's first draft of *Watt.* Mercier also mentions to Watt another Beckett character: "I knew a poor man named Murphy, said Mercier, who had a look of you, only less battered of course. But he died ten years ago, in rather mysterious circumstances."

After leaving Watt, who has caused a stir in the bar by his raucous behavior, the two once more find themselves unwillingly together, sitting on a bench by the canal, gazing up at the stars. Then Mercier leaves. Camier, alone on the bench, looks up at the sky: "And in the dark he could hear better too, he could hear the sounds the long day had kept from him, human murmurs for example, and the rain on the water." After another fruitless voyage, another moment of lyrical beauty.

This first Beckett couple experience many of the same problems of those who follow in the plays: they think of leaving each other, but hesitate; they suffer together but fear suffering alone, without a partner to hear them speak; they talk, as in all Beckett's later works, to fill time while waiting, yet they recognize that words fail; they have a sense of being watched, of eyes looking down upon them and their plight; they feel they are being punished by God. The two offer the most blasphemous invectives any Beckett characters hurl at the heavens. At one point, Mercier lifts his convulsed and streaming face, "as for thee, fuck thee." While both suffer in the present, they, like the others, remember an earlier time "when they were young, and warm, and loved art, and mocked marriage, and did not know each other." Yet such memories are vague and difficult to recapture. Mercier sees a chain on which he played when a child, but cannot remember specific details of a more idyllic life.

Although *Mercier and Camier* is a flawed fiction, with abrupt shifts and gratuitous characters and situations that do not seem to forward the action, it does present in stark terms the central image of the major plays Beckett would soon write, and it does create two memorable avatars supporting each other—"On the less weak let the weaker always lean, for the course to follow." They offer companionship but not salvation. "I can help you, said Camier, I can't resurrect you." Adrift in a hostile world, they are presented as two small creatures, less laughable than their predecessors, more pathetic in their suffering.

The fiction is pared down from *Murphy* and *Watt,* but the narrator is still aware of the impossibility of ever recording all the events that constitute a life: "Even side by side, said Mercier, as now, arm to arm . . . we are fraught with more events than could fit in a fat tome, two fat tomes, your fat tome and my fat tome. Whence no doubt our blessed sense of nothing, nothing to be done, nothing to be said." *Mercier and Camier* is Beckett's first attempt to say nothing in French.

*Mercier and Camier* also provides some clue as to why Beckett began writing drama after the completion of *Molloy* in 1947. Having created two people, he naturally found things for them to do—meet, leave, open umbrellas, push bicycles, comfort each other. If a pair provides physical respite from language, why not create the pair in the natural genre of action: drama? *Mercier and Camier,* the first French fiction, also marks the beginning of a phase that will flourish in the major plays of Beckett's career. After this novel, the fiction will take a different direction. Rather than two together, Beckett will chart the course of one alone.

## Four *Nouvelles*

In *Dream of Fair to Middling Women* Smeraldina asks Belacqua about a word that is troubling her: "Monologue? . . . What's that? Something to eat?" He replies, "Oh . . . words that don't do any work and don't much want to. A salivation of words after the banquet." In July 1946 the French journal *Les Temps Modernes,* edited by Jean Paul Sartre, published a short fiction (called in French a *nouvelle,* indicating a form longer than a short story, but shorter than a novel). It was entitled "Suite," and it was written by Samuel Beckett, his first published work in French and his first monologue. In earlier fiction Beckett had experimented with embedded monologues—Arsene's long lecture to Watt, Mr. Madden's interrupted story to Mercier and Camier—but unlike these partial uses, the *nouvelle* emanated directly from the mind of the speaker, omitting the dichotomy that Beckett had previously employed between a character and a storyteller who tells about him. Gone is Sam who records Watt's story; Sam and Watt become what they in fact were: voices of an author who created them both. The "salivation of words" is the reconstruction of the experiences of the past reflected, as the speakers often remind us, "with the celebrated advantage of tranquility" after the less than sumptuous banquet Beckett characters call their lives.

The technique was hinted at in *Watt,* where, in Part 4, the narrator talks of "a disquieting sound, that of soliloquy, under dictation . . ." The self telling itself stories—Sam in the head of Watt or the reverse—becomes the dominant mode of narrative representation in the subsequent writing. Beckett uses the word *soliloquy,* but I have used the word *monologue,* with which it is often interchangable, because soliloquy is more closely associated with dramatic speech, embedded in plays and not in fiction.[3] While these monologues take place within the skull of the speaker, they are not to be confused with what is often called in literature interior monologues or streams of consciousness. The voices in the *nouvelles* and the fictions that follow tell stories: they are constantly editing, sorting, organizing. Beckett is not trying, as James Joyce did, to tap the inchoate inner voice; he is trying to illustrate how the inner voice competes with the speaking voice, regales it with tales, and how the two voices, usually represented as *I* and *me* or *you* vie for the position within the self of a single, thinking, speaking, recording figure: the author.

The four short fictions date from the second half of 1946, that prolific period that also produced *Mercier and Camier.* Although written in the following order—"The End" by July; "The Expelled" from 6 to 14 October; "First Love" from 28 October to 12 November; and "The Calmative" begun on 23 December—they were published in a different order. In the English collection entitled *No's Knife,* they follow the order established in the original French edition: "The Expelled," "The Calmative," and "The End."[4] Beckett withheld publication of "First Love" until 1970. It first appeared in English in the collection entitled *First Love and Other Stories.*

In "First Love" a man describes his first experience with love at twenty-five, although the emotion is more clearly associated with another experience that runs through all the tales: exile. "What goes by the name of love is banishment, with now and then a postcard from the homeland," he says, starting his story with a long description of his father's death and his subsequent remove from the family home, two events that fuse in his mind with the advent of love. Alone on a bench near a canal—the town, he says, has two making it most likely Dublin—he is joined one evening by a woman he first calls Lulu and then renames Anna. After several encounters, the speaker finds that "she disturbed me exceedingly, even absent," and consents to join her in her room providing she first rid it of excessive furniture, which he abhors. So lethargic is the lover that he experiences what he calls "my night of love" while asleep. "One shudders to think of her exertions," is all he says of the experience.

Life seems to settle down into a routine for the pair, resembling the lives of Murphy and Celia: the woman once more a prostitute, the man desiring a return "to the slow descents again, the long submersions." Tranquillity is destroyed not by imprecations over work but by pregnancy. The speaker denying responsibility—"If it's lepping . . . it's not mine"—abandons the woman in the throes of childbirth, recounting that her cries "pursued me down the stairs and out into the street." Though the event is past, the cries linger on in his mind.

In "The Expelled" the speaker again begins by recounting an expulsion from the home "I would gladly have died in . . . . " Like Watt his first act is a fall, tumbling down the steps he has climbed "a thousand times," and his first feeling confusion since he still cannot say with certainty how many stairs there are. He also has the recognizable Watt walk: "Stiffness of the lower limbs as if nature had denied me knees, extraordinary splaying of the feet to right and left of the line of march." He attributes the condition to early incontinence that continued, like his education, to the third form.

He attempts to walk on the sidewalk but narrowly misses "crushing a child," no great evil, he thinks, since "I loathe children and it would have been doing him a service, but I was afraid of reprisals." Finding the way too hazardous, he enters a cab to continue his meandering through the city, and shares lunch with the driver, who invites him home at dusk to spend the night. When they arrive, the man decides he would prefer a night in the stable and makes his bed in the now-unhitched cab, watched over by the suspicious horse. Toward daybreak, he attempts to leave the stable, finds the door bolted and exits through a small window.

"The Calmative" is a story about storytelling, making it a model for the trilogy which follows, most particularly *Malone Dies,* whose central theme, as here, is the calming effect of fiction. Like that novel, it describes a man telling himself stories so that he won't have "to listen to myself rot." Stories may bring the hoped-for calm of the title, a condition all Beckett characters desire. Like *The Unnamable,* the fiction he tells comes from beyond the grave: "I don't know when I died," is the first line of the *nouvelle.* The story befits the interior landscape, "for we are needless to say in a skull": vague locales, spectre people, images of dens and ruins seemingly interchangeable. The speaker is another outcast with no fixed address, again in Dublin (unnamed) "the city of my childhood." He is clothed in the familiar greatcoat and hat, attached, like those of the trilogy men, with a string. And like them, he follows a similar route: "For me now the setting forth, the struggle and perhaps the return."

Beginning by emerging from a wood, in search of human contact, he sees a man in a brown suit entertaining an audience of men and women. Much as he would like to linger with the assemblage, he reminds himself, "But it's to me this evening something has to happen." The things that do happen are few: he wanders to the harbor and thinks of boarding a vessel undetected; meets a young boy with a goat who offers him candy before retreating "like a young centaur," becoming one with his animal; sees a cyclist going his way. "All were going the same way as I was," he thinks, sounding a theme Maddy Rooney will repeat in *All That Fall.* Finally, after taking temporary refuge in a church, climbing to the top on narrow, winding stairs, he returns to the street in search of contact, and meets a man who desires to hear his life's story, tells him his own as an example, and offers to sell him a phial from the case he carries. Convinced that the speaker has no money, the man agrees to exchange the calmative for a kiss which is bestowed on the forehead. The speaker then continues on his way, falling to his knees in a crowd, content for a time to be among humans. At the end, however, he finds himself back again, alone in the skull, with his own voice relating the fiction that he has concocted to dispel the dark, "in the same blinding void as before."

The last of the three collected stories, "The End," is the longest in the English edition of *No's Knife*—twenty-three pages compared to fifteen pages for "The Expelled," and seventeen pages for "The Calmative." It is also the most developed and lyrical of the three. It begins with the speaker being ejected again, this time from an unspecified type of hospital where he has been a patient. He is given clothes from a deceased man and some money. Reluctantly bidding goodbye to the doctor, whose name is Weir, and leaving the grounds, he goes out in pursuit of lodging, as in "The Expelled," pained again by his contact with society: "My appearance still made people laugh." He finally finds a basement room in the home of a woman who provides him with food and chamber pot. After the woman asks for six months' rent in advance, she disappears, and her place is taken by a new owner who evicts him, needing the room for his pig. Again on the street, he wanders lost in the city and country. Abruptly he mentions seeing his son—"the insufferable son of a bitch"—and later a man he has known in the past who invites him to share his lodgings in a cave near the sea where he lives with his ass.

After residing there for a time, the man finds it intolerable because of the proximity of the sea, and takes up residence instead in his friend's shed in the mountains, a dilapidated hut but "nevertheless a roof over my head." Needing food, he takes up begging with a tin hung from the button of his greatcoat, and his terrible condition provokes a street speaker to use him as an example for his diatribe against capitalism. The man returns once more to his shed, seeking refuge in an overturned boat he finds there. He sleeps in it, protected against rats by a wooden cover he fixes to the opening. The boat becomes even more secure and comforting than the cab in "The Expelled." The last image is of the speaker in his boat/bed, repeating the word *calm,* taking a phial—presumably obtained in the preceding story—and imagining that the boat is filling with water and he is going to sea. His final memory is of being with his father on a height and seeing the gorse burning on the side of the mountain. "The sea, the sky, the mountains and the islands closed in and crushed me in a mighty systole, then scattered to the uttermost confines of space."

In the *nouvelles* we find the beginning of a compulsion that runs through Beckett's later fiction: the need to tell stories, particularly the story of one's life. Beckett has his speakers reconstruct a past and a self that lived in that past, a way of creating calm and killing time in the present. Composition also becomes a way of avoiding the horrors of decomposition, as the speaker in "The Calmative" recognizes.

Since they are consciously creating the fiction of their lives, all four speakers are aware of the fictive process, editing as they go along. "But how describe it? Some other time, some other time," the speaker in "The Expelled" says. In "The End" he begins to describe his hut but finds the task impossible: "Only the ground-floor windows—no, I can't." After a particularly florid description in "The Calmative," he thinks "phew, if that's not clear." They are also involved with decisions about tense and person. "I'll tell my story in the past none the less, as though it were a myth, or an old fable," the man in "The Calmative" decides (although Molloy will use the same notion of myth to tell his story in the present). Since Beckett's speakers always feel themselves split, they have equal difficulty fixing on a pronoun that will cover the two voices of the self. In "The Expelled" the character refers to his past self as "he." No matter what the form, however, the speakers are continually reminding the reader that what is being told is an arbitrary collection of details, as well this as another. "The Expelled" ends with: "I don't know why I told this story. I could just as well have told another. Perhaps some other time I'll be able to tell another." "The End" concludes with the speaker thinking "The memory came faint and cold of the story I might have told, a story in the likeness of my life, I mean without the courage to end or the strength to go on." And in "The Calmative" the voice cancels the entire narrative: "All I say cancels out, I'll have said nothing." The constraints of the narrative form require some sort of cessation, while the speaker finds that his life continues. Fiction can be rounded off, shaped; life, since it is still being experienced, cannot be caught in the confines of a formal fiction. The dichotomy between fiction and life, first expressed in these short fictions, goads the subsequent Beckett speakers who also wish to capture themselves and their lives in stories, but cannot.

Another dichotomy between fiction and life in the *nouvelles,* which appears later in Beckett texts, is the pull between misanthropy and need for human succor. The character in "The Expelled" expresses his abhorrence of children; if children represent hope for the future, they are painful reminders to characters who reject such possibilities. Their death, as the speaker in "The Expelled" says, would be "a service" since it would shorten the inevitable and painful journey to death. Yet at the same time, the parallel need for companionship is so strong that the man in "The Calmative" is touched by the offer of candy from the young child with a goat. The act proves the man is still alive.

Characters feel a similar abhorrence for adults. "I felt them hard upon me, the icy, tumultuous streets, the terrifying faces," the man in "The End" thinks. Against such a hostile world, similar to the world of quid pro quo that Murphy eschewed, the protagonist in "First Love" is content to sink into his own private world, the speaker in "The End" pleased that his basement retreat allows only the image of feet to disturb his isolation. The kindness of the old man in the cave is rejected; he prefers to exist alone. In "First Love" he succumbs to Lulu/Anna but only to gain again the peace she has disturbed.

What holds the *nouvelles* together is that in all the speakers still need some sign of their own existence, some human contact. They are less misanthropic than isolated, their retreats more self-protection and survival than choice. For all, the overriding condition that causes the contradictory tendencies is the experience of exile, displacement from home. Having lost their shelters, the figures seem wary of renewing human contacts, yet are constantly pursuing some sort of womb substitutes—closed, dark places such as the cab, the boat, narrow stairways—as a way of compensating for the primal expulsion: birth. Comfort is short-lived, however; they are once more ejected by the imminent birth of a child, a new landlord, a physician making room for another patient. Only their stories bring temporary calm, but they too must end, bringing the storytellers back to the world where they can find no haven.

## The Trilogy

The trilogy stands at the center of Beckett's oeuvre, the most thorough depiction of the particular world in which his mature fiction is based: the skullscape of a loquacious speaker attempting to talk himself into existence. Characters and situations, reconstructions of memories, flights of fancy, snippets of facts, and descriptions are filtered through the consciousness of a first-person storyteller. All voices are his voice, all stories his stories. The only fixity is the *I* alone in a dark, closed place—a room in the first two stories, an "empty space" in the third. The reader may travel outward along the path of the narrative, but is forced to return again and again to the point of departure, the consciousness of the speaker who remains "the teller and the told."

They work in darkness and confusion, their "sense of identity . . . wrapped in a namelessness often hard to penetrate." In desperation they create a persona, a "little creature," the better to study and know themselves. But when the creation seems too paltry, too unlike its creator, or when it becomes so compelling that it threatens to subsume the creator in its own veracity—a veracity he knows is not his own—the creator destroys it, only to begin again with another name and another voice. The godlike writer creates an image he hopes is his own, devouring it when the creation fails to replicate the self he imagines.

The dilemma for the storyteller/writer is fourfold. First, "How can I recognize myself who never made my acquaintance," the Unnamable asks. Second, how can I bring the *me* and *I* of self together under one name and one voice? As the Unnamable also recognizes, "But enough of this cursed first person, it is really too a red herring . . . . Bah, any old pronoun will do, provided one sees through it." Third, how can I find words to express the selves I do not know? "It, say it, not knowing what," the Unnamable says. Finally, how can I speak my way to the desired end: silence? Only in the cessation of the creative act or in death can such silence be achieved. The speakers know these options and reject them. While the Unnamable may say "Talking of speaking, what if I went silent," he continues talking for talk is life, and in life exists the only hope they have: the hope that they may find the words that will finally lead to themselves.

That is not to imply that all the characters in the trilogy, or in the subsequent fiction, speak in one voice. "Prime, Death, and Limbo," were the words Beckett used to describe the three *nouvelles* in *No's Knife*.[5] The words are appropriate for the three time periods charted in the trilogy. Molloy, while already toothless and hairless, is probably as "prime" as he ever was; Malone, confined to his deathbed, is nearing ninety; and the Unnamable, that disembodied, gelatinous form wearing puttees, is in a state beyond life, in limbo. Their voices and concerns reflect their age and situation, a literary triptych of the stages of man: Molloy seeks himself in his relationship with his mother; Malone is interested only in having his stories carry him to the threshold of his life; and the Unnamable frantically searches for an end to the struggles that have followed him beyond the grave.

Read as a unit, the novels offer a panorama of the interior world of the mind; however, each is a discrete work. When the first novel was written between September 1947 and January 1948, Beckett seemed to have only two works in mind. The original French version reads, "this time, then once more I think then it'll be over." In the English translation, completed by the author in 1951, he adds, "perhaps a last time" to indicate his additon of a third novel. The only references Beckett makes between the novels are those examples of intertextuality common to most Beckett fiction, references to past characters alive in the consciousness of the present speaker. The effect of crossreferences is to point to the outline of a creator behind them all who has spun them in an attempt to spin himself. Thus, the individual failures of characters are not anomalies; they become part of the human struggle to transcend the limits of language and the limits of self, engaged in by them and by the one who created them. While each character may fail, the creator achieves a kind of success in his ability to realize their failures in fiction, to wrest meaning from language and give them life.

***Molloy.*** *Molloy* is divided precisely into two eighty-four-page sections. The first is the story of a speaker, Molloy, no first name, who finds himself in his mother's room, is unsure of how he arrived, and chronicles the beginning of the path that led him there. Unlike former Beckett characters, with no fixed profession, he is a writer, and is parceling out the story of his journey to a man who comes on Sundays, takes the pages, and requests more. The story Molloy tells and the story he writes are the same, problems with the act of creation interspersed periodically with the story being created, so that the two experiences—writing and searching—become reflections of each other. Chronologically, we enter the narrative at the end, the events described already over, with only the recounting to complete. "What I'd like now is to speak of the things that are left, say my goodbyes, finish dying," Molloy begins.

After a two-page introduction that acts as a kind of preface—a technique repeated in the following two novels—Molloy turns, without transition, to a description of two men A and C (in the French version A and B) seen approaching, passing, and moving away from each other, A "back to town," C "on by-ways he seemed hardly to know . . . for he went with uncertain steps . . . ." Like the opening story of Mr. Hackett in Beckett's novel *Watt,* the introductory image foreshadows the central action of the novel: Molloy's journey toward his mother, and Moran's journey, in Part 2, toward Molloy. A and C become icons, prefiguring these tedious travels toward unknown destinations, the observed and the observer equally shrouded in doubt. The opening images also offer Molloy a means of introducing himself through the only device he has when talking of the self: indirection. By learning about C, we learn about Molloy: that he is "a sorry sight," does not smell good, wears a hat attached to his greatcoat by a string tied to a buttonhole, is lame and maneuvers on crutches, prefers to sleep in the mornings.

Moving from his revery about A and C, with the physical outlines of his own person now etablished in the narrative, Molloy returns to the subject of his mother, whom he calls Mag, explaining that the gutteral *G* obliterates the preceding "Ma." He calls her Mag and she calls him Dan, although that is the name of his father. He also describes the elaborate semiotic code he has developed for communication with her "by knocking on her skull": "One knock meant yes, two no, three I don't know, four money, five goodbye." He concludes his evocation with the thought, "And if ever I'm reduced to looking for a meaning to my life . . . it's in that old mess I'll stick my nose to begin with, the mess of that poor old uniparous whore and myself the last of my foul brood . . . . "

"Now that we know where we're going, let's go there," Molloy thinks, anxious to set off on the way he has charted. He travels on a bicycle, the favorite mode of transportation for Beckett characters, none described with more love and relish than Molloy's. A familiar obstruction to bicycles and bicyclists appears immediately in the omnipresent figure of authority, the policeman. He asks the question Molloy cannot easily answer, "What are you doing there?" and he requires something Molloy finds difficult to produce, proof of his identity. The only papers Molloy has are "the bits of newspaper used to wipe myself." These he offers, and for his pains, is taken to jail.

Having survived incarceration, Molloy proceeds, spending the night by a canal, probably indicating Dublin, under the watchful eye of a shepherd, a figure who also appears in Part 2. With daybreak Molloy shakes off his "raglimp stasis," once more astride his bicycle, until he accidentally runs over and kills a dog belonging to a woman he first calls Loy or Mrs. Lousse, or Sophie, and settles on Lousse. He is taken to her home to help bury the animal and stays on to become a surrogate for the lost pet. Molloy accuses her of poisoning his beer, to "mollify Molloy," and he becomes in her care "nothing more than a lump of melting wax, so to speak." The interlude allows Molloy to recount past sexual experiences, with a chambermaid and with a woman identified by the tripartite name Ruth/Edith/Rose. From these experiences Molloy concludes that all women become "one and the same old hag, flattened and crazed by life.

And God forgive me, to tell you the horrible truth, my mother's image sometimes mingles with theirs."

After escaping Lousse's house, but leaving his bicycle behind, Molloy painfully wanders the streets of the town seeking refuge in a shelter and an alley. Evicted from both, he enters a chapel and plans to kill himself, but is dissuaded by the thought of pain and the belief that "death itself must be a kind of backsliding." Dismissing suicide as an option—"So much for that"—Molloy leaves the town and heads toward the sea. While walking the strand, he launches into a five-page description of the various ruses he has used in order to rotate the sixteen sucking stones he carried on his person to assuage hunger. The section is one of Beckett's most hilarious parodies of the elaborate procedures people invent for achieving ends that they never question, an indictment of Western logic comparable to the ratiocinations of *Watt.* Why the stones must be alternated is never discussed, why sixteen stones are needed is unchallenged. Exhausted from the sheer weight of calculation, Molloy says: "And the solution to which I rallied in the end was to throw away all the stones but one, which I kept now in one pocket, now in another, and which of course I soon lost, or threw away or gave away, or swallowed." So much for the plans and organization of man. In the wake of the collapse of logic Molloy remains "the black speck I was, in the great pale stretch of sand."

Leaving the sea and the few people who have furtively viewed him there, he turns once more toward land, and is forced to cross a swamp to enter the town, unable to go directly there since "they never had heard of Watt," that inveterate walker of straight ways. Molloy's physical condition deteriorates as he painfully draws himself forward: "I hobble, listen, fall, rise, listen and hobble on," he thinks as he is reduced to crawling through the forest on the edge of the swamp. While there he encounters a charcoal burner who, much like the old man in "The End," offers him kindness and lodging, but whose love is repellent, and Molloy, bracing himself on his crutches, strikes the man with his swinging feet. He dismisses the event which has "no interest in itself, like all that has a moral." Attempting to proceed in a straight line, but moving in a circular fashion—direction through indirection, he hopes—Molloy hears the distant sound of a gong and a voice "telling me not to fret, that help was coming. Literally." The season is spring, and Molloy rests in a ditch. His chronicle ends with "Molloy could stay, where he happened to be."

Part 2 shifts without any explanation to another speaker, his name "Moran, Jacques. That is the name I am known by." It is midnight and he is at his desk writing; his son, also named Jacques, sleeps nearby. Unlike the narrative of Molloy that flows in two gushing paragraphs, Moran's report is orderly and precise, befitting the character who says of himself: "I like punctuality"; "I had a methodical mind and never set out on a mission without prolonged reflection as to the best way of setting out"; who "found it painful at that time not to understand"; and who says of his writing, "I write . . . with a firm hand weaving inexorably back and forth and devouring my page with the indifference of a shuttle." Despite his apparent differences from the disorderly, indecorous Molloy, Moran finds himself in a similar situation as his predecessor in the novel. He too is writing for a man who arrives only on Sundays and is always thirsty, as is Molloy's visitor. Perhaps reflecting the logical mind that shapes the section, the visitor in this section is given a name, Gaber, and an employer, Youdi, for whom Moran also works as an agent—some sort of detective—given to tracking down people, who turn out to be, with one exception, characters from earlier Beckett novels: "What a rabble in my head, what a gallery of moribunds. Murphy, Watt, Yerk, Mercier and all the others," Moran writes. To this list is added the name of Molloy, the latest person Moran is asked to find.

Bearing orders from one Youdi, Gaber appears on a quiet Sunday afternoon in August disturbing Moran as he is about to leave for church to receive communion. "It was impossible for me to refuse," Moran explains, although the sudden assignment on which he is required to leave that evening causes him discomfort: "I felt a great confusion coming over me." After drinking a beer with Gaber, he goes to church alone, his son having gone earlier, and takes communion from Father Ambrose, not disclosing his earlier imbibing. The two have an insipid conversation about hens and neighbors, and Moran returns home feeling more disturbed. Before his evening meal he lies in bed thinking of his new case and reveals that before Gaber's arrival, the spectre of Molloy had already haunted him: "Perhaps I had invented him, I mean found him ready made in my head." He describes Molloy as "Just the opposite of myself in fact."

Reluctantly aroused, Moran begins the preparations for the journey on which he is to be accompanied by his son who is ill the evening of departure, but who obediently, if sullenly, does as his father orders. After deciding on his attire—shooting suit with knee breeches, stout black boots, stockings to match, straw boater, yellowed by rain, carrying massive-handled winter unbrella—and his means of transportation, an autocycle, Moran bids goodbye to Martha, his maid, and leaves, keys in hand, morphine tablets in pocket, and son trailing behind. Unlike Molloy, who cannot stand to see anything receding behind him, Moran turns "a last time towards my little all, before I left it, in the hope of keeping it."

As he travels his knee, that had begun to ache the evening before, stiffens, and he is reduced to hobbling, much like Molloy. Unable to go further, he sends his son to a nearby town to purchase a bicycle and a sidecar, while he waits in a forest. Alone for three days, Moran meets a man with a club and white hair who asks for bread, but whom he gives sardines. On the second day another man appears dressed in a blue suit, black boots, with a fishhook in his hat, "his face resembling my own," Moran thinks. The man talks brusquely and inquires after the first man, whom Moran denies seeing. Moran attacks him, without explanation. "I am sorry I cannot indicate more clearly how this result was obtained, it would have been something worth reading. But it is not at this late stage of my relation that I intend to give way to literature," is all he says of the matter, passing it over as quickly as Molloy does his confrontation. He notes that the dead man has stopped resembling him. Alone on the third day, Moran passes time by asking himself questions until his son arrives with the bicycle, and the duo continues once more.

After continual bickering with his son, Moran wakes one day to find the boy, his money, and the bicycle gone, and himself alone "with my bag, umbrella, and fifteen shillings." Undaunted, he painfully moves on until he reaches Molloy's land, Bally, where he also hopes to find someone he calls Obidil "whom I so longed to see face to face." However, in the forest outside Molloy's town he is met by Gaber, who delivers the following message from Youdi: "Moran, Jacques, home, instanter." After questioning Gaber and learning that Youdi has said "Life is a thing of beauty . . . and a joy forever," the bedraggled, crippled Moran turns and retraces his way to his own land, Turdy. "It was August, September at the latest that I was ordered home. It was spring when I got there." On his way he encounters a big ruddy farmer, possibly the same one he has seen on the way out, and tells him that he is on a pilgrimage to the Turdy Madonna, a ruse Moran thinks necessary to forestall any questions. He arrives at his own home, finds his bees and hens dead, Martha gone, his home in darkness, and a letter awaiting him from Savory tellng him his son is well. After describing the summer he spent in his unkempt garden, his narrative switches to the future tense and Moran indicates that he plans on "clearing out" and that his son has returned. He ends by describing the voice that had come to him: "It told me to write the report . . . . Then I went back into the house and wrote, It is midnight. The rain is beating on the windows. It was not midnight. It was not raining."

Going even further than in *Watt,* Beckett fragments the narrative structure of *Molloy,* beginning each section with a different writer whose story has already ended, moving the former toward the latter and the latter toward the former, but never completing the lacuna between Molloy and Moran; the circle—like the one pictured in Erskine's room in *Watt*—remains incomplete. As the above summary indicates, the plots in both sections concern quests: Molloy's for his mother, Moran's for the spectre that has haunted him, the "massive, hulking" figure of Molloy. Both quests seem to be undertaken in the region of the mind, what Molloy calls "the within, all that inner space one never sees." Beckett's accomplishment in the novel is to offer a picture of this "space one never sees."

Molloy, who opens the novel, sets the limits of this inner world whose dimensions can only be approximated since they must be drawn in words that exist for Molloy "as pure sound, free of all meaning." Molloy's concern is centered on the means to articulate the experience he has, the search for language paralleling the search for his mother, both—if found—keys to the self. In rhythmic, melodious prose Molloy describes the problem of a language-centered existence: "Yes, even then, when already all was fading, waves and particles, there could be no things but nameless things, no names but thingless names . . . . All I know is what the words know, and the dead things, and that makes a handsome little sum, with a beginning, a middle and an end as in the well-built phrase and the long sonata of the dead." Murphy wanted to escape the world, Watt to understand it, Molloy wishes to articulate it. His quest is for means to bring forth life in language. Like his forerunners, he too is an inhabitant of "the little world" who "misjudged the distance separating me from the outer world," but more than they, he struggles to embrace the levels of human experience where "all things run together in the body's long madness."

By contrast, Moran is the quintessential material man, defined by the possessions he has acquired, at ease as long as he can remain on schedule and in surroundings he can control. He is, he says, "so patiently turned towards the outer world as towards the lesser evil." And had Beckett created a lesser novel, it would be enough to say that the two provide mirror images of each other, the two sides of human experience. While Moran does begin as a direct antipode of Molloy, during the course of his journey and reports he becomes captive of his quarry, prey to the victim who eludes him. Molloy is presented not only as counterforce but as the inchoate voice in the mind of the punctilious respectable Moran, that material goods, church observance, and paternal prerogatives cannot quell, a voice which finally leads to "a crumbling, a frenzied collapsing of all that had always protected me from all I was always condemned to be." Moran never finds Molloy, but he does experience "my growing resignation to be dispossesed of self." Molloy, nascent within him, usurps the reasoned, rational Moran, making him "unrecognizable."

Searching for roots, losing self, and finding selfhood through struggle: these are the themes of myth, the "mythological present," Molloy says, for which the past tense of his writing is suited. Woven through both stories are threads of traditional mythoi. Molloy's search for his mother, his arrival at her room/womb embodies the psychoanalytic oedipal connection between selfhood and mother. With language acquisition tied to the Freudian primal experience, Moran's desire to see Obidil—libido backward—is associated with his shift toward the less-structured presence of Molloy. Using traditional Freudian terms, Molloy might be seen as the id that the ego and superego in Moran are unable to cauterize and that must be united to them and acknoweldged in order for the whole individual to merge.

References to literary myths of quest, particularly those of Ulysses, can be found in *Molloy* as well: Lousse an ample Circe, offering the moly of forgetfulness to a malleable Molloy; a young woman on the beach a shadowy Nausicaa leaving her group to gain a glimpse of Molloy; and the proliferating policemen Cyclops, fixed with one-eyed tenacity on impeding the path of the traveling hero. It is also possible to find, as it is in all works of art, the quest of the artist after his art, the attempt to break with the past—here the mother figure—and find a vehicle to bring forth a personal view of the world.

Religion myths can also be traced through the meanderings of Molloy/Moran. Both are under the employ of Youdi—from which *Youpsin* comes, a colloquial epithet for *Jew* in French—perhaps the Old Testament God, who sends his messenger Gaber or Gabriel to deliver his orders. The two protagonists may also replicate the two thieves crucified with Christ, one of whom—according to the Gospel of St. Luke—is saved, a tempting average to taunt all Beckett couples from Mercier and Camier on. The presence of the shepherd and his flock in both sections of the novel reinforces the religious reading, as does Molloy's image of cargo of nails and timber "on its way to some carpenter" against a horizon "burning with sulphur and phosphorous," to which Molloy thinks "I was bound." For Moran, who begins by performing hollow rituals he further falsifies, the teleological questions he asks himself on his journey lead him to a revised paternoster: "Our father who art no more in heaven than on earth or in hell, I neither want nor desire that thy name be hallowed, thou knowest best what suits thee. Etc." The pilgrimage to the Turdy Madonna, with its scatalogical associations, is diversionary not actual.

While all these readings of *Molloy* are possible—even encouraged by Beckett's use of quotation and direct reference—it is a mistake to single out any one and doggedly follow that, allowing it to subsume all others. To do so is to limit the scope of the parable of quest, too narrowly ascribing it to one fable when the power of the novel comes from its ability to inscribe all human explorations: psychological, religious, literary, or unnameable.

More than anything else, *Molloy* must be approached as a work of fiction, a narrative about narrative, where two storytellers struggle for the words and phrases that will bring their journeys into being, since the travels of Molloy and Moran exist only in the travelogues each creates. More directly than in "The Calmative," but less than in *Malone Dies,* Beckett attempts to make the fictive process the central issue, a model for any other quest. By having Moran negate the report he has written ("It was not midnight. It was not raining.") Beckett illustrates that any attempt to capture the past will become, of necessity, a fiction. The experiences of the dual protagonists are clouded by the unverifiable nature of the past and by the distortions of language. To make the point in earlier works Beckett resorted to lapses in the narrative, question marks, addenda. In *Molloy* and the following fiction he builds the disjunctions directly into the fiction, with no signposts to warn of pitfalls. The reader shares the experience of the speakers, stumbling as they stumble because there is no hand but theirs, shaky and unsure, to point the way. Their inabilities to reach their goals are a reflection of the difficult way all must tread, the whey of words.

Such a journey could be unbearable were it not for the Beckettian humor. Beckett is still able to call up the grotesques and grotesqueries of society. Molloy's account of his communication with his mother, his experiences of lovemaking, his forays with police and do-gooders, his struggles with the logic of ordering sucking stones—all produce the grim humor of a world askew. More overt irony is leveled at the smug, complacent Moran and his entourage: the maid Martha, the banal priest Father Ambrose, the sadistic/masochistic relationship between father and son. With the deft hand of the caricaturist, Beckett, using few strokes, brings forth the central foibles of contemporary life.

Yet, as in all Beckett's works, irony is not an end, merely a means to make the going easier, a hiatus offered against the tedium and pain of the way. Were Molloy and Moran viewed from above, we could well laugh as we remember that, while Moran crawls, he is still dressed in a hunting suit with matching socks, that while Molloy rolls on, presumably his greatcoat flaps behind him. But the vantage point Beckett provides in the trilogy is not from without, but from within, forcing the reader to share the interior view of the protagonists who are less aware of the ridiculous shadow they cast before them than of the pain they endure within their self-enclosed world.

***Malone Dies.*** A man alone in a room, confined to a bed, unable to move more than a few inches, retrieving objects with the aid of a long, hooked stick; a notebook and two pencils—one of them unseen within the folds of the covers—his only means of diversion, writing himself stories while waiting to die. This is an outline of *Malone Dies,* the title in the present tense: Malone not dead but in the process of dying. "I shall soon be quite dead at last in spite of all," he begins his diary one April. In order not to watch the progress—"Have I watched myself live?"—he, like Molloy, tells stories, hoping that they will provide distraction and calm, the effects desired by the speaker in the short story, "The Calmative," from which the novel takes its theme. Molloy and Moran wrote of their pasts, Malone writes in the present, of fictional characters, in a diary form, with breaks indicating the end of entries or the intrusions of the writer who revises, edits, and comments on the fiction he creates. He calls the process of storytelling "a game," one he had not been able to play in the past but hopes now to master.

Since Malone remembers little of the past, we learn few facts about him. He says he is "nearly a century old," is presently in a room—not in a madhouse or hospital—and can't remember how he arrived, echoing Molloy on the same subject. Molloy said, "Perhaps in an ambulance, certainly a vehicle of some kind." Malone says, "In an ambulance perhaps, a vehicle of some kind certainly," the adverb qualifiers now affixed to the end of phrases as befitting a fiction designed to end life. We also learn that Malone, like all Beckett characters, once wore a greatcoat, with his hat attached to it by a string, a hat he "should rather like to be buried with," he says. Although inert, he once "wandered in the towns, the woods and wilderness and tarried by the sea," knew a man named Jackson who had a parrot, was "a great man for apples," but now is toothless, and "emits grey." Explaining this small store of biographical information, he says, "I have lived in a kind of coma."

He can only speculate on the reason for his present condition, again resorting to his favorite word, "perhaps": "But perhaps I was stunned with a blow, on the head, in a forest perhaps, yes, now that I speak of a forest I vaguely remember a forest." The image calls forth the dual assaults of Molloy and Moran on ill-defined gentlemen in forests, in the preceding novel. He does recall that at first a woman came into his room, bringing food and taking away his chamber pot, but now he has only his stick to retrieve the food an unseen person pushes through an opening in the door. "How great is my debt to sticks!" he says; however, such gratitude does not extend to humans. "Let me say before I go any further that I forgive nobody. I wish them all an atrocious life, and then the fires and ice. . . . " Despite this early outburst, spleen is not Malone's humor. He has few complaints or regrets, beside his inability to crawl anymore and is "not much given to nostalgia."

Having established his condition and his setting—his name will have to wait for forty-three pages, as opposed to the fourteen it took for Molloy to reveal his—Malone turns to making a plan for himself as Molloy did, a kind of outline that will allow him to see where he is going. He will tell himself stories, he says: "One about a man, another about a woman, a third about a thing and finally one about an animal —a bird probably." If these do not prove sufficient, he will add "an inventory" of his possessions.

The preface and exposition over in three long paragraphs of eight pages, Malone turns to his first story, about a family named Saposcat, and particularly the son, called Sapo by his friends, to whom Malone attributes his own problems of apprehending the world: Sapo "could make no meaning of the babel raging in his head, the doubts, desires, imaginings, and dreads." After the first paragraph, however, Malone begins to edit. Continuing for one more paragraph, he interposes with "What tedium," a phrase he repeats after several sections of narrative about the family. Malone is also wary about the use of inappropriate words, for example, the description "gull's eyes." "I know these little phrases that seem so innocuous and, once you let them in, pollute the whole of speech." Constantly richocheting between fiction and commentary, Malone makes clear the purpose of his characters: "And on the threshold of being no more I succeed in being another." Yet success would obliterate him and end the creative act, so Malone adopts a different strategy. While holding to the motto "live and invent," he writes "no longer in order to succeed, but in order to fail," thereby forcing himself to foist another story and another persona, suspending the end of fiction and the end of Malone.

Failing with Sapo, Malone switches to the Lamberts: man, wife, and two children. Big Lambert, the father, is a bleeder and disjointer of pigs. While he works, often aided by his son, Sapo appears and sits in the squalid kitchen with the mother. She is a figure Beckett describes with particular sensitivity. The other characters are often caricatures of rural brutality; she is depicted sympathetically in several striking images: trying to separate grit from lentils, and in frustration finally pushing both piles together, knowing her labors in vain; worrying about her maturing daughter; sitting alone in the silent kitchen during the night, her mind "a press of formless questions, mingling and crumbling limply away." She does not possess the ability to enter the "little world" of Beckett's male personae, but life has provided for her, as for Celia in *Murphy,* experiences that lead to a desire for the surcease of the physical world. Malone writes, "She set down the lamp . . . and the outer world went out."

After the extended interlude with the Lamberts and Sapo, Malone reenters decrying the ruse of fiction: "All the stories I've told myself, clinging to the putrid mucus, and swelling, swelling, saying, Got it at last, my legend." Undaunted, however, he dips a third time into his storehouse of stories, bringing forth a new character, Macmann, who usurps the discarded shape of Sapo, "Because in order not to die you must come and go, come and go." Macmann whose name means son of man, is introduced on "a true spring evening" while riding in a cab, a conveyance used by the speaker in "The Expelled." After a long aside in which Malone talks about his own condition, he returns to his fictive creation, giving him a setting, a hospital of some sort called "the House of St. John of God, number 166." Macmann is an inmate, like his creator, but mobile, and is served by a woman named Moll whose most distinguishing feature is the pair of ivory earrings in the shape of a crucifix she wears. A love affair develops between the two—sucky Molly and Hairy Mac—with love notes and poems exchanged, until Malone tires of the description because "Our concern here is not with Moll, who after all is only a female." She is replaced by another keeper, Lemuel, who "gave the impression of being slightly more stupid than malevolent."

Having created a fictional world that in many ways resembles his own, Malone interrupts the narrative to say that he has had an unexpected visitor—a man with a black tie, suit, white shirt ruffled at the wrist, oily black hair, and the tightest rolled umbrella he has ever seen. He also comments that the food supply has stopped. The two events seem to presage the end for him. Returning to his diary and Macmann, he describes one April morning, Easter Sunday, when the hospital is visited by Lady Pedal who desires to take the inmates—known in the neighborhood as Johnny Goddams or the Goddam Johnnies—for an outing to the islands. Lemuel proceeds to round up four, three of whom bear strong resemblances to Murphy, Watt, and perhaps the composite Molloy/Moran.

With no transition, Malone describes the boat they take, the island on which they land, Lemuel's murder of Lady Pedal and the attendants, and his return to his charges. The narrative closes without Malone's intervention. The last image is of Lemuel's hatchet, and the last refrain is of cessation: "he will not hit anyone, he will not hit anyone anymore, he will not touch anyone anymore, either with it or with it or with it or with or . . . ," the words trailing off, without punctuation into single-line phrases describing the objects Lemuel—and presumably Malone—will no longer use. The story, the diary, and Malone end.

Both Molloy and Moran are writers, but neither displays his craft so conspicuously as Malone. In none of Beckett's other novels is the art of writing held up to the close scrutiny it receives in Malone's diary. We actually watch the words form on the page, sometimes single words standing alone on a line, poised to be cancelled out in the following paragraph; sometimes fragments, such as the agonized phrases that end the narrative, positioned like the tail end of monologue, arduously being squeezed out. The novel thus brings together two themes alluded to in earlier works—the problem of writing and the problem of living—and provides the exact vehicle to ally them. The struggle to find words to describe selfhood becomes part of the struggle to live.

A special rapport and a special verisimilitude are created by the process of watching a writer write. Rather than the finished product, free of mistakes, an artifact produced in some fictive past, we are privy to the present act of composition, watching—as it were—over the shoulder of Malone as he seeks for the words that will allow him to continue his chronicle. The persona becomes more human and more real as a result. When, after presenting a fact about his character Sapo, he writes, "no, that won't do," we gain a glimpse of the hesitations involved in the creation of literary figures. While *Molloy* is a more ambitious and challenging book and *The Unnamable* is more painful, *Malone Dies* is the most accessible work in the trilogy.

It is also the most immediately apprehensible. Malone says he will attempt to "die tepid," having reached "the final tot" clear and calm. Yet we are not surprised when he does not "go gentle into that good night." While the "rail" comes from the persona, Lemuel, it indicates the all-too-familiar tendency of human nature to hold tenaciously to consciousness. The internecine events that end the novel may shock; they do not puzzle the reader who understands that Lemuel is the embodiment of the violence with which Malone struggles to maintain life. Earlier Malone had used sea imagery to describe what he believed would be the condition accompanying his death: "I want to be there a little before the plunge, close for the last time the old hatch on top of me, say goodby to the holds where I have lived. . . . " The end he experiences is quite different; it comes unannounced, gratuitous, as Lemuel's sudden attack, and leaves no time for the sentimental fond goodbyes, for closed hatches, or explanations.

Since the only action in the novel is the action accompanying word choice, it is appropriate that Beckett creates the struggle for self through his manipulation of words. In the lyrical passage below he describes Malone's experience: "the rapture of the vertigo, the letting go, the fall, the gulf, the relapse to darkness, to nothingness, to earnestness, to home, to him waiting for me always, who needed me and whom I needed, who took me in his arms, and told me to stay with him always . . . , whom I have often made suffer and seldom contented, whom I have never seen." The repetition of the six articles and the accompanying nouns leads directly to five prepositions, which in turn are replaced by four pronoun forms, forming a linked grammatical sequence that mirrors the sequence of personae and stories that create the fiction. The final "him" in the quotation is unseen, but his presence is given shape through Beckett's careful crafting of the syntax. Malone may experience the self as an inchoate buzz alive in his head, but Beckett has wrested from such murmurs an order that shapes "the spray of phenomena."

The technique is paralleled by Beckett's larger manipulation of the character of Malone who becomes, through his own admission, one in a sequence of characters, the M's: "Murphys, Merciers, Molloys, Morans and Malones, unless it goes on beyond the grave." As Malone discards his Sapos and Lamberts only to introduce Macmann, Beckett discards his previous M's to bring forth Malone who will, in turn, be replaced by yet another figure—the Unnamable "from beyond the grave," one more in the unending search for a final persona, the true persona. By having Malone remember his fictional predecessors, even place them within the fictional walls of St. John of God hospital, Beckett makes Malone's attempts at fictionalizing a microcosmic reflection of Beckett's parallel struggle. Each novel thus describes the process of self-actualization and becomes one in a larger sequence, like the sequence of servants in *Watt,* without perceptible beginning and without discernible end. Malone is a mask, discarded by an unseen hand, leaving yet another mask in place still hiding the identity of the creator of all.

What is also significant about the novel is its pared-down canvas. Gone are the numerous characters and situations that teemed through earlier works, even as recently as *Molloy*. *Malone Dies* creates a single image—a dying man, inert, writing—and omits the busy history that led to his present condition. By focusing on one figure, the novel points to the talking heads that follow. It also bears a resemblance to the play Beckett was writing at the same time, *Waiting for Godot,* where characters, through lack of volition, are inert, waiting as much for death as for Godot.

***The Unnamable.*** *The Unnamable* begins, "Where now? Who now? When now? Unquestioning." Three questions followed by the renunciation of questioning. The dichotomy introduces the dichotomies that follow. A speaker who appears dead talks; someone who says, "Talking of speaking, what if I went silent?" retorts, "I shall never be silent, never"; one who describes his body as having the consistency of mucilage, adorns his gelatinous form with puttees; who bemoans the time he has wasted spinning stories in the past—"All these Murphys, Molloys, and Malones do not fool me. They have made me waste my time"—proceeds to speak of himself by inventing three more fictional characters: Basil, Mahood, and Worm. These are just some of the puzzling contradictions in *The Unnamable,* the most difficult book in the trilogy to read and—most probably—to write. *Molloy* and *Malone Dies* each took five months to complete, *The Unnamable* ten. In an inscription on the cover of draft A, Beckett wrote, "Beyond words?" The question is reflected in the form of the work. While the earlier novels had scraps of plot and characters for the reader, and perhaps the writer, to cling to, *The Unnamable* virtually scuttles the traditional stuff of fiction. For one hundred and twenty-three pages, the central concern is with a character who speaks an unending litany on his inability to speak.

More than any of his predecessors, even Malone, the unnamed speaker in the novel is aware of his predicament and talks incessantly about it. As if words were barriers between him and the truth he wishes to capture, he hurls himself at them in order to bore a hole through the partition that separates him from himself. But the obstruction does not give. Murphy talked of silence as "that frail partition between the ill-concealed and the ill-revealed" and desired to pass through it in order to enter the inner world. The Unnamable seems caught between worlds, unable to move outward or inward, capable only of incessant speech that leads in neither direction.

His talk reflects his desperate attempts to achieve silence. Although he tells himself stories, his are less structured than those of Molloy, Moran, and Malone. He can barely provide his three characters with situations, and he blurs the details until the narrative dissolves into his own plaint for an end. We have only to look at the structure of the opening lines to notice the deterioration. Gone are the carefully crafted sentences of Molloy, the precise formations of Moran, or the droll prose of Malone. The Unnamable's words become fragments that disintegrate further through the course of the novel until they end in one long shriek, a fifteen-hundred-word sentence, with ideas separated only by the brief respite of a comma. In both form and content, *The Unnamable* is the tail end of the trilogy.

To indicate the disintegration, Beckett uses the same basic outline, even some of the same situations employed earlier, and illustrates through their transformation how reduced his present character is. There is the familiar opening that marks all the stories in the trilogy: a brief introduction or preamble that establishes the characters' situation and intention. Just like Molloy and Malone, the Unnamable speaks of the difficulty of opening, but unlike them he offers almost no explanation for his difficulty: "I seem to speak, it is not I, about me, it is not about me. These few general remarks to begin with." Ironically, while the preceding prefaces lasted only a few pages, the Unnamable rambles on for fifteen. Confused, but in need of a beginning, he says: "But I have to begin. That is to say I have to go on." Eleven pages later he is still in the throes of his introduction: "I hope this preamble will soon come to an end." The inability to begin mirrors his basic dilemma: the inability to do—or say—anything at all. While Molloy and Malone could force themselves into some sort of narrative, the Unnamable continually wanders around a dead center he cannot bring to life.

Finally, shifting from introduction to exposition, he makes a stab at those concerns that filled the preceding novels at the outset: locale, physical descriptions, clothing. He states categorically that the place is "the inside of my distant skull where once I wandered, now am fixed." He is able to make out some spectres that seem to inhabit his space, particularly Malone who appears to be orbiting him, and a couple who collide, that make him think of the pseudocouple Mercier-Camier; yet the comfort of physical description seems closed to him. Unable to describe his dress, he can only assume he is lightly clothed because he can feel tears "coursing over my chest." He has a bit more luck with his body. As much as he would like to describe himself as an egg, he still has indications of a human form: "I know I am seated, my hands on my knees, because of the pressure against my rump, against the soles of my feet, against the palms of my hands, against my knees." The resistance of the outer world gives him or at least his skeletal structure a sense of physical existence. Whether he has a nose, penis, teeth, he discovers during the course of the narrative. At first he gives himself a beard, but thinks better and omits all hair: "it is a great smooth ball I carry on my shoulders, featureless, but for the eyes, of which only the sockets remain." Of the familiar objects that comforted other characters, there are none: no umbrellas, bicycles, or sticks; the "days of sticks are over," he says.

There are the ubiquitous "they" that plagued Molloy and Moran. The Unnamable's "they" seem to merge with these earlier tormentors, a group he says at one point issued reports from Bally, Molloy's land, and spoke to him of his mother, and of God, among other subjects. The most frightening of this group, he gives a name Basil, the first of his fictive characters. But rather than concentrate on this new persona, the Unnamable almost immediately abandons him in favor of yet another name and figure, Mahood.

"Perhaps I shall be obliged, in order not to peter out, to invent another fairy-tale, yet another, with heads, trunks, arms, legs and all that follows," the speaker states as he begins the process of externalizing himself through Basil and then Mahood. By telling Mahood's story he hopes to tell his own. Beckett, as he has done in earlier works, attributes to his opening tales the central dilemma embedded in the larger fiction: struggle for "home." A journey that ends in defeat echoes the story of the Unnamable, who uses the language of travel to express his plight: "I invented it all, in the hope it would console me, help me to go on, allow me to think of myself as somewhere on a road, moving, between a beginning and an end, gaining ground, losing ground, getting lost, but somehow in the long run making headway."

When mobile Mahood fails, the speaker takes him off the road and establishes him "stuck like a sheaf of flowers in a deep jar, its neck flush with my mouth, on the side of a quiet street near the shambles." The head in the jar is described as a kind of relic but, as Beckett may be indicating of all such relics, ultimately employed in commerce. His light points the way for the restaurant across the street, his position provides illumination of the nearby menu. Finally, even this story, vague and static as it is, fades with the speaker substituting the non-mammal Worm—"the first of his kind"—who also fails to merge with the self the Unnamable is trying to capture: "I'm Worm, no, if I were Worm I wouldn't know it, I wouldn't say it, I wouldn't say anything, I'd be Worm."

In the last section of the book the speaker continually vacillates between Mahood and Worm, hoping that by the friction produced in the struggle of the two he can bring forth himself. Finally, he gives up even this ruse: "I'm something quite different, a quite different thing, a wordless thing in an empty place." Having brought himself to this recognition, the speaker attempts to go on giving shape to the wordless thing in the black place. Sentences collapse of their own weight; ideas, separated by commas, drone on with heightened intensity and difficulty, almost subjectless until a final paroxysm marks the end of *The Unnamable,* which is not an end but a statement of continuation. It is one of the most often quoted passages of the Beckett canon: "I can't go on, you must go on, I'll go on, you must say words, as long as there are any, until they find me. . . . " "I" talking to "you" about "me," the tripartite form of self doing battle against the unnamed "they": that is the final image of *The Unnamable* and in many ways the ironic image that lurks behind all Beckett's fiction. A self that is split, talking aloud, trying through language to coalesce and to continue against the "they" that thwart it.

Having scattered his few puppets to the wind, the speaker stands without a story, unable to find sufficient fictional forms to cover himself, reduced to "The image of a vast cretinous mouth, red, blubber and slobbering, in solitary confinement." The "flitters of mind" have ceased to produce even the remnants of fiction. And yet the voice refuses to acknowledge its own fictional impasse. It will continue, even when there is nothing left to say. "Would it not be better if I were simply to keep on saying babababa, for example, while waiting to ascertain the true fiction of this venerable organ?" it asks.

Yet it is a mistake to assume that any words would suffice in order to fill the pages of *The Unnamable,* that Beckett has been reduced to the AEIOU of Eugene Ionesco's *The Bald Soprano.* On the contrary, while the speaker can find no fiction to express his dilemma, Beckett presents this dilemma in the most graphic terms. For page after page he describes the situation of one in a void, unable to realize himself or find a language to articulate the pain he experiences. The difficulty in reading *The Unnamable* does not come from confusion about the situation; if anything, it arises from the all-too-clear articulation of the horror of life in a "hard shut dry cold black place." It is possible, as Molloy and Malone recognize, to forget their situation because of the compelling nature of their stories. With *The Unnamable* there is no such danger. The scantiness of his fictions allows the clarity of his situation to break through. As comic as the head in the jar may be, it diverts but little from the overwhelming horror of the speaker in limbo.

Having discarded the apparatus of fiction almost entirely, in order to bring forth the unencumbered, unnamed speaker in the void, Beckett moves in his following fiction into this black hole of consciousness from which subsequent speakers try to extricate themselves, with less and less narrative support to sustain them.

# *Chapter Five*
# Skullscapes
## Fiction: 1950–1969

Samuel Beckett concluded *The Unnamable* in 1949 with the words, "I don't know, I'll never know, in the silence you don't know, you must go on, I can't go on, I'll go on." The sentence ends with a period, but it might just as well have paused with a comma, because in the next year Beckett again tried to record the antithetical desire for cessation and continuation expressed by an unnamed, first-person speaker. *Texts for Nothing* picks up, almost uninterrupted, the struggle: "Suddenly, no, at last, long last I couldn't any more, I couldn't go on. Someone said, You can't stay here. I couldn't stay there and I couldn't go on. I'll describe the place, that's unimportant." If ferreting out one unified self from behind numerous pronouns is impossible, yet going on is desired—even required—then a place description may suffice; for if place can be delineated, perhaps a person alive in that place may emerge.

The nine works written between 1950 and 1969 share a preoccupation with locale, albeit difficult to discern because of the conditions described in "Text I": "Glorious prospect, but for the mist that blotted out everything." The *Texts* of 1950, for all their "mist," are still awash in physical detail; the following fictions, however, jettison proper names and are reduced almost entirely to binary structural oppositions: light/dark, hot/cold, day/night, below/above, in/out. The obliteration of description is accompanied by abandonment of familiar graphological and syntactic structures. In *The Unnamable* Beckett began to move away from paragraphs. The last 110 pages of the 123-page novel are written in one unbroken unit. Sentences too collapse. The vast, compulsive rush for closure that issues forth from the speaker comes in unbroken streams, the last five pages one continuous sentence. *Texts for Nothing* restores punctuation but omits paragraphs, breaking only to distinguish sections. The following work, *How It Is*—one of Beckett's most radical departures from traditional syntactic form—abandons all punctuation and uses capital letters only for proper names and for emphasis. Later works like *Imagination Dead Imagine* and *Ping* reintroduce punctuation but omit paragraphs. Through these experimentations and variations Beckett places on his reader the very state of ambiguity his personae experience. For example, it is virtually impossible to understand a work like *How It Is* without carefully reading aloud and sorting slowly through the punctuationless phrases, trying to find some pattern and direction in a work bereft of traditional guides. Such reading elicits a reader response that approximates that of the protagonist hesitantly moving through an unmarked terrain "in the mist."

Even the titles of the works of this period are ambiguous. They eschew the proper names of past fiction which implied a self, unified and identifiable as a focal point. Instead they describe conditions: *Texts for Nothing, How It Is, Imagination Dead Imagine, All Strange Away.* These tripartite titles offer several possible pairings and possible meanings. For instance, the word *text* by itself implies a particular form, with scriptural origins; yet when coupled with the pivotal preposition *for,* the word becomes uncertain: are they texts on the subject of nothing or texts for no end, texts elucidating the nothing or meaningless writing? Similar ambiguities can be found in the juggling of the other three-word titles. Even when Beckett employs a single word, confusions abound. The title *Enough* may indicate sufficiency or the desire for cessation; *Ping,* a sound stripped of all lexical meaning—onomatopoetically approximating the sound of metal struck—can imply the clang of affirmation or the clack of defeat, depending upon how the title is "heard."

While French is Beckett's dominant language in the period (only *All Strange Away* and "From an Abandoned Work" were first written in English) there is no dominant fictional form. Of the nine works, only two, *How It Is* and *The Lost Ones,* are sufficiently developed to be called novels. While *Enough* bears some resemblance to a short story, "From an Abandoned Work," as the title indicates, is an aborted fragment; *Texts,* a composite; and *Imagination Dead Imagine, All Strange Away, Ping,* and *Lessness* impossible to categorize in traditional terms. The critic Ruby Cohn has called all the works "lyrics of fiction."[1]

Whatever general term one uses, the fact is that the writings are strikingly different from those Beckett fictions that precede them. They grow progressively shorter; the briefest, *Ping,* is only 3-1/4 pages. Gone are the traditional vestiges of plot; no bildungsroman of a young man trying to lose his fortune in London, as in *Murphy,* or of a man's search for his mother or his double, as in *Molloy.* There is still travel—the Beckettian requisite for continuation—but the direction is inward, back to the skullscape home. The skull becomes the circumscribed center from which the fictions emanate, a place from which the speaker attempts the triple task of defining the inner and outer world and of coalescing the two.

Beckett indicated the difficulty of such demands and of such confines when he commented in the sixties about his fiction of the preceding decade: "For me the area of possibilities gets smaller and smaller. . . . At the end of my work there's nothing but dust. . . . In the last book, *L'Innommble (The Unnamable),* there's complete disintegration. No 'I,' no 'have,' no 'being.' No nominative, no accusative, no verb. There's no way to go on."[2] The fictions of the next two decades are the "no ways" that Beckett created in order to "go on."

***Texts for Nothing.*** The texts are a series of thirteen individual sections, each complete in itself and only tangentially related, totalling sixty-five pages, and ranging in length from 2-3/4 pages (in "Text X") to 5-1/4 pages (in "Text III"). All are in the first person, the words of an unnamed speaker, never physically described, whose only possession, "a traditional hat," is gone. The speaker, punning on the preceding novels, recalls, "I was attached to it." But if physique is unmentioned and hat is absent, the familiar duality of mind and body still persists. The speaker in "Text I" says, "let them work it out between them, let them cease." But he immediately rescinds the wish, remembering that their end would be his own, since they are he: "Ah, yes," he muses, "we seem to be more than one."

The *Texts,* although repeating the familiar Cartesian split Beckett has described before, add to it. Whereas Malone is either storyteller or the tale told, and the Unnamable transforms into a succession of selves, the speaker in this sequence—if one speaker he be—acknowledges the duality present in any given moment. "I'm up there and I'm down here, under my gaze." "Up there" is a place of light where "life was babble," a "then" as compared to "now," the macrocosm, as compared to the dark below of the microcosm or, as he says in "Text II," that "ivory dungeon" of the skull. It is from the present location within the skull that the speaker ranges over the past, recollecting "life above" and images of people he knew there: Mother Calvet, also a rummager, accompanied by her dog and "skeletal baby-buggy"; Mr. Joly, late of *Molloy*; and Mr. Graves, a figure from *Watt* and *Mercier and Camier.*

They are not the only references to preceding fiction. The speaker directly mentions "a vulgar Molloy, a common Malone" in "Text IV." In "Text V" he poses the question: "Why did Pozzo leave home?"—recalling the figure from *Waiting for Godot,* the play written two years earlier. While not directly cited, the spectre of Murphy is present in "Text VI," invoked through locales around London where he trod and male nurses and keepers of the hospital where he worked. Dublin and Paris are also described: the former in "Text III," where the speaker remembers two old cronies, sitting on a bench watching the canal—an image from *Mercier and Camier*—and the latter in "Text VIII," "IX," and "XI."

Of all the shadowy images from "above" perhaps the most significant is one that appears in "Text I": the image of a father telling his son the nightly story of a "Joe Breem, or Breen," a tale of heroism that begins unhappily and ends happily. "The same old story I knew by heart and couldn't believe," the voice says. It is an image that first appeared in Beckett's earlier short story, "The Calmative." A variation is described in the same text as father and son are shown walking silently hand in hand. This picture from the past will surface in several subsequent fictions, particularly in *Company* and in *Worstward Ho,* where it becomes one of the three images still alive in the greatly reduced skullscape of the speaker.

The significance of the father/son image in *Texts* is less in the paternal ties it evokes than in the fictional process it introduces. The desire for a story with a happy ending is somehow connected with an earlier time and may explain the narrator's desire to turn his experience into stories. "There's going to be a story," the speaker in "Text III" proclaims as he begins the process that so many Beckett storytellers go through—getting himself going, begetting the story of himself. He employs the present continuous tense, the repeated "-ing" form generating the needed velocity to thrust his story into motion: "getting standing, staying standing, stirring about, holding out, getting to tomorrow."

At the start, the storyteller in "IV" is faced with the dilemma of direction: "Where would I go, if I could go, who would I be, if I could be, what would I say, if I had a voice." Objectifying himself and his quest for self by turning the process into fiction does not help; the speaker-cum-narrator is still stalled in his search: "It's the same old stranger as ever, for whom alone accusative I exist, in the pit of my inexistence, of his, of ours, there's a simple answer," the speaker in "IV" admits.

Not "simple," and not "an answer," the speaker tries other ruses to tease the self into confession. In "Text V" he creates a courtroom scene in which the narrator is both scribe and clerk, and presents a series of questions in an interrogation. Yet ironically, in this section, Beckett omits question marks and has the speaker/writer remind himself only near its conclusion: "don't forget the question-mark." Questions asked of self are less interrogative than declarative, just another device to prod the self into confession of its being. The device does not work.

The major concern of the remaining *Texts* is with the dilemma carried over from the trilogy: the task of articulating what remains hidden in silence, or the pull between language that conceals and silence that reveals. "Nothing ever but lifeless words," the voice in "Text XII" concludes. This "farrago of silence and words" is all the speaker in "VI" has to create his "little story," and it seems insufficient for his task. The man in "X" identifies himself only as "the head and its anus the mouth," an image reminiscent of that which closed *The Unnamable*. The words of "Text XI" could well have appeared in that former fiction: "I don't speak to him any more, I don't speak to me any more, I have no one left to speak to, and I speak, a voice speaks that can be none but mine, since there is none but me." Gone, however, is the frenzy of failure. In "Text XIII," the final text, Beckett offers an image to concretize the dilemma, "the screaming silence of no's knife in yes's wound." To indicate the significance of the image, Beckett called his collection of shorter prose of 1945–1966, which includes *Texts for Nothing, No's Knife.* The physical act of piercing "yes" with "no," of stabbing surety with doubt, can only be accomplished, he says, in a "silent scream." Again, the artistic problem of how to give voice to what is without voice is unsolvable. It is a problem that literally threw Beckett into silence in fiction for the next ten years. With the exception of the fragment "From an Abandoned Work," Beckett wrote no prose until 1960 when he once more attempted in *How It Is* to shape the "silent scream."

**From an Abandoned Work.** In the decade that separates *Texts* from *How It Is,* Beckett wrote only one prose piece, the aborted "From an Abandoned Work," written in English in 1956. Its closest companion piece is probably the short fiction *Enough,* written ten years later in French. Both are more firmly placed in the macrocosm than the skull. Like earlier characters, these avatars are still upright—though in *Enough* just barely—walking in the larger world. Both works are reminiscent of the *nouvelles.* Like "The Expelled," the fragment begins with a man speaking in the first person, describing his exit from his home. The "they" of former fiction becomes mother hanging out the window, not indifferent, but on the contrary weeping and waving. The weather is like that described in *Murphy, Mercier and Camier,* and those texts with Irish locales, where it rains until just before sunset "then blue and sun again a second, then night."

Like earlier travelers, the speaker indicates that while he has no destination, he is "on my way," his progress marked either in bursts of speed or in slow steps: "with me all was slow, and then these flashes, or gushes," he explains. "Vent the pent," is the inner phrase that marks the pace. Of earlier costumes that attire wayfarers in Beckett, only the stick remains. There is no mention of hat or boots, and of the long coat he says only, "I turned against it."

While dress is altered, the personality of the speaker is familiar. He has the attentive eye of a painter who frames scenes into still-life sketches. Mother at the window "white and so thin," becomes part of a composition framed by pale green window frame and grey house. He also has the accusatory plaint of Malone: "No, I regret nothing, all I regret is having been born." Garrulous, like all Beckett's figures, he is given to sore throats, thus reduced to whispering his diatribe. No Celia or star charts, no bicycles: this time the persona loves only the color white, a foreshadowing perhaps of the all-consuming whiteness that will pervade *Imagination Dead Imagine* and *Ping.* "White I must say has always affected me strongly," he explains. The first image the man encounters as he travels from home is a small boy—or perhaps a small man or woman—preceded by a white horse.

For all its similarity to works before, there is, in nascent form, an image that will dominate Beckett's plays in the 1970s and 1980s: a woman—here identified as his mother—whom he hears at night talking to herself, praying or reading out loud. This image will become the central one in *Footfalls, Not I,* and *Rockaby.*

Having ejected his speaker from home, got him moving and talking, Beckett abruptly ends the piece, leaving him fallen among great ferns with "my body doing its best without me," the last words of the text. In 1956 Beckett seemed unable to supply a destination; in 1960, in *How It Is,* he gives his speaker a fixed point and a line of movement: toward Pim in a straight line "wending its way eastward."

***How It Is.*** *Texts for Nothing* had been an attempt to break the impasse Beckett encountered at the end of *The Unnamable,* but the attempt failed. "Text XIII" trails off with the obstacles in place: true/not true, silence/not silence, no one/someone unreconciled. "No's knife in yes's wound," but *who* the wielder and *how* the thrust still remain hidden among the plethora of possible pronouns: "it and me, it and him, him and me." In 1950, unable to answer or to continue framing the questions, Beckett turned from prose to drama, completing six plays in the next decade. Only in 1960, after *Endgame, All That Fall, Krapp's Last Tape, Embers,* and *Acts Without Words I & II,* and immediately before *Happy Days* did he return to fiction. The result, *How It Is,* is a 133-page work divided into three parts of 41, 48, and 44 unpunctuated verse paragraphs each, an elliptical prose poem—referred to as a novel for want of a better term—devoted to telling what appears to be a simple tale of "how it was I quote before Pim with Pim after Pim how it is three parts I say it as I hear it."

"The end is in the beginning and yet you go on," the Unnamable observed. Like that earlier narrator, the speaker here, another nameless "I," tells a story already finished before he begins. He employs the present tense when talking of the past in the hope that by reconstituting the past in the present he may indicate not only "how it was" but, more important, "how it is" now. In the French the title *Comment C'est* precisely echoes the word *commencer* (to begin). The technique of adopting the present tense is appropriated from *Molloy* and *Malone Dies;* yet *How It Is* is different from those novels in several ways. First, the narrator is not writing his memoir alone in a room, at a desk, or in a bed. Instead, he is "on my face in the mud and the dark," the position of the unnamed speaker in *Texts for Nothing.* He shares with the earlier fictive writers an ignorance of how he arrived at his present station, but he finds himself more physically impoverished than they, with no bicycle, no son, no stick, not even pencil and paper. His only possessions are a sack tied around his neck with a cord, in which he keeps tins of fish and a can opener, a pun on the possibility of beginning. The origin of his narrative also differs. Unlike Molloy and Malone, he is not the initiator of his tale. Echoing a phrase first used in "Text V," he reminds the reader that "I say it as I hear it," and he underlines his function as recorder by interjecting "I quote," and periodically describing a "brief movement of the lower jaw," indicating speech. The teller in this fiction is himself being told, the narrator directed by unseen, unheard voices identified only as "they," who control the movements and possibilities open to the character.

*How It Is* is Beckett's most insistently auricular book, presenting a series of speakers breathing messages into the ears of listeners, heard first by the narrator who relays the words to a reader who, of necessity, must join the procession, speak aloud, and "hear" the text in order to decipher and make sense of the unpunctuated prose. For example, in the following passage—"all I hear leave out more leave out all hear no more lie there in my arms the ancient without end me we're talking of me without end . . . "—questions immediately arise that force the reader to say the words in order to decide how they are to be "heard." With which of the repeated "leave outs" does "more" go? Is one to "leave out all" or "all hear?" Does the speaker "hear no more lie" or "lie there in my arms?" And how is one to know? The difficulties of the reader replicate those the speaker describes on the first page of the work "ill-said ill-heard ill-recaptured ill-murmured in the mud brief movements of the lower face losses everywhere."

Despite his problems, from the beginning the speaker says that he will not detour, double back, circle. He commits himself to a narrative with beginning, middle, and end: "before Pim with Pim after Pim." There will be, he insists, "no callers this time no stories but mine no silence but the silence I must break." *How It Is* thus sets itself up as a narrative about the posssibilities of narrative through its insistence on linear discourse "languidly wending from left to right straight line eastward," the direction the reader's eyes travel across the printed page. What is at stake in the work becomes more than the character's search for Pim; it is also the writer's search for form.

In Part 1, the narrator begins his journey toward Pim with a description of both his present condition—crawling slowly through the mud "right leg right arm push pull"—and brief "bits and scraps" of images remaining from the "life in the light" which he, like the speaker in *Texts for Nothing,* has renounced: "no going back up there." Through the darkness he sees a youth in a crib scissoring the wings of a butterfly, a young boy or "a small old man," hands covering a tear-stained face, and a more detailed image of a young boy, kneeling on a pillow gazing up into the downturned face of his elaborately hatted mother (a picture taken from Beckett's own childhood where, however, the child cast his eyes down). The longest word picture in Part 1 is of a young couple at a racecourse on an April day, hand in hand, walking, talking, eating, turning toward each other, blue sky and white clouds above. It is a central image, fragments of which return in greatly abbreviated form in Parts 2 and 3.

True to his intention to eliminate "stories," the narrator omits the usual references to preceding Beckett fiction. "Belacqua on his side," and an image from "The Calmative"—a crocus nurtured by a disembodied hand in a basement retreat—are the only traces of earlier works. "I'm not like that any more they have taken that away from me this time all I say is how last how last," the speaker explains. The few proper names are from mythology, philosophy, literature, or biology—Erebus, Thalia, Heraclitus the Obscure, Malebranche, Klopstock, and Haeckel—and appear in Part 1.

Yet, however scrupulously the narrator rejects devices of the past and tries to follow his narrative agenda on his quest for Pim, erosions take place, almost immediately. First, he indicates that his divisions so carefully guarded and repeated are at best arbitrary: "divide into three a single eternity for the sake of clarity." Then he questions his own senses and asks for an additional witness and scribe, Kram and Krik. Finally he discloses that his very quest is a sham, that Pim doesn't exist. But if only a contrivance, Pim is still sought, and when found offers temporary comfort. Running through the narrative is the repeated phrase "something wrong there." It is uttered five times in Part 1, three in 2, and nine times in 3. The distribution points to the fact that while Pim is present, surety is temporarily gained, but when he "abandons" (the narrator's word) "how it is" is even less sure.

Although denying his reality from the beginning, the speaker still moves toward Pim. The central action of Part 2 is their encounter and the tortuous method the speaker devises for wresting communication from him. Even more elaborate than the technique perfected by Molloy for communicating with his mother, the speaker recounts the long process of goading Pim into speech: nails in armpits cause song, blade of opener gouging arse elicits speech, thump on skull indicates stoppage, pestle on kidney causes loudness. Pim's speech coincides with the speaker's identification with Pim; for, despite the disclaimer in Part 1, the quest appears to be another quest for self, gained through the office of the fictive persona. The speaker naming his victim, names himself: "I too Pim my name Pim." Or, as he boasts, "I can efface myself behind my creature." As Pim finally begins to issue sounds—"hey you me what don't hey"—the narrator begins to write. A symbiosis is formed; the sounds of Pim merge with the written words of the unnamed storyteller. Instead of paper, he carves his capital letters on his captive's back. Yet he soon recognizes that the words and the writing emanate not from another, but from himself. Refusing to admit his own isolation, he prevents the slippage by immediately creating another, Bom, who will take Pim's place. "The one I'm waiting for oh not that I believe in him I say it as I hear it he can give me another it will be my first Bom he can call me Bom." The tormentor replaces the tormented, creating a progression, either of three or millions in a series; the speaker is not sure. Part 2 moves toward closure with the words emblazoned on Pim's back in capitals: *"YOUR LIFE HERE"* with *"HERE"* repeated eleven times in one paragraph near the end. Locked into a present that denies beginning and end, the narrator refuses to admit his condition, holding still to his narrative plan, and to the search for Pim, or Bom. The last paragraphs of the section end with yes and no vying for dominance, no's knife again attempting to thrust in yes's wound. But the speaker is still unready to accept the nullity such a thrust brings. His concluding paragraph returns to the narrative design, to forestall the truth he cannot yet face.

The calm voice of the speaker begins the last part as it ended the former, but quickly the order and composure break down. Resorting to a ploy that earlier characters have used when all else failed, he takes solace in arithmetic, which in Part 1 he said, "I always loved . . . it has paid me back in full." Numbers of Pims and Boms proliferate, but to no avail. The section ends with another yes/no dual, this time culminating in the awareness averted at the end of Part 2 but now no longer denied: "only one voice here yes mine yes when the panting stops yes." All else, the speaker says, is "balls." The penultimate paragraph also provides one other awareness: first the word "DIE," then "I MAY DIE," and finally, in a scream, "I SHALL DIE." Having reached the conclusions that he is alone, one voice, and shall die, the speaker attempts yet again to return to the shattered narrative he decimated in the process of discovery, ending with "good good end at last of part three. . . ."

The central image of *How It Is,* a man scratching his words on a fictive surrogate—or on himself—has been used by two other twentieth-century writers: James Joyce in *Finnegans Wake* and Franz Kafka in "In the Penal Colony." In Joyce's novel Shem the Penman, using his own body as the only foolscap available, writes upon himself and produces "mood-moulded cycle wheeling history." Beckett's unnamed "I" scratches his roman capitals on Pim's back, but finds after Pim that he is alone, still without voice, unable to structure his experience. His scriptural exercises bring him closer to those described by Kafka in "In the Penal Colony" where language provides no enlightenment, only gratuitous pain and senseless death. Joyce, using a similar image of self-effacement, finds coalescence; Beckett—like Kafka—finds failure.

The failure is not only in finding a fictive surrogate, but in using the narrative form. *How It Is* holds steadily to a beginning, middle, and end, yet the tale told is one in which the linear collapses under the weight of the truths it must convey. In the novel Beckett seems to lay linear narrative to rest; it cannot suffice in the world of the skullscape. Having done so may have freed him to return to fiction—a different type of fiction. While able to complete only this one sustained prose work from 1950 to 1960, after *How It Is,* Beckett had, if not the burst of creativity of the late 1940s, at least a resurgence of fictional production. From 1963 to 1969 he wrote six works. While different, they have one point in common; all are spatially constructed, none "wind their way eastward," and all give up the ghost of Pim for the reality of life after Pim and after linear narrative form.

***All Strange Away.*** The first line of *All Strange Away* contains the title of the prose piece that follows it, *Imagination Dead Imagine.* The two short fictions can be seen as companion works, the first written in English in 1963 but withheld from publication until fourteen years later, the latter originally in French and published in 1967 in a collection entitled *Residua,* along with *Enough,* "From an Abandoned Work," and *Ping,* all collected in English in *No's Knife.*[3] *All Strange Away* is the longer—37 pages—and contains more details, humor, and clearly discernible setting than the 3-1/2-page distillation. Both works, and in fact all those in *Residua,* take their point of departure from *How It Is.* After the complete collapse of the temporal, Beckett turns to a spatial fiction.

All Beckett's prose works, as far back as the trilogy, begin by placing a speaker in a particular environment. Initially *All Strange Away* seems to promise the same. "A place, then someone in it, that again." As in *Molloy,* that begins with "I am in my mother's room," the narrator describes the area: "Five foot square, six high," with a stool, bare walls covered with a few "tattered syntaxes." Yet this space is different; there is "no way in, none out." No specific locale, no generalized terrain; it is the inside of the head, the "ivory dungeon" first mentioned in *Texts for Nothing,* the "vault bone-white" described in Part 2 of *How It Is.* In that novel, when the speaker finally admitted his failure to find himself through his fictive surrogate Pim, he marked the awareness with an image—a mouth, lips clenched, teeth and gums hidden in a face—and a question: "Where am I flown?" *All Strange Away* provides the answer: behind the clenched mouth, where the "gibberish garbled six fold" that overwhelmed the previous speaker is reduced to "a sound too faint for mortal ears."

Within the skull a third-person narrator resorts to the imperative form to describe a self enclosed in an ever-narrowing space. Even though he is well aware that his choice of pronouns is a ruse and that he is still "talking to himself in the third person," the device seems to alleviate the prior agony of multiple voices vying for dominance. At the outset, catching himself falling into old ways, he asks, "No where is he," but immediately rejects the obvious pitfalls such questions bring, and counters with a vehement, "no," and the statement, "Now he is here." Yet for all this vehemence, the voice is still not a sure one; it indulges in the editing, shifts, and reworkings that all Beckett narrators go through, responding, it seems, to some unheard voice. The effect is a kind of dialogue, only one part of which is reported, a technique that Beckett will employ repeatedly in subsequent works.

The unheard voice is less storyteller than director, dressing and undressing his character, positioning him, shifting the space, the lighting, and the props. First he gives his creation "the old hat and coat," but soon amends the costume, dressing him in a black shroud. Light continually "ebbs" and "flows," the area five foot square, six high, gradually is reduced to two by two. Into this shrinking playing space the narrator first wedges the body of a male figure who fantasizes about a woman embossed on the walls, and then replaces him with the woman herself, named Emma. First there is a self imagining itself as object, then a self objectifying the object of its fancy.

Akin to the shrinking space is the diminished sound described in the work. If *All Strange Away* can be said to be about anything, it is about the steady movement—or better the desired pull—toward silence and the nothing it denotes. Other Beckett characters have sought the same, but in this work Beckett focuses not on the idea of silence but on the process. While the dominant sounds in *How It Is* are plosives—words like Pim, Bom, Kram beginning with the phonemes */p/*, */b/*, and */k/*—the words in *All Strange Away* move perceptibly away from such strongly articulated sounds to more muted sounds produced by spirants or fricatives, marked by the proliferation of words beginning with the phonemes */s/*, */f/*, and */v/*. For example, lines such as "for old mind's sake sorrow vented in simple sighing sound," indicate that Beckett is self-consciously employing repeated spirants to reinforce his theme: the desire for silence, to "say a sound too faint for mortal ear." The speaker makes direct reference to the process when he says, near the end of the piece, "Fancy dead, try that again with spirant barely parting lips in murmur and faint stir of white dust . . . ." The fiction ends with "faint sighing sound for tremor of sorrow at faint memory of a lying side by side and fancy murmured dead." As the sounds fade into a sigh and murmur, the light fades, the space collapses: all is directed toward the desired, still elusive end: silence.

Besides employing spirants and phrases indicating diminished sound, Beckett also has his character refer to "faint tremors," "ruffles," "turmoil," and "black soundless storm," all phrases that imply breath movements in the production of speech sounds. Even more directly, he offers an image that represents the workings of the lungs. When he places Emma within the ever-narrowing cube, he places in her hand "a small grey punctured rubber ball or ball from a bottle of scent." The important fact seems not which it is but the similar function of both. Three times the speaker describes the same motion: "squeeze firm down five seconds say faint hiss then silence then back loose two seconds and say faint pop." The motion and accompanying sounds parallel the movement of the lungs, filling and emptying, allowing sound to be made. Within the dome of the skull, with "no way in one out" the mouth and vocal apparatus become central; along with eye and ear they provide connection to the outer world. As Beckett's fiction continues to become more refined and spare—the 1966 one-minute play *Breath* is only the action of the lungs—such sensory functions fill the page and stage. *All Strange Away* is a transitional piece, from the still macrocosmic-centered world of *How It Is,* with its mud, can openers, and sardines, to the self-enclosed vault where the very act of breathing becomes an activity over which one ponders and wonders. Within the head, looking out, the figure may be describing the voice box when he talks of the continuously narrowing "room" seen in the process of making ever softer sounds as it moves toward silence.

***Imagination Dead Imagine.*** If *All Strange Away* relies on auditory structure, *Imagination Dead Imagine* concentrates on visual sense. Read as its companion piece, this work becomes what is left of the limited world of the skullscape, now shown to be fading into some all-consuming whiteness, that promises finally to obliterate all: "No, life ends and no, there is nothing elsewhere, and no question now of ever finding again that white speck lost in whiteness." In the previous work Beckett sought to collapse his fiction in a flurry of fricatives or */s/* phonemes. The characteristic feature that marks fricatives is called "white noise" because on a spectrograph, an instrument for measuring the speech wave spectrum, the */s/* appears almost as a solid, devoid of individuality since it covers the whole band within a continuous section of the spectrum. The white of *Imagination Dead Imagine* visually describes what Beckett orally presents in the preceding work.

Again, there is a rotunda, three feet by three, but this time the space is segmented into two semicircles, wherein two bodies, a man's and woman's, are confined simultaneously. Their only identifying physical features are the long hair "of strangely imperfect whiteness" on the white body of the woman, and the "piercing pale blue" of the left eyes of both that at "incalculable intervals" suddenly open wide and gaze in unblinking exposure long beyond what is humanly possible—a technique Beckett will use in the image of the unblinking spectre of woman in the television drama . . . *but the clouds* . . . . They are silent—"Only murmur ah"—and do not move. The speaker can tell that they are alive by placing a mirror to their lips. The sole actions in the piece are the alternating shifts of light—source unknown—and temperature, which in intervals of twenty seconds move from brightness and heat to darkness and cold. Although the process is repeated, the movement is not consistent. As the speaker explains, "The extremes alone are stable."

The unnamed narrator still employs the third person, as in the preceding work, but he has less tendency to indicate that it is a ruse. Only in the first line does he allude to an unheard "other" dictating or conversing within him, prodding him along in his narrative: "No trace anywhere of life, you say, pah." There is an attempt at objectivity, even beyond that of *All Strange Away,* a calmness, as the voice intones the alternations of light/heat and dark/cold. Yet for all the concentration on the climatic conditions, the central concern of the piece is the gradual fading of what is left of the human forms, seen passing into an obliterating whiteness, not—this time—to be retrieved. The reader is told near the end to "Leave them there, sweating and icy, there is better elsewhere." Yet the immediate disclaimer of an elsewhere, and the sense of irrevocable loss concludes the fiction, the two reduced to "a white speck" consumed in "the black dark for good, or the great whiteness unchanging." The starkness of the scene and the lack of human comment on the loss makes the fading image—the speck that remains of life and love—a poignant residue of life.

***The Lost Ones.*** Whether in "the black dark" or the "great whiteness," the space enclosing the two figures at the end of *Imagination Dead Imagine* is lost to the narrator who holds no hope of recapturing it. Beckett's next fiction, written in 1971, no longer tries to describe the world of the skull by objectifying the self and the object of desire, but rather creates within the "globe of ivory" a world not of two but of two hundred, a teeming, imaginative construct, a mythical universe of "lost bodies . . . each searching for its lost one."

*The Lost Ones* is Beckett's most sustained fiction between *How It Is* in 1960 and *Company* in 1980. Rather than settling on the world of one individual, he offers a third-person, omniscent narrator who, in fifty-five pages, makes no comments, but only describes the world he sees, a Dantean hellscape.

Precisely, as if constructing a medieval tapestry, the narrator describes the physical conditions in the enclosure. The white light that bathed earlier fictions is replaced by "yellowness" that remains constant, while only the temperature varies "between hot and cold" at intervals of four seconds. Periods of "dead still" punctuate these shifts. The result of such constant fluctuations is dryness: bodies "like dry leaves." The world is also one of near silence because of the solid rubber "or suchlike" that lines floors and walls. Only the sound of ladders can be heard, fifteen of them, used periodically by the inhabitants to reach the niches in the upper part of the walls.

Of the inhabitants, the narrator describes four types: those "perpetually in motion"; those who sometimes pause; those who are sedentary and remain frozen unless forced to move; and those called the "nonsearchers" or the "vanquished" who, having given up searching, sit along the walls. All but the vanquished continually scan the adjoining faces, freed from their searching only during the brief respites of temperature variation. Of the vanquished, the speaker describes three: a woman still young with white hair and a small "Mite" at her breast; another woman with red hair, who is designated "north" by the moving horde, and a man. Only he still moves round though vanquished as the others "recognize him and keep their distance."

In this world all is orderly, and rules control action. For example, only one person may climb a ladder at a time; the ladders are to be moved in designated zones, a belt of one meter, by the next to ascend—labeled the carrier—followed by the line that has formed behind the ladder; once in line a climber may not leave until his turn has come; and, having once climbed and dismounted, a climber may join another line or leave the area and rejoin the general horde of searchers in motion in the center of the floor.

The narrator makes one direct comment about the created world of the novel: "For in the cylinder alone are certitudes to be found and without nothing but mystery." Continually describing the demarcated areas, the activities of the four groups, and the climatic conditions, the narrator is intent on depicting the hell of the cylinder as a world that can at least be delineated and understood as opposed to the world that Beckett has drawn in preceding fiction: the world of the "outside," mysterious and finally undepictable in fiction. Yet having drawn his world so clearly, Beckett was unable to conclude it, and *The Lost Ones* was abandoned in 1963, at the end of paragraph fourteen. Only in 1971 did Beckett return to it, add a final paragraph, and allow it to be published. The concluding paragraph describes "this last of all if a man," and his final search before lapsing into immobility. Peering one last time into the sightless eyes of the woman with the white hair, he too becomes vanquished. With this last human act, silence descends, and darkness finally comes, along with cold. The most allegorical of Beckett's works, *The Lost Ones,* is also one of the most final. No "perhaps" lingers on; the story, although without a beginning or middle, is brought to a clear close: all are vanquished even in this inner world.

***Ping.*** Richard Admussen, in his study of Beckett's manuscripts, indicates that the ninth version of *Bing,* the French title for *Ping,* is prefaced with this statement by Beckett: "*Bing* may be regarded as the . . . miniaturization of *Le Dépeupleur (The Lost Ones)* abandoned because of its intractable complexities."[4] Despite its brevity (1030 words) *Ping* is a complex piece, combining many of the preceding motifs into a tightly structured work.

Its setting is an indeterminate area of whiteness, this time with planes meeting invisible walls and floor; the ceiling is not seen. Light and heat are no longer varying; they remain fixed. The figure is upright, but is described like some inanimate nonhuman scarecrow sewn together, legs and arms placed at varying angles. The only functioning part is the eye, "blue fixed front." It remains the one physical indicator that life—to use the neologism that Beckett creates—is "unover." "Unover" too are other traces of the past: nature, albeit diminished to mere splotches of color "blue and white in the wind"; a desire for meaning; a hope of company "perhaps not alone"; an image "dim eye black and white half closed long black lashes," the scattered traces of the face of Emma, the woman in *All Strange Away* whose eyes are similarly described; and a murmur, never reaching the level of sound, invariably stilled by the silence.

While these shards of detail—too brief to call story—remain, Beckett is able to give them shape and structure. In fact, it seems that as he progressively jettisons more and more content, he pulls in the structural core compactly, just as he does the walls in the decreasing space of *All Strange Away,* until form fits snugly around his figure.

In this work the key structural word is "ping," which appears thirty-four times—eleven times in each of the three sections plus a final "ping" that closes the work. After the appearance of the first "ping," the phrase "fixed elsewhere" appears. It is repeated between sections one and two, but at the end of the third section, the speaker presumably no longer looks for—or has hope of finding—what is "fixed elsewhere." This "ping" is followed by the word "silence." As if to underline the cessation, the work concludes with a final "ping" and the word "over." Yet, as the rush for closure occurs, there is the familiar Beckettian search for means to keep the search going. For example, while in section one there are four variations of words that follow "ping," in section two there are six, and in the final section there are eight, an indication that as less is seen more words are dispatched to keep the fading image present.

While the piece begins with "All known" and describes the place "all white" and the figure "bare white body," Beckett indicates that even in such a place with such a human—with all known—all is not over, that even in greatly diminished form life continues "unover." Variations abound most in section three, with the pings demarcating the continuing struggles within the ever-obliterating white.

***Lessness.*** This work carries the formulaic permutations of *Ping* even further. After a three-year hiatus, when Beckett once more turns to fiction with *Fizzles,* he will introduce the scuttled "I," and details of place, time, and situation that he has omitted in the last three works. *Lessness* is, therefore, a culmination of the highly structured form Beckett had experimented with in fiction following the impasse of *The Unnamable;* it is another attempt to describe the landscape of the skull. The enclosed "bare white body" described in *Ping* with "only the eyes only just" becomes "Grey face two pale blue little body heart beating." No longer enclosed, it is the "only upright" in a world fallen into decay, a world not of white or black, hot or cold, but of "grey air timeless." Images are of decay, ruin, collapse. There is "no stir," no other living creatures, little differentiation of nature: "Earth sky as one all sides endlessness." All descriptions of place and condition return to the central image and fact: "little body only upright."

In 1971 the BBC Radio 3 entered the work as a radio play, for the Italia Prize. In his notes for the contest Martin Esslin, then head of Radio Drama for the BBC, wrote that as Beckett had envisioned it, the piece was to be read by six voices, each voice as an "indicator of different groups of images," with a central image for each group.[5] Esslin lists them as "the ruins; the vastness of earth and sky; the little body; the fact that the enclosed space is now forgotten 'all gone from mind'; a *denial* of the past and future; and opposed to is an *affirmation* of past and future."

Esslin concludes his notes by remarking that "each voice is a strand of color" and that it is "only by *hearing Lessness* that we can become fully aware of its structure and . . . meaning—which is expressed by its formal pattern."

While the formula may sound arbitrary and limiting—six groups of ten sentences repeated twice in different order—the resultant 120 sentences are a powerful distillation of the world of the preceding fiction. Besides the repetition of lines, there are repeated phrases such as "true refuge," echoing words of negation ("never," "no") and words whose suffixes indicate either negation ("issueless") or continuation of the present state of being ("endlessness"). These, combined with the specific images of ruin, desolation and stasis, create a bleaker, more devasting skullscape than either *Ping* or *Imagination Dead Imagine.* Words and phrases of hope ("dream," "calm," "imagination," "love") are all described as vanquished; "figments" present in the past, they are now "long last all gone from mind." The future tense is invoked to indicate continuance of the same condition, offering no respite from the unremitting present. The character will "curse God"; "On him will rain again . . . the passing cloud"; "it will be day and night again over him the endlessness." While "He will go on his back face to the sky," he will encounter only "the sand the endlessness." As in all Beckett's works—but here the starker because of the formal presentation and the limited variables—there remains only "Heart beating little body only upright. . . . "

*Lessness* is significant, not only for the stark image of this human form, but also for its lyrical, poetic depiction. It moves further than preceding Beckett works to obliterate the lines between genres. More poem than prose, it employs many of the conventions of poetic form: assonance, alliteration, ellipsis, repetition of words and images, and brevity. The music of the phrasing—what Esslin referred to when he said the work must be heard—is created by the omission of punctuation other than periods. Phrasing is determined, as in *How It Is,* by the voice structuring and combining as it goes over the lines, an act akin to the slow movement of the figure traversing the world of grey. The variations in the ordering of the sentences indicate slight permutations in the ongoing grey world of the little figure. The only respite possible, the form indicates, is in alteration, but not cessation.

***Enough.*** Although *Enough* was written in 1966 before *The Lost Ones* and after *Imagination Dead Imagine,* I have placed it here because it differs from those works and stands closer to the more detailed world of *Fizzles* that follows. Actually, *Enough* backtracks to a world before *How It Is,* the speaker upright in the macrocosm, not yet reduced to crawling in the mud. Light is not "above" but behind, in an unspecified past, when all was "calm" and there were flowers. The seven-page story is a reverie, told in the present about the past, a reconstruction of a life now over: "It was then I shall have lived then or never." The function of the fiction is to superimpose the "then" on the "now" in order to give life once more to the writer.

The first-person narrator is unnamed and of indeterminate sex.[6] More important than gender is the relationship between the speaker and a "He," a figure who acts as mentor, lover, and fellow traveler. The speaker is of "an entirely different generation" and is passive in the relationship. "I never asked myself any questions but his." The older figure is described through his physical infirmities: bent over, seemingly blind—although the narrator reveals that what was taken for blindness was "merely indolence"—"left hand lingering over his sacral ruins." The relationship between the youth and the aged one began when the former was six, but the central memories concern a ten-year period demarcated by two events: the day when "He" shared the confidence that "his infirmity had reached its peak" and the day of the narrator's "supposed disgrace." What illness and what disgrace are never revealed. Also omitted are details describing the two figures or the locale. Their connection alone is important: the shared walks "side by side hand in hand," the shared confidences emanating always from the old man, delivered when the two were bent over, heads touching.

The subject of these confidences often concerns the constellations rather than the earth, and this dichotomy between earth and sky helps structure the story. In Lucky's monologue in *Godot* stones thwart human desire for flight, and in *Happy Days* Winnie constantly feels the pull between earth, that "old extinguisher," and the heaven toward which she desires to float. So too in *Enough:* while the pair walk the plains, their eyes scan the "mansions" of the sky; while the actual scenes of disgrace and separation are on the flat ground, the narrator wishes to remember them as taking place on a rise, on "the steepest slope." Age and youth are shown as equivalents for earth and sky. The old man in the story makes his "prognostic" that his infirmity "had reached its peak" but he is nevertheless pulled down, bent toward the ground. The speaker, now even more aged than the remembered "He," may also wish to escape the temporal grip of earth represented by the stones of the landscape he/she treads. The only possible way to avoid the grip of age and earth is to have the ability to seek in memory for lost time and to transplant past events on the present inhospitable stones. Thus, at the end of the story, the speaker says: "No I'll wipe out everything but the flowers." Flowers grafted onto stone become a visual equivalent for the imaginative process of re-creation and for the desire to, if not fly up, at least hide the stones that bear us down.

## Fiction: 1972–1984

Those prose pieces beginning with *Fizzles,* while more heterogeneous than the preceding group, are marked by certain shared characteristics: more visual detail, general lack of fixity of place, greater length, and comminglings from the outer and inner worlds. Still experimental, they do not eschew paragraphs and punctuations as do those of the preceding group. Rather than presenting a fixed world, they weave past and present together, often emphasizing the former rather than the latter. There is still the scramble for pronoun control, but less frantic than in earlier works. These pieces take place in the mind, but the narrators do not generally describe the terrain. Rather, they fix on some object perceived by the mind and continually return to it or to some fixed memory or image that they weave into their reveries.

***Fizzles.*** *Fizzles* are eight short prose pieces, three with separate titles: "Afar a Bird" ("Fizzle 3"), "Still" ("Fizzle 7"), and "For to End Yet Again" ("Fizzle 8"). They range in length from approximately eight pages ("Fizzle 1") to 1-3/4 pages ("Fizzle 6"), with Fizzles "7" and "8" 4-1/4 and 6-1/4 pages long, respectively. They were first published together in English in 1976, although their composition goes back further. In appearance the collection may recall *Texts for Nothing* since both works are composed of discrete sections only tangentially related. In form the eight parts of the work have even less relation than the paragraphs of *Texts* since there is no central voice that connects them. "Fizzle 1" is in third person, describing "he"; but Fizzles "2," "3," "4," and "6" are in first person, with no indication that the person is the objectified self of the first section. "Fizzle 5" returns to a third-person description of a place, "Arena bare vast," that bears some similarity to the "closed place" of *The Lost Ones;* and Fizzles "7" and "8" are told in the implied second person first used in *All Strange Away,* created by an observer seeming to stand aloof from himself, describing his actions and his observations without recourse to pronoun.

The title is another example of Beckett's play on words. While the word *fizzle* is the onomatopoeic form for a hissing or bubbling sound—a less strident sound than the onomatopoeic title *Ping*—it also implies "the breaking of wind" from the obsolete frequentative of the word *fist,* while its informal meaning is "to fail or die out especially after a hopeful beginning," or "to create a fiasco." The thematic—if not formal—element that does seem to hold the group of prose pieces together is the last sense of the word, the new beginning leading eventually to another defeat or fiasco with Beckettian sound effects. The recurring words in *Lessness* were "not" and "never"; the repeated word at the beginning of "Fizzle 1" is "again." "He is forth again," the narrator says, describing a figure slowly moving after long inaction, once more squeezing along between the walls, attempting to draw "closer and closer to the open." This picture of hope, however, is balanced by the figure in "Fizzle 8"—the same person or another—"Fallen unbending all his little length . . . not a breath. Or murmur. . . . "

In "Fizzle 1" he is seen in the familiar position—on his way—although the way is narrower than that offered other Beckett walkers, with continuous turns, steep rises, sudden drops. Unlike the speaker in *Enough* who willfully cancels out the tale just told, the speaker cannot remember any past prior to this leave-taking. Moving, he begins to piece together a brief history, developed in these limited straits. Gaining resolution as he progresses, he even tentatively suggests, "perhaps he was wrong not to persist, in his efforts to pierce the gloom."

"Fizzle 2" is an abrupt shift, moving from third to first person, and introducing an abbreviated sentence structure. While the first sentence in "Fizzle 1" contained forty-one words, the first sentence of "2" contains only five: "Horn came always at night." It is a description written in the present about a time in the past that marked yet another beginning, this time the character beginning to leave bed and receive visitors, or a visitor, Horn. He is not yet ready to "see" himself, he says. All the meetings occur at night, with the aid of a flashlight trained only on Horn's face, while Horn consults his notes and answers the questions the speaker asks. The "I" makes a point of saying that Horn is not a part of himself and exists "in the outer space, not to be confused with the other."

"Fizzle 3" and "Fizzle 4" shift, making it clear that the "I" and "me" are not "other" but the same, fighting for control of a singular pronoun. The problem of the "me" is to find words: "he is still, he seeks a voice for me, it's impossible I should have a voice and I have none, he'll find one for me, ill beseeming me," the voice in "Afar a Bird" says. While the subjective self may be guardian of words, he is unable to employ the first-person pronoun comfortably. "He will never say I, because of me," the imprisoned microcosmic self recognizes. These two Fizzles are Beckett's most direct statement of the schism of self. More than the traditional mind/body dichotomy, they depict what Austrian philosopher Fritz Mauthner described in his *Critique of Language.* "We have bodily organs and senses for the observation of the movement of bodies; but we have no senses besides our organ of thinking for the observation of thinking. The so-called self observation has no organ."[7] It is with what Mauthner labeled "this rascal of an ego" that "cannot project its feelings, cannot throw them outside, cannot utter them"[8] that Beckett is concerned in "Fizzle 3" and "Fizzle 4."

Unable to find a voice, the inner self threatens in "Fizzle 3" to "put faces in his head, names, places, churn them all up together." "Fizzle 5" may well be one of the embedded images the mind produces. It is a pared down version of *The Lost Ones.* Again, a Dantean world is described, only this time without people. The closed place consists of an arena, ditch, and track with "Room for millions. Wandering and still." Despite the number, each inhabitant is, as in *The Lost Ones,* condemned to be alone: "Never seeing never hearing one another. Never touching." All is dead and dry; light that once was bright progressively fades to dark. The impersonal tone, without recourse to comment from the narrator, distills the earlier landscape into a harrowing few pages of desolation.

"Fizzle 6," the shortest section in the group, acts as a culmination of what has preceded and a transition to the remaining two sections.

It builds on the I/me dichotomy and points to the objectification and acceptance of self projected in "Still." Beginning "Old earth, no more lies, I've seen you, it was me, with my other's ravening eyes," the speaker no longer plays the pronoun game, but describes himself as object, seen gazing out the window, viewing not the immediate scene but "faces, agonies, loves, the different loves, happinesses too." This short piece introduces a technique that will be central to Beckett's theater in the 1970s and 1980s: the use of a virtually silent or inert figure presented along with a voice—presumably his own—that describes his memories in the second or third person. The technique will be used in *That Time,* the two television plays *Ghost Trio* and *. . . but the clouds . . .*, *A Piece of Monologue,* and *Rockaby.* "Fizzle 6" and even more "Still" introduce the form.

In "Still" the self becomes totally objectified, the narrator describing the figure of a man both sitting and standing, staring out a window. The figure's main action is the raising of his hand and the lowering of his head to meet the waiting fingers. Seen from behind, the figure seems without motion, but on closer inspection the narrator recognizes that he is "trembling all over." Beckett is able to capture both the stasis and the shaking by employing the word *still* and its modifiers. Twenty-four times in the 4-1/4-page piece the word is used with the adjectival meaning "subdued, calm, without sound" or the adverbial "a picture up to the present time." Beckett then modifies *still* with the adverb *quite.* If *still* means "no motion," to modify it with a word that may mean "entirely" or "somewhat" begins to blur the originally clear linguistic picture. Is the figure without motion or only somewhat still? Beckett continues the word games by often combining *quite* with *quiet,* again through modification making what appeared clear confusing.

More than the verbal play, however, it is the image itself that gives power to the "Fizzle," making it the most forceful of the collection. Never emerging from behind the guise of the second person, the narrator draws the lonely man unmoving and moving all over, wordless, yet eloquent in his misery.

The last work in the collection is entitled "For to End Yet Again," and it completes the circle begun in the first. The hoped-for beginning leads once more to the "fizzle" and the inert figure stretched full-length in the sand, in a position of crucifixion. Like *Lessness,* it is a world of "greyness." But the narrator also makes clear that the true locale is the head "place of remains," the "Sepulchral skull" in which appears an image of two white dwarfs carrying between them "the dung litter of laughable memory." This image rises from the "skull alone in a dark place pent bowed on a board to begin." The double meaning of *pent*—both past participle of *penned* and *confined*—tie together the figure fallen in the sand and the writer who conceived him, making the fizzles of the title apply not only to the persona but to the writer unable to bring his work to the conclusion he desires.

**"Sounds" and "Still 3."** The two brief prose paragraphs "Sounds" and "Still 3" date back to May and June 1973, immediately following "Still" but they were first published in *Essays in Criticism,* April 1978.[9] Both are highly compressed, resembling in their brevity, imagery, and assonance the poems "dread nay," "Roundelay," "thither," and "Something There" *(hors crâne)* which Beckett completed between 1974 and 1976. Like the poetry, and like "Still," the prose piece they most closely resemble, "Sounds" and "Still 3," are works of balance: sounds balancing stillness, past/present, mind/body, stasis/movement. In the first, a seated figure first avers and then denies his desire for sound. After describing the listener's intent position, the narrator employs the imperative, casting him into motion: "for catch up the torch and out up the path." This action is described as happening "now," a reconstruction of the actions of "he" in a prior time. Up a path by torchlight to a tree and back "in the chair quite still as before." Whether the figure actually moves or imagines himself moving is not clear, just as it will not be clear if the woman in *Ill Seen Ill Said* is on the path outside her house or within, imagining herself moving. What is apparent in both prose works is the isolation of the figure: in "Sounds" "listening trying listening," creating and obliterating himself in his mind. In *Company* the speaker will recognize that "there is no such thing as no light"; in "Sounds" the narrator seems to acknowledge that there is no such thing as no sound. As long as life continues, consciousness precludes silence. The mind and the body sit poised listening if only for the silence they hope will come. Again, as in *Fizzles,* the authorial hand is present, shown in phrases such as "as shown" and "better still," thus placing the writer beside the straining listener of his creation.

Less than a page, "Still 3" has a figure "Back in the chair at the window before the window head in hand," and an author "as shown," back from "some soundless place" still unable to tell "where been how long how it was." Only the faces are sure: in dark and sudden whites, moving one by one, not detailed, only described as "dead faces" with "no expression."

Together the two brief works reinforce the important image of "Still": activity within the mind of a figure who is inert, turmoil masked by an outward immobility, a desired ending but a continued struggle. All three works offer yet another I/me dichotomy, this time seen from without.

***Company.*** *Company,* written between March 1977 and September 1979, is the first novel since *Watt,* thirty-three years earlier, that Beckett composed first in English; it is his first extended piece of fiction since *How It Is,* seventeen years before; and—most important—it is the culmination of the experimental works of the 1960s and 1970s, a novel of extreme compression and precision, yet one of great scope and power. Not since *Malone Dies,* in fact, has Beckett so successfully and parsimoniously melded form and content.

In fifty-eight paragraphs spread over fifty-six printed pages, he offers both the story of a life and the condition of living. The paragraphs are of two sorts: forty-two tell about a figure "lying on his back in the dark" and fifteen offer up memories of the life the figure has lived. Like the man in the play *A Piece of Monologue,* written at the same time, he is silent, referred to as the listener or hearer, mute while the voices alive in his head vie for dominance. At one point he is given a name, "H. Aspirate Haitch," a play on sound since the three parts of the name refer to the ejaculation or blowing out of air: the letter *H* marks the movement, *aspirate,* the act, and *aitch,* preceded once more by *H,* the nominative for the letter. The name also points, in typical Beckettian fashion, to the irony of the physical situation. The aitch-bone is the name of the large bone of the buttocks on which the silent figure reclines as he blows out air and *aspires* to achieve some goal. The pun conveys the situation so many Beckett characters have faced: on their asses, in the dark, without words, aspiring to clarity and an understanding of the experiences that constitute their lives.

A man lying mute in a world of darkness, this is his present condition that remains a constant in the work and is established in the nine words of the first paragraph: "A voice comes to one in the dark. Imagine."

In paragraph 2, while the narrator explains these parameters of action, he also sets the theme that will affect the physical states of the listener and of the memories he spins: doubt. "Only a small part of what is said can be verified." Empirical evidence can corroborate, but only up to a point. The narrator may be certain of the physical position of the figure—"on his back in the dark"—but when he tries to ascertain more about his surroundings or about the voices he hears, all slowly dissolves into uncertainty until he is not even certain if the voice he hears is addressed to him or another.

Verification is only part of a larger *aspiration* expressed in the work—the desire for company. Thirty times in the novel—not including noun, adjectival, and adverbial variations—the word *company* is evoked as a kind of incantation used to ward off loneliness. Descriptions and memories are seen as attempts at "devising it all for company." "The voice alone is company but not enough," the narrator remarks. Were the first-person singular to be assumed by the figure "what an addition to company that would be!" But in lieu of this, anything will do, even doubt. "Confusion too is company up to a point," the voice repeats. So, too, memories and the constant reshaping of details concerning the physical condition of the listener: from supine "on his back in the dark" to "crawling creator," whose altered physical state is a source of company.

The opposition between company and alone is one of several binary oppositions that structure the work. There is the balance between reports of the present and the fifteen memories of the past interspersed throughout the text and divided chronologically: seven of childhood, two of "the bloom of adulthood," and six of old age. The movement is from youth—the topic of the early ones—to old age. Of the fifteen sections, only two present scenes of adulthood, although both are among the longest recollections in the work. The following chart details this distribution:

| YOUTH | ADULTHOOD | OLD AGE |
|---|---|---|
| 1 | | |
| 2 | | |
| | | 3 |
| 4 | | |
| 5 | | |
| 6 | | |
| | | 7 |
| 8 | | |

| YOUTH | ADULTHOOD | OLD AGE |
|---|---|---|
| 9 | | |
| | | 10 |
| | 11 | |
| | 12 | |
| | | 13 |
| | | 14 |
| | | 15 |

Memories of childhood dominate the beginning of the work. They are not presented in the expected chronological order, however; the memory of birth is preceded by a memory of youth. The ordering is significant because in this first scene the dominant theme of doubt is struck. A young boy is walking home from town, hand in hand with his mother, moving west and climbing toward the fading sun. Looking up at the sky, he poses a question about the distance of the sky as opposed to how "it appears." Getting no response, he rephrases his sentence, still trying to distinguish reality from appearance. For his pains, he receives no reply from his mother; instead, "this question must have angered her exceedingly" since she shakes off his hand and "made you a cutting retort you have never forgotten."

The small boy is in many ways like all of Beckett's figures: in motion, moving westward toward the end of day, questioning the space between the self and the not-self, between the microcosm within and the sky without; and for his troubles he receives only reproof, still left in doubt. Mother and child are first described as they "broach the long steep homeward." *Broach* and *steep* both have multiple meanings that allow Beckett to create complementary situations. The former in its transitive form, now rare, indicates "piercing or thrusting through to obtain liquor" or, figuratively, "blood." The more common usage is associated with speech: to utter or bring up something. The broaching of the hill becomes a physical equivalent to both the thrust for surety and the verbal forming of this need.

*Steep,* meaning "height" and "incline," as well as "depth or precipitous falling off," indicates yet another dichotomy echoed in the following three memories of youth: the desire for elevation or ascendancy thwarted by the inevitability of descent. In memory four the voice tells of the young boy returning from school on his "tiny cycle" and seeing "An old beggar woman" who "Could fly once in the air." Left unexplained, the act of the old woman is allied to two later acts of the boy. In memory five he is pictured "at the tip of the high board," his father entreating him to jump. In the following memory the boy is again pictured in flight; however, now the act is deemed "naughty," not heroic, and he is rebuked by his mother for throwing himself out of a tree in the presence of a Mrs. Coote, possibly the woman who herself attempted flight earlier. The desire to soar is checked, it seems, by the pull of the earth—or by parental displeasure.

Horizontal movement also offers a dichotomy in the book. All figures in motion are shown to be moving from east to west, indicating their common journey from birth to death while against this directional pull there is an attempted rebellion or variation in course. In memory seven the figure, now old, after following the familiar way, suddenly cuts through a hedge "hobbling east across the gallops." Twice in other memories the word *withershins* is used, a word that means movement in a counterclockwise direction. In old age, near the end of the work, the figure, no longer able to go out and traverse the countryside, sits staring at the hands of a clock. Withershins now is impossible.

The pull of directions is a corollary to the pull between youth and age, another structuring dichotomy in *Company,* as it was in *Enough.* Yet Beckett handles the generational pull in a special way. Rather than having son usurp father, son becomes one with father; the father exists as a spectre in the mind of the son, accompanying him as he moves westward, melding into the same aged figure.

As the memories dip toward old age, and move toward the west, they also shift away from light toward darkness, the last oppositional pair in the work. Light has two modes in *Company.* It represents both the macrocosmic, physical world and also the inner world of the imagination. Whereas the youth moves in the light of the sun, his birth room suffused in light from a window looking west, by memory eight in the middle of the novel, a perceptible shift occurs. The light is that created by the imagination, imposed on the physical world which no longer is its source. The boy in his memory looks not west but east, and returns from his travel to re-create—in tranquillity—a light he never actually sees. Rebuked by the adults, as the young boy in the first memory is rebuked by his mother, he takes refuge alone "on his back in the dark" and is "back in the light," the light of his memory.

However, the light that suffused the early sections—emanating for instance from a beautiful scene—becomes more difficult to capture as the boy matures. In the last image of youth, a young boy attempts to save a hedgehog by confining it, and discovers days later that he has condemned the animal to death. A variation on the ascent/descent dichotomy, here the youth learns the difference between desired ends and actual ends or between good deeds conceived and their less satisfactory results. This memory, the last picture of youth, is a powerful culmination of the growing sense of doubt and isolation.

While the light in youth becomes progressively more internalized, stored for future use, the memories move toward old age, and the physical light almost totally fails. The last three memories take place at night or in darkness. In memory thirteen the figure stands on a strand in evening. In fourteen he is in a room with only the artificial light above his desk. In the last memory, where present and past fuse, all is in physical darkness, the only light now possible is the light provided by the voice recounting its memories: "What visions in the dark of light," the voice says.

As the external light fades, so too the light the memory creates. However, unlike the physical light, it never totally disappears while "a certain activity of mind however slight" is present. As long as the voice supplies memories to a conscious mind, that is, as long as there is life—there is light.

***Ill Seen Ill Said.*** *Ill Seen Ill Said,* written two years after *Company,* first in French under the title *Mal vu mal dit,* is the first Beckett fiction that focuses on a woman. In his dramas women protagonists have been numerous. Yet in the fiction, with the possible exception of the "I" in *Enough,* whose sex is cast in a deliberately obscure fashion, most women are relegated to ancillary roles. In the early works they are predominantly grotesque sex partners engaging in grotesque sexual couplings; in the shorter fiction they appear usually as unnamed and disembodied objects of desire, fading into some all-consuming void. The one exception is Celia, in *Murphy,* a rounded, compassionately drawn woman.

"This old so dying woman" presented in the fifty-two-page, sixty-one-paragraph prose text, is not drawn in such detail; in fact, she is barely described. Her hair is long and white, surrounding her like a fan; her eyes—or rather "one staring eye"—is "washen blue"; her dress black with a hint of lace at collar and cuffs. She wears stockings and boots fastened with a hook in the shape of a fish. In her cabin are pallet, chair, and coffer placed within an open space. She is described as more spectre than flesh, a ghostlike inhabitant of a barren scene, making a habitual path round the confines of her cabin, and from it to a tomb and back, traversing en route a pasture and a "zone of stones" that is rapidly encroaching on the terrain. Wishing to be "pure figment," however, she is still body. At the end of the work there is "still life," a pun on the rustic images that are described. "Not another crumb of carrion left" she may wish; but body still remains, for without life and consciousness the figure could not appreciate or enjoy that moment when being becomes nothing. Recognizing this insoluble dilemma, the speaker concludes with a renunciation of cessation. "No. One moment more. One last. Grace to breathe that void. Know happiness." Once more a persona reaches the awareness that all Beckett figures eventually reach: to know the happiness of non-being—as opposed to simply not being—a figure must still live and be. The woman in *Rockaby,* written soon after, reaches the same conclusion and clings to life.

Existence here is subsistence existence at best. Several times in the text there is even the suggestion that the old woman is already dead. While the eye stares out on the physical world unseeing, it is the other world "in the madhouse of the skull and nowhere else" where the action of the piece is set and where the mental eye is fixed. More than in earlier works, here the differentiation between the two worlds has been obliterated. The speaker talks of the dichotomy between "reality and—how to say its contrary" as "the old tandem" that in the present fiction has been reduced to "a confusion." The demarcation between what the old woman sees and what she imagines is impossible to determine; so, too, the distinction between where she goes and where she imagines herself going. For example, in one paragraph there is description of a field filling with snow, and superimposed on the scene, the figure of the woman. However, Beckett purposely leaves unanswered the question "Whither in her head while her feet stray thus?" and begins the next paragraph with "All dark in the cabin while she whitens afar." It seems of little import whether she moves or imagines herself moving. Both the world of the body and of the mind are verging on coalescence as they verge on cessation.

It is not even certain that she is herself the activator of her text or herself the creation of yet an "other" who conjures her and her madhouse skull. From the beginning of the work there is the mark of a narrator spinning the tale. The first line reads "From where she lies she sees Venus rise." Like the mythic goddess slowly rising from the foam, the figure of the old woman emerges from the words of the sentence, accruing detail. The third sentence reads: "From where she lies she sees Venus rise followed by the sun." Between the two the single word "on." It is never clear who is saying "on" or the other narrative prods—"careful," "enough," "gently gently"—that keep the words and images flowing. Whether the woman is speaking to herself telling the story of her life as in "Fizzle 6" or is a figment of another person's thought is impossible to determine.

One hint that there is an implied observer observing the creature and her inner world comes from the title. While the adverb "ill" when combined with adjectives forming attributive modifiers always employs a hyphen—"an ill-defined idea"—when "ill" modifies a predicate adjective before a noun, the two words appear without hyphens—"she is ill defined." Since all hyphens are omitted in the title of this piece, Beckett may be pointing to the ellipsis "she is" implied before *Ill Seen Ill Said.* However, even here there is ambiguity since she could be ill seen to herself. Whether seen by self, other, or both, the important point in the text is the difficulty of all seeing: "Haze sole certitude," the text reads and "Incontinent the void."

The dominant action in the work is concerned with sight. The narrators in *Texts for Nothing* and *How It Is* repeated "I say it as I hear it"; the silent woman, were she given to speech, might say, "I say it as I see it." References to sight and eyes abound: "iris," "pupil," "occulted," "opaque." The eye becomes the primary sensory means through which the world is perceived and through which the perceiver is known. "Fit ventholes of the soul that jakes." The emphasis on sight is also apparent in the variation of a phrase from "Text 7" of *Texts for Nothing.* There the line reads: "the farrago of silence and words"; here "the farrago from eye to mind."

The image of the spectre woman in *Ill Seen Ill Said* is connected to the condition of her locale: a world being innundated by stones. The "unspeakable globe" of her eye merges with the dying globe of the earth, and perhaps the entire universe where her celestial surrogate, Venus, makes her morning and evening appearance in a sky that is cold and dying. The dichotomy between earth and sky that Beckett used in the past is here connected to the paths that humans and stars make through a fixed cycle. "The twelve" above who appear to circle the woman may be the twelve constellations of the zodiac. Twelve is also a recurrent number in the text. "On" punctuates the text twelve times in paragraph one. A central image of the woman's clothing, the fish boothook, is the sign representing the twelfth zodiac figure, Pisces. Yet the number is shown to be arbitrary, "for twelve is only a figure come what may," the speaker in the text remarks. It explains nothing.

The world Beckett creates in the fiction is a world on the brink of death, death of the woman, of the stone-strewn earth, and of the sky. All subsides into what the text calls "a slumberous collapsion" which is marked not by a bang, ping, or fizzle, but an almost soundless crumbling away, a vision almost gone but not quite yet.

***Worstward Ho.*** *Worstward Ho,* Beckett's last fiction to date, written in English in 1983 and not translated into French by the publication of this book, is an appropriate coda for the works that precede it. Having given up the possibility of plumbing the secrets of the outer world or of coalescing the dual aspects of the self alive in this world, Beckett writes of the only subject still viable for the artist: rather than "bestward" toward some understanding, he will document the way "worstward," making a fiction of the impossibility of making a fiction. This time the speaker, unnamed and totally hidden behind the varying verb forms, will not try to understand but to "misunderstand," will not "say" but "missay," will only go "on" by going "back." In *All Strange Away* Beckett coined the word "unover" to indicate the continuance of what cannot be ended; in this fiction, the process is made more explicit. While the attributive modifier of the last title may be read as either comparative or superlative, in *Worstward Ho* the superlative is clearly indicated, the suffix "ward" pointing the way toward the desired end: "worst." The repeated recognition that there is "nohow on," no way "how," and nothing to show "how" becomes the structural underpinning for the narrative. If toward "nothing," there is at least some goal.

The prose opens with some of Beckett's most pared-down sentences: "On. Say on. Be said on. Somehow on. Till nohow on. Said nohow on." For readers of Beckett's preceding fiction, the words can be deciphered as tracings of what in the past have been elaborate edifices built on the same foundation: doubt. The first line indicates an imperative form, the familiar Beckettian command to continue, or at least to "say" the continuing, to articulate the direction. Next the elliptical phrase moves to the passive form. What will be said is unknown, and the phrase indicates this uncertainty by not only omitting an auxiliary verb that would indicate tense and case, but also by omitting person. Who is speaking and what is said are not known. The next lines reflect the lack of content the "say" will have. On is all that matters, until "nohow" is reached. And that in turn will be yet another way to go on—"nohow on"—pushing to the final form. It too will be rendered into a past act, although the lack of auxiliary calls both tense and perfective once more into question. All the trials of past struggles to continue and to "say" or write the continuation are summarized in these fourteen words, shards of the monumental thrust forward and the commensurate awareness of the meaninglessness of the attempt. One thing seems certain: if the "say" can become the "said," the act of life still has possibilities if only in the fictional creation that the struggle engenders.

Never before has Beckett's work tottered so close to extinction, had so few variables to begin, so little room to move. Yet forty pages and ninety-six paragraphs later, the speaker can look back and state in the last line "said nohow on" and point to a fiction that concretizes the statement, a fiction overcoming the insurmountable "nohow" of the introduction. The work, perhaps more than any other Beckett fiction, is a testament to human tenacity and to creativity. Given nothing, the artist—Beckett—can still shape that nothing.

*Worstward Ho* is not a difficult work to read once the neologisms and ellipses are translated and completed. It is more comprehensible than the dual world of *Company* or the analogical equivalencies presented in *Ill Seen Ill Said.* It begins with the standard Beckettian givens: a body and a place. "Nothing else ever," the speaker says. The place is only delineated by light; it exists in a dimness surrounded by a void. Both dimness and void may diminish, but they can never totally disappear: "at most mere minimum."

What variables there are in this seemingly fixed world come from the shades, so called, that the speaker introduces. Again, they are remnants of more elaborately drawn figures in preceding fiction. First there is a body. Rather than the birth accorded the old woman in *Ill Seen Ill Said,* equated with the mythic Venus rising from a foam of phrases, here only bones remain, fulfilling the wish expressed at the end of the last fiction: "not another crumb of carrion left."

The bones, referred to first as "it," slowly rise, "somehow up and stand." Yet, even as vestiges of physical form, they are still attached to feeling and to mind: "remains of mind." So even in this drastically diminished form, Beckett offers the familiar dichotomy—a center of sense attached to a skeleton body. Continually seen from the back, the figure is first dressed in a greatcoat from head to pelvis and wearing a black hat. An "it" in familiar apparel, the body becomes "one," then "he," and finally "she," an old woman, who during the course of the work diminishes until she is mere stance: "stooped as in loving memory . . . "

The second image consists of two figures, an old man and child, also seen from the back, dressed initially in black greatcoats from head to foot with black boots. They too are reduced in the fiction until torsos remain. The "twain," as the voice calls them, hold hands, an image that brings to mind the pair in "The Calmative" and *Enough,* and the father/son in *Company.* Whenever their shades are recalled, the hands are described: "joined by held holding hands." Only near the end of the fiction are they separated: "Vast void apart old man and child dim shades on unseen knees."

The final image is a familiar one, taken from *Fizzle 6,* "Still," and the recent television dramas: a "head sunk on crippled hands." The eyes are clenched. It is called, when first mentioned, "the seat of all," and it is from this skull that the other spectres emanate. While they may be obliterated, turned on and off, the head remains. The narrator contemplates obliterating skull as well, but at the end of the text he recognizes that such destruction is impossible. "What left of skull not go."

*Worstward Ho* mixes these three images, alternately describing and diminishing them. When the speaker seems at a loss to say more—or rather less—about the three, the "dim" or "the void" replace them, just long enough for the narrative to rest before continuing "worstward." All may be altered and shifted, except the skull. "In the skull all save the skull gone." This seems a given. Another given is the impossibility of ever fixing the source of the words in the skull. In fiction of the middle period, Beckett seemed interested in affixing the voices to particular pronouns: I/me, you/he. In this diminished world there is "no saying." The pronoun *him* is suggested but only as an unanswered question to be immediately replaced by *one* and finally *it:* "no words for it whose words."

The work ends with the voice saying "enough" and the images "Sudden all far," finally only "Three pins. One pinhole." The final words, almost contentless, offer no physical images. "At bounds of boundless void. Whence no father. Best worse no father. Nohow less. Nohow worse. Nohow naught. Nohow on." Then in a paragraph by itself, the last three words take the text back to the hoped-for end stated in the beginning: "Said nohow on." The "nohow" has been said, and the work ends not with "no," but with its graphological opposite "on," the obverse of negation still proclaimed in this "boundless void." It seems an appropriate place to leave Beckett's fiction, a fiction that began with the recognition of failure and committed itself to continuing to do what it knew never could be done: to "say the unsayable." *Worstward Ho* still makes the attempt and still goes "on," its last word.

# *Chapter Six*
# Two Together

Samuel Beckett is a literary anomaly: a novelist who is a playwright, a playwright who has produced a canon of fiction. The fiction came first, but just barely. In 1937, one year after completing his first novel *Murphy,* Beckett set for himself a new goal—to dramatize a romantic relationship he intuited between Dr. Samuel Johnson and Hester Thrale, the wife of his patron. The result was a fifteen-page opening scene at Johnson's Bolt Court home on the evening of Mr. Thrale's death, while the assembled residents wait for Johnson—who does not arrive. Beckett's relocation to Paris soon after the aborted attempt at drama and the six years during the war when he was in hiding in Roussillon, France, severely inhibited his writing. *Watt* was his one completed work from the war period. However, once resettled in Paris in 1946, Beckett embarked on the most fertile writing period in his career, producing, among other works, four plays.

*Eleuthéria,* written in 1947, is his first completed play, aside from the college parody *Le Kid,* written sixteen years before. Both have never been published and remain to date unproduced.[1] The title, *Eleuthéria,* taken from the Greek, means "freedom," and refers to the attempted rebellion of thirty-three-year-old Victor Krap (an early model, minus one *p,* of the hero of *Krapp's Last Tape)* who has moved from his family home and, despite entreaties, refuses to return. The subtitle of the work is "drama bourgeois," and Beckett creates both the serious struggles of his hero and a comedy of manners depicting the life of the Krap family and their society. The play breaks with naturalism. Two settings, Krap family home and Victor's lair, vie for dominance until in act 3 the latter forces the former offstage. Names are chosen for scatalogical effect: Krap, Piouk, Meck (prostitute in French), and Skunk. The separation between audience and performance is shattered at one point when a spectator jumps on stage to entreat the hero to abandon his isolation, in another when Victor is attacked by a Chinese torturer with the same intent.

Beckett submitted *Eleuthéria* to the director Roger Blin, along with another play he had written soon after. Since the latter work called for only one set rather than two and five rather than seventeen actors, Blin decided to try and stage it, which he finally did several years later on 5 January, 1953 in the small Left Bank Théâtre de Babylone. The play was *Waiting for Godot*.

"I began to write *Godot* as a relaxation to get away from the awful prose I was writing at that time," Beckett said in response to the question of why he turned to drama.[2] The prose was *Malone Dies*, the second book of the trilogy. Given the constraints of the book, and of *The Unnamable*, which followed, it is possible to imagine how drama afforded Beckett's characters and Beckett "a relaxation" and a way out of the impasse of depicting being with words. No matter what else characters may be on the stage, they are always there. Devising stories of their past, lost in reveries of the future, they still present palpable, physical bodies that testify to their being in the present. Theater also has access to sign systems that do not rely on words. The physical gestures of the actors, the lighting, music, costumes, and tone of the voice can convey a meaning apart from the language of words, and may at times even undermine or contradict the verbal component of a play. Rather than "speak and say nothing"—the Unnamable's wish—physical movement can, as theater theoretician Antonin Artaud believed, obliterate the "transition from a gesture to a cry or a sound," allowing all the senses to "interpenetrate as if through strange channels hollowed out in the mind itself."[3] One of the great strengths of Beckett's theater is precisely the visual images that exist on the stage: two tramps huddled together against the fearful approaching doom; Winnie buried in her mound; Krapp sitting under his desk light, listening to the whir of the tape recorder before him; May pacing on her little strip of floor; and, the most powerful and horrific of all, Mouth spewing out sounds barely audible as words. Artaud called such images "animated hieroglyphics" not reducible to representational meaning but embodying multiple interpretations in their configurations. Beckett used the same word in his 1931 monograph *Proust* when he said, "The only reality is provided by the hieroglyphics traced by inspired perception (identification of subject and object)."

While these images could have been described in prose, the impact of their presence could not have been conveyed with the same power. Beckett recognized this very problem at the beginning of his career in *Dream of Fair to Middling Women* when he bemoaned the fact that his characters could not be portrayed as musical sounds—a simultaneity of sounds played at one time: "how nice that would be, linear, a lovely Phythagorean chant-chant solo of cause and effect." The theater, while it still may not explain characters, can do what prose cannot: present the "chain-chant" directly to audiences who are free to react without the necessity of explanation, who can apprehend life being presented. Vladimir and Estragon in *Godot* are there; they can be seen in all the multiplicity of their being and of their power. The stage allows for such verisimilitude and transference from life without the obligatory words that never quite say it right.

Besides being there, Beckett's characters share other characteristics. Despite their physical presence, they are uncertain of themselves. They often answer to several names, trying them on as they try on hats, searching for a fixed self. They also suffer from faulty memories; even the present sinks before their eyes—and the audience's—into a past that cannot be verified. When Vladimir says, "So there you are again," Estragon replies, "Am I?" Immediately after chewing his carrot, Estragon begins to lose the surety of its existence. Beckett's most direct articulation of the vagaries of memory and the resultant uncertainty of being can be found in *Proust,* where he speaks of the "unceasing modification of . . . personality, whose permanent reality, if any, can only be apprehended as a retrospective hypothesis." One function of the Beckett couple is verification of self through the testimony of an "other." If a character cannot remember yesterday, there is always a companion to act as witness to another time and another place.

Habits and rituals also provide some protection against the tenuousness of existence. Although habit, Beckett wrote in *Proust,* is "ballast that chains the dog to his vomit," it also provides "the guarantee of a dull inviolability." Taking off shoes, peering into hats, opening windows, circling rooms, making yearly birthday tapes keep characters from thinking. There are moments, Beckett recognized, when habits slip or fail. Such moments are marked in his plays by silence, when characters are most painfully "there." The commonly shared locale in Beckett's early plays is at that juncture when old habits are about to run out, and the characters frantically perform them, knowing they soon will cease to provide comfort. Although the activities are often comic—dropping pants, pratfalls, funny stories, pantomimes—what keeps Beckett's personae from becoming ludicrous figures is their total awareness of the ruse of habit. A "tragicomedy" is the subtitle for *Godot,* but it could serve as subtext for all the plays: comic because the habits are funny or are performed in humorous ways; tragic because the figures recognize the pathos of their feeble attempts to ward off anguish. There is, as the first couple recognize, "nothing to be done" but they and subsequent pairs still "do." And audiences who have never worn bowler hats or dropped pants can still empathize with the situations they see, because they have performed other habitual acts that constitute their lives, and they too have waited—for something or someone. Seen in this way, the plays of Samuel Beckett are not intellectually foreboding but immediately human since they are concerned with the most basic of experiences: life lived with uncertainty, with repetition, and with hope.

## *Waiting for Godot*

Two men of indeterminate age wait on a country road by a tree for a man named Godot with whom they believe they have an appointment. While waiting, they talk, tell stories, reminisce, joke, sing, sleep, eat, caress, urinate, contemplate suicide, meet two other men, think. Their wait is divided into two acts; the second, repeating the activities of the first in a different order, is shorter and ends with the pair in the same place, still waiting. Godot did not come, does not come; perhaps tomorrow he will come.

The theme of waiting is not unique to Beckett; it is one of the dominant motifs of modern drama: Chekhov's characters in *The Three Sisters* wait to go to Moscow, where life will have meaning; Tennessee Williams's in *The Glass Menagerie* wait for the Gentleman Caller who will make everything right; Arthur Miller's in *Death of a Salesman* wait for the success that will heal all wounds. In the case of the few who get what they wait for, like the bill-sticker in Strindberg's *The Dream Play,* they may find the item—in this case a green fishing net—"is all right but not quite what I expected." What makes Beckett's waiting pair different from the others is that they are totally absorbed in their waiting. While Chekhov's characters wait, they live; while Beckett's characters live, they wait.

The simplicity of the action has fostered many readings of the play; the brief details have been kneaded, shaped, and patterned to fit endless interpretations and persuasions. Far too often discussions focus on "Who is Godot?" a question Vladimir and Estragon don't ask. When Beckett was asked the question, he replied, "If I knew, I would have said so in the play."[4] Far from explaining his work, he sees the critical sleuthers as misdirected. In conversation with director Alec Reid, Beckett stated: "the great success of *Waiting For Godot* had arisen from a misunderstanding: critics and public alike were busy interpreting in allegorical or symbolic terms a play which strove at all cost to avoid definition."[5]

That is not to say the play is formless, far from it. *Godot* is a highly structured work balanced as carefully as its central characters, Vladimir and Estragon. The play opens on a barren scene: a country road, a tree, near sunset. The first to enter is Estragon, usually played by a fat, squat man. It is he who has trouble with his feet, worries about food, sleeps and dreams. Of him, Beckett has said: "Estragon is on the ground, he belongs to the stone."[6] Vladimir usually is tall and spare, his physical ailment his prostate, his trouble his hat. Of the two he is more contemplative, the dispenser of food, the initiator of action, and of the meeting with Godot. "Vladimir is light, he is oriented towards the sky. He belongs to the tree," Beckett observed.[7] Stone and tree become visual hieroglyphics for the pair, and their actions are skewed to their signs: the body and the mind, the earth and the sky.

In this and following plays action precedes words. Before Estragon speaks he performs a pantomine with his shoes. Not only do actions precede words, in *Godot* they supersede them. Although Estragon says, "Nothing to be done," he continues to struggle with his shoes. At the end of the play while he says, "Yes, let's go," the pair "do not move." Words and actions are constantly disjunctive and discontinuous throughout the work. What ties the first and last lines together is that Estragon speaks them and his gestures belie their intent. "I take no sides. I am interested in the shape of ideas," Beckett once remarked.[8] The recurrent shape in *Godot* is the circle. Like the song that Vladimir sings at the beginning of act 2, it is a circle that turns in on itself—more a spiral—never completed, diminishing like the action of the play, but never reaching a center of absolute zero.

Repetitions reinforce the circular pattern with each permutation somewhat diminished from what has preceded. We enter the action in medias res—in the middle. Vladimir's first words to his friend are "So there you are again," and his following questions indicate recurrence: "And they didn't beat you?" "The same lot as usual?" After Pozzo and Lucky leave in act 1, he indicates that they have been there before. In act 2 the audience can corroborate the cycle; they have become witnesses to the recurrence, albeit diminished, of Pozzo and Lucky, Godot's messenger, and the couple themselves.

Echoing the circularity are the numerous word games the pair play to keep themselves going. One of the more common is the rhetorical device of stichomythia, antithesis and repetition by two speakers. For example, Vladimir's bush becomes Estragon's shrub and returns to bush again. The game is replayed with other words in act 2. Vocabulary is also repeated. Estragon's "help me" is echoed by Pozzo in act 2; "blathering" and "calm" also appear in both acts. There are repetitions in the responses after certain words. In every case but one, when Estragon is reminded that they are "waiting for Godot," he responds with the sigh "Ah." It sets up an expectation in the audience, a familiar sound that marks recurrence. In a similar way Beckett as director of his work, insists on specific movements that are to be repeated when the couple leave and meet each other, move across stage, and hold each other.[9] Gestures signal repetitive situations, just as tones of voice indicate a familiar situation once again being faced.

Sometimes repetitions signal the impossibility of fixing an experience in language. For example, at the beginning of act 1, Estragon is in pain and Vladimir inquires "It hurts?" Almost immediately Estragon asks the same of his friend. Neither can answer, for, as Ludwig Wittgenstein argued in *Philosophical Investigations,* it is impossible to definitely convey one's private pain; meaning can only be inferred from one's own experiences with pain. Therefore, each can only approximate the meaning of "hurt" by substituting his own experience with pain—just as the audience must do.

To circumvent such ambiguities caused by words, Beckett returns to action, creating visual images that offer in their clarity a meaning that transcends the limits of language. One example of the technique appears in act 1, when Estragon tries repeatedly to ask about their relationship with Godot, about whether they are "tied to Godot." The questioning is interrupted by the appearance of Lucky who enters with a rope around his neck. He covers half the distance of the stage before the audience and the pair see who is holding the rope. A man held by an invisible power, tied to an unseen element, is a visual concretization of the very question Estragon has been trying to ask. "Tied" in the person of Lucky becomes palpable: Estragon tied to Vladimir, the pair tied to Godot, as Lucky is tied to Pozzo, and this pair tied to the force that keeps them walking. In the same way other visual images transcend simple definitions of words: Vladimir comforting Estragon as he sings him to sleep, Estragon hiding frantically behind the narrow tree, Vladimir rummaging in his pockets spilling those items modern people use to verify appointments, the pair embracing after conflict, the four men in act 2 prone on the ground.

Beckett goes even further to make the point that meaning is not easy to deduce even from firsthand experience. At the beginning of the play Vladimir talks of the testimony of the Gospels, only one of which reports that one of the thieves crucified with Christ was saved. "But all four were there," Vladimir says angrily as he tries to explain to a bored Estragon the problem that perplexes him. Besides cutting the percentages for salvation to one in four, the discrepancies cast doubt on human observability and possibility. This doubt is reinforced soon after in act 1 when Pozzo and Lucky appear. Although direct witnesses, Vladimir and Estragon are still unsure of the culprit in the relationship and vacillate in their reading of the events before them.

Not only are situations at any given moment subject to misinterpretation, but series of events alter because of the havoc wreaked by time and circumstance. Pozzo, the dominant master in act 1, enters in act 2 led by the very rope he wielded. How then can humans answer ontological questions, if daily occurrences shift before the eyes of the observer? The word *perhaps* thus becomes the unspoken word that runs through *Godot,* more painful than the word *never* because it ties the pair to their agony of waiting. When Colin Duckworth asked Beckett if Lucky is so named because he has found his Godot in Pozzo, Beckett replied, "I suppose he is Lucky to have no more expectations."[10]

Although Lucky is freed of expectations, his monologue offers a composite of the philosophy that has brought him to his awareness. It is also a parody of human attempts to deny the human condition. Often described as gibberish, the speech is actually a carefully structured tripartite critique. Talking to the German actor who played the part, Beckett indicated that the first section describes "the indifference of heaven," ending with the line "but not so fast"; the second, starting with "considering what is more" is about "man who is shrinking—about man who is dwindling"; and the third fixes on "the earth abode of stones," starting from the line "considering what is more, much more grave."[11] The monologue summarizes the position of the two tramps, Lucky, his master, and all people: condemned to shrink and decline on a dying earth under an indifferent sky. Having spewed out his message—the verbal dance of the net—Lucky becomes dumb. There is nothing left to say. Having heard the words, however, Vladimir and Estragon ignore the speech and continue waiting. To reinforce the idea that all the characters share the same fate, Beckett in his own direction of *Godot* has blurred the distinctions among the four, dressing them in similar mismatched clothing, the top of one suit combined with the pants of another. Even Pozzo loses his dominance; his human vulnerability is stressed more than his tyrannical bent.

The radically altered and decaying state of Pozzo and Lucky in act 2 presages a commensurate decline in Vladimir and Estragon, also subject to the vagaries of time and fortune. Act 2 indicates the movement toward such a decline: word games are shorter, actions fewer, despair greater. The two even begin to play at being Pozzo and Lucky, with Vladimir using such words as "hog" and "pig" to call his friend. Although it almost seems as if time has stopped, as Pozzo reminds them in act 1, "Don't you believe it." Continual erosions take place. Those who see the blossoming of the tree in act 2 as an indication of hope misread the message. The leaves are less a sign of regeneration than of the cyclical process that promises no respite but only further waiting and suffering in time. Despite the repeated cries for help issued in act 2 from Pozzo and Vladimir who wish to rise and from Estragon who wishes to take off his shoes, there is no help for the central abiding condition that Hamm in *Endgame* describes: "you're on earth, there's no cure for that!"

The last image of the play is both comic and tragic: Estragon with his pants around his ankles contemplating suicide. Working toward closure, Beckett has Vladimir echo his initial comments about shoes in act 1, substituting three "on"s for the earlier "off"s. Looking down at his dropped pants, Estragon utters the word *true.* Of that much he—and we—can be sure. Pants must be pulled "on" if not "off." The former choice at the end of the play also indicates the direction of the two, performed at some later time after the conclusion of the play entitled *Waiting for Godot.* The characters will go on, the actors playing them will go on again, though as the lights fade the pair stand mute and inert, hoisting up pants and courage before continuing "On."

## *Endgame*

In a desperate attempt to keep the conversation going in act 1 of *Godot* Vladimir appeals to Estragon: "Come on, Gogo, return the ball, can't you, once in a way?" Coming perilously close to cessation in act 2, he once more chides his friend: "Will you not play?" *Godot* is a play, an imitation of an action, in which the actors play at playing; the game is "Filling-Time-While-Waiting-For-Godot." The pair fulfill many of the Oxford English Dictionary definitions of *play,* both as substantive and verb: They engage in "free bodily exercise," exhibit "a boiling up or ebullition," are "actively engaged" and employed as they "briskly wield or ply," and even—taking their leave from *Hamlet*—"play on each other" and "would seem to know the stops."

Play becomes even more central in Beckett's second dramatic work, *Endgame,* where the title is taken from the last section of a chess game and indicates that time when two basic options are still open to the players: checkmate—entrapment of the king—or stalemate—a draw. To emphasize the play as a game, the first words of Hamm, king on the board, are "Me to play," a phrase he repeats three times, as various sections of the repartee move him toward closure. After the last repetition, he continues "wearily": "Old endgame lost of old, play and lose and have done with losing." Not chess game but endgame because, as in *Godot,* the acting begins in medias res, this time close to the conclusion, the endgame, of what the audience must assume has been a long battle, one already predetermined from the start but of necessity to be played out. "The end is in the beginning and yet you go on," Hamm recognizes.

Play is a human need, basic to civilization, argues J. Huizinga, in his book *Homo Ludens: A Study of the Play Element in Culture.* It is voluntary, removed from real life, limited in time and space, and able to create order. "Into an imperfect world and into the confusion of life it brings a temporary, a limited perfection," Huizinga says.[12] Play becomes a controlled microcosm of life where participants may freely engage in activities whose results are only irrevocable in the course of and the time of the game. A finite portion of life is demarcated and within it an ordered segment of life, complete with its own rules and penalties, is acted out. The word *play,* used to describe the dramatic form, comes from the idea of imitation of life in a given substruct. The similarities between the literary play and life parallel those between game and life. Both remove a segment of life from the flux of time, establish rules, impose order. Life seen as a game and also as a play are common metaphors. Hamlet has the players ape the life of the play to catch a king, Macbeth equates life to a stage, a person to a poor strutting player. Prospero becomes director moving the actors on his island stage.

*Endgame* employs the metaphor of life as game and as stage drama, using Shakespearean examples to bolster the image. Hamm is the ham actor, demanding stage center. He is also Hamlet, desiring to end but unsure of what lies beyond the surety of his cell. "Will there be sharks, do you think?" he asks of that "unknown land." He is also a director like Prospero in *The Tempest,* and echoes his line "Our revels now are ended." The parallel to *The Tempest* is even more clearly drawn, since in it Miranda and Ferdinand sit playing a game of chess, imitating Prospero who attempted to make chessmen of the other characters. Further, Clov indicates his associations with the servant Caliban when he complains to his mentor Hamm, "I use the words you taught me," repeating Caliban's plaint, "You taught me language; and my profit on't Is, I know how to curse" (1. 2. 363–64).

*Endgame* is a play about play, where the participants do not speak of winning but of merely finishing. Clov's first words that begin the play are "Finished, it's finished, nearly finished, it must be nearly finished." The four verb phrases retreat from absolute certainty to a questioning of the irrevocability of ending. Clov never specifies what will be finishing since he uses the indefinite pronoun "it." Hamm does the same: "Yes, there it is, it's time it ended and yet I hesitate to . . . to end." Later he asks, "Have you not had enough . . . of this . . . this . . . thing." The "it" or "thing" become the "something" that is taking its course.

Some "somethings" are finished when the play begins. There are no more turkish delight, bicycles, or coffins. During the course of the play pain killers, pap, and perhaps Nell are added to the list. Most things, however, remain incomplete, not yet finished. Hamm's dog has only three legs and no sex; Nagg's story concerns pants not yet finished. When the punch line is finally delivered, Hamm inquires of his father, "Have you not finished? Will you never finish?" Later Hamm asks Clov, "Why don't you finish us?" and offers the combination of the cupboard "if you promise to finish me." Most significant of the "unfinished" are Hamm's chronicle and Clov's leave-taking, both incomplete at the end of the play. Hamm cannot finish his story because it is the story of his life, and while living it he cannot end it. Clov, from the beginning of the play, repeats "I'll leave you"; yet he returns after each exit to complete tasks or in answer to the whistle Hamm blows to herald a new round of activities. When Clov asks why he stays and follows Hamm's commands, the only answer Hamm offers is "The dialogue." Without Clov Hamm could not move or see since Clov provides mobility and sight; but more important for their particular game, without Clov Hamm would be forced to talk to himself.

While dialogue provides comfort, the fear of isolation hovers about the cell. Clov's four climbs up his ladder bring the same report: "Nothing." Within the enclosure, images repeat the dreaded loneliness. The two ashcans touch, but they isolate Nagg and Nell from each other. Nell threatens further separation when she tells Nagg, "I'll leave you," and seems to carry out the threat by presumably dying within the course of the play. The threat of isolation is indicated in Clov's attempted retreats to his kitchen, a sanctum Hamm cannot enter. Abandonment and loneliness also shape Hamm's chronicle: the abandonment of child by father.

The father/son relationship is central to *Endgame.* While Nagg and Nell recall sexual love, their relationship is overshadowed by Nagg's role as father to Hamm, and Hamm's as father/mentor to Clov. Both pairs are fictionally represented in the father/son story in Hamm's chronicle and reechoed in the child spectre that ends the play. Hamm is master to Clov's servant, a reminder of the Pozzo/Lucky connection, but rendered less harsh because of the domesticity of the comings and goings. Hamm also reminds Clov that he has been like a father to him, and Clov concurs. Nagg similarly reminds Hamm of their paternal link. Calling himself "as happy as a king in the past," Nagg appears as a dispossessed ruler condemned to the ashcan by the scion.

These human patriarchal ties, in their cruelty and indifference, mirror the relationship between God the father and His children. A religious motif runs through the play. As Ruby Cohn has shown, Clov's introductory word "Finished" echoes Christ's on the cross according to St. John and Hamm's call to his father parallels Christ's words according to St. Matthew, while his "mene mene" translates to "God has numbered thy kingdom and finished it."[13] Of that first father, Hamm, after seeking him in prayer, says—in language that caused Beckett problems with the English censor when it was first produced—"The bastard! He doesn't exist!" If God is a "bastard," he avoids the patriarchal chain that binds all characters in *Endgame:* son becomes father and is himself at the mercy of his own son.

Ennui and despair mark this constant grinding down of the generations, one into another. The physical movements of the play reinforce these habitual patterns and frustration. Clov's opening struggles with windows, ladder, and telescope seem to endure forever; so too the attempt to get Hamm in the center of his universe, a physical concomitant to Nagg's endless story, and Hamm's unending chronicle. Any new additions or complications only exacerbate the situation. Since defeat is determined from the beginning, a flea, rat, or young boy can only be greeted with horror and require extermination. "More complications," Hamm says when Clov announces the boy.

Why play a game lost from the beginning or continue a life whose end is vividly manifested in the preceding generation? Several answers are provided in the play. First is the fear of ending, facing the abyss of silence and death. Then there is the human desire to understand. "All life long the same questions, the same answers," Clov says, and Hamm echoes soon after, "Ah the old questions, the old answers, there's nothing like them." Much of the action of *Endgame* is structured on questions. In the first exchange, which concludes with Hamm's "we're getting on," Hamm asks twenty-seven questions, Clov five. Few are satisfactorily answered, often receiving immediate, perfunctory replies that are then qualified. Other times questions are answered with other questions or merely repeated. While Hamm is the primary questioner at the beginning, Clov outquestions him by the end. The central question that Hamm raises is, "We're not beginning to . . . to . . . mean something?" To which he gets no answer, merely a scoff. Yet questions, even those without answers, keep the dialogue going. They become the linguistic habitual equivalents to the physical movements. However, question marks are not the only punctuation marks in *Endgame.* Exclamation points also abound, more than in any other Beckett work. As less occurs, more is made of it.

Despite its dearth of detail, *Endgame,* like *Godot,* has been subject to unending interpretations. Some have read the cell as a fallout shelter after a nuclear attack, the ashcans as a commentary on what society does with its old people. Less limiting are readings that connect Hamm with Noah (Hamm is the name of Noah's second son), the cell with the ark, the last habitable place for "the creatures." None of these readings should be taken as the only one, for each can easily be subsumed under a more general state of human affairs. In a series of letters Beckett wrote to the director Alan Schneider prior to the first production of *Endgame* in America, he talked about the starkness of the play, comparing it to *Waiting for Godot:* "Rather difficult and elliptic, mostly depending on the power of the text to claw, more inhuman than *Godot.*"[14] *Endgame* claws because of its images and because of its refusal to conform with dramaturgy that dictates that answers be supplied in last acts and themes be reduced to simple explanations.

Beckett calls direct attention to the dramatic underpinnings of the work by having Hamm, near the end of the play, refer to his "soliloquy," a possible "underplot," and the use of an "aside." With its form thus exposed, the play becomes itself object, and Beckett can include it with those items that remain "unfinished." Clov, in the last tableau, remains frozen still in the playing range, and Beckett purposely leaves unanswered the question: "Does Clov leave?" By so doing, he offers the possibility of the game continuing and the play form circling back upon itself to work out yet another move in an ongoing, unfinishing game.

## *Act Without Words I and II*

Printed along with *Endgame* in the Grove Press edition is the short mime play *Act Without Words I* which Beckett in a note to his American publisher called "in some obscure way, a codicil to *End-Game.*"[15] It and *Act Without Words II,* written in 1959, dispense with language, making their impact through the visual images on the stage. Beckett's early plays begin with mime; in these pieces he offers a series of physical movements that allow the struggles of the actors to appear unimpeded by the words that would seek to explain them.

Like all Beckett's plays, the action in *Act Without Words I* begins in the middle: "The man is flung backwards on stage from right wing. He falls, gets up immediately, dusts himself, turns aside, reflects." Responding to a whistle from left, he repeats the same action. The whistle blows fourteen times—twice from right, three times from left, and nine times from above—calling the man to seven props: a palm tree, a carafe of water, three different sized boxes, scissors, and rope. Each activity leads to frustration. Sitting under the shade of the tree, the man attempts to cut his nails with the scissors, and the tree "closes like a parasol." Desiring the water, he attempts to stand on the boxes and the water is moved out of his reach. He climbs a rope and it collapses. In the process of his struggles the man shows intelligence. He learns that small boxes cannot support large ones. He also shows ingenuity. Unable to climb the rope, he attempts to fashion it into a lasso. Despite his accomplishments, however, he cannot defeat the force that whistles him into the next foray and continually impedes his victory. All he can do is pause, brush himself off, and wait for the next whistle. The mime ends with the man still looking at his hands, suspended—as are Estragon and Vladimir, Hamm and Clov—between cessation and the next round.

Endurance and repetition are also central to *Act Without Words II,* where A and B are prodded not by sound but by light, a goad that becomes progressively more mobile, forcing them to emerge from their respective sacks and go through the motions of the day. A is a pill-taking, nervous, sloppy person; B is an organized, efficient clock-watcher. Both, however, are controlled by the light and perform rituals, albeit differently. In the short mime Beckett reduces the routine of daily existence to a few gestures appropriate to the personalities. Reminiscent of Molloy/Moran, the pair are antithetical in habits but identical in their lack of freedom and their enslavement to routine and repetition.

Artaud, recognizing the limits of language, saw the possibility of movement creating "a new physical language." He based his description on a performance of Balinese dance, where gestures represented not imitations of actions in the conventional sense but movements standing for a complex series of experiences. "A kind of terror seizes us at the thought of these mechanized beings, whose joys and griefs seem not their own but at the service of age-old rites, as if they were dictated by superior intelligences," he wrote.[16] Beckett's pantomimes do not create terror; they do, however, create modern versions of "age-old rites": the rites of survival, at the will of "superior intelligences."

## *Krapp's Last Tape*

Fritz Mauthner, Austrian philosopher of language, whose *Critique of Language (Beiträge zu einer Kritik der Sprache)* Beckett read in 1929 at the suggestion of James Joyce, described the impossibility of individuals coalescing parts of the ego. Because the "I" is constantly changing in time, the individual cannot be apprehended whole. "We know of no enduring ego, we only know of moments of the drive of living and the memory of each individual moment," Mauthner wrote.[17] In his monograph *Proust,* written two years after reading Mauthner, Beckett used many of the same ideas, particularly the lack of continuum in selves held "victims and prisoners" of time, and of the "unceasing modification of his personality, whose permanent reality, if any, can only be apprehended as a retrospective hypothesis."

Twenty-five years after writing *Proust* Beckett was introduced to a machine that could call forth images of the past unbesmirched by time, that could resurrect the self of the past and superimpose it on the present. The mechanical marvel was a tape recorder—more accurately called a memory recorder—since the verbal images it records remain as recorded. Introduced to the recorder when he received a tape of his BBC radio play *All That Fall,* Beckett two years later wrote *Krapp's Last Tape* that employed its recollective properties. The play was originally called *Magee's Monologue* since it was written for the Irish actor Patrick Magee, whose cracked voice was the model for the cracked sounds of "wearish old" Krapp.

The play is set on "A late evening in the future," to explain the anachronism of a tape recorder in the past. The setting is Krapp's den. Only the central lighted island surrounding his writing desk is visible; the rest is in darkness. Into this darkness Krapp ventures to drink, get his dictionary, and, in the stage productions Beckett has directed, get the tape recorder and microphone that are not on the desk in the beginning. Yearly, at the moment of his birth, Krapp repeats a ritual: taping a birthday message. He is always alone, often preceding the tapings with a visit to a pub. Before commencing the new tape, he eats bananas—"Fatal things for a man with my condition"—drinks, and listens to a tape made at an earlier time which begins with reviling a still-earlier Krapp. An old man listening to a younger self talking about a still younger self unlocks a procession of selves emerging, as Mauthner called it, from "the black nothing of the past."[18] If not the infinite regress of dogs described by Vladimir's song in *Godot,* there are a succession of beings going back in time till the moment forty-five years before when the recordings began.

Just as the figures are variations of one self, each tape mirrors the others, bearing traces of similar habits and character, though marked with progressive deterioration and decline. Each begins with a renunciation of the past and a resolution for the future: less drinking, fewer bananas, more work. Each describes the present isolation and silence. Each concentrates on a woman: Bianca, the girl on the railway station, the nurse in the park, the woman in the punt, the fictional Effie, and the "bony old whore." While each talks of life, each contains an image of death: the death of a father, mother, and finally Krapp, whose last tape is never made. "Nothing to say, not a squeak. What's a year now? The sour cud and the iron stool," he says in his last, uncompleted tape. Unable to record, Krapp prefers to return to a younger self, at age thirty-nine, and to replay "farewell to love" choosing to "be again be again" in the past rather than continue to record for the future.

Each tape also contains imagery of light and dark, which James Knowlson has described as the central dichotomy in the play, citing Beckett's 1967 notebook for the German production, in which he calls the light "spiritual" and the dark "sensual" with Krapp attempting to coalesce them through his intellect. The attempt is ethically correct, Beckett writes, but a transgression since "the duty of reason being not to join but to separate (deliverance of imprisoned light)."[19] The action takes place in a small section of stage lighted by the lamp above Krapp's desk, a small island carved out of the circling darkness. Although he ventures into the dark, Krapp feels reassured when he returns once more to the light and finds "me. (Pause.) Krapp." In the tapes light also plays against dark. Krapp at twenty-nine lives with Bianca (white) on Kedar Street (dark). At thirty-nine, while awaiting his mother's death, he sits in a park and sees a woman dressed in white pushing "a big black hooded perambulator, most funereal thing." His first act after the death is to give a black ball to a white dog.

The central image of the play is that of the woman in the punt, the image recorded as "farewell to love." Begun in the middle, the scene is replayed in its entirety, the old Krapp tearing off his present tape and returning to it at the end of the play. The woman is not described, rather it is her eyes that are mentioned, an echo of the eyes of the preceding women. Not "incomparable!" like Bianca's or "crysolite!" like the unnamed nurse's, they are mere slits. The scene takes place in glaring sunshine, and Krapp must provide a circle of shade, reversing the original light/dark symmetry. Yet even as he provides dark, Krapp makes clear that "it was hopeless."

Balancing this image is the one that precedes it titled "memorable equinox." An equinox indicates the time of year when light and dark are equal. On this day Krapp records his revelation, never totally articulated in the text, but greeted with impatience and derision by the old Krapp. The fragments point to a resolution of contraries, the dark "held in check." Whatever the "miracle," it has produced little: "seventeen copies sold" of the "opus . . . magnum" and seems of less importance to the listener than the love it replaced. It is to the dark that the aged Krapp is still drawn.

Beckett is not the first to use a tape recorder as a central prop in a play. Arthur Miller, in *Death of a Salesman,* has the machine overshadow the live Willie Loman in a scene with his young boss Howard. The new gadget depersonalizes human relationships. "Speak into it, it's running," Howard cajoles his reticent wife. In *Krapp's Last Tape* the machine is not depersonalized; on the contrary, it provides the only life left for the lonely figure who bends over it, caressing it as he attempts to recapture the life he has rejected. The same hands, now gnarled with age, that touch the machine touched the girl. The young voice that wondered at Old Miss McGlome singing of her girlhood, now is old and his prophecy fulfilled: he does not sing. The superimposition of the sounds of youth on the decrepit figure in Krapp's den creates a powerful image of age, the deterioration of time, and the inevitability of death.

What keeps the picture from being too painful is the comedy of the play. Like all preceding plays, *Krapp* opens with an extended pantomime, here taken directly from vaudeville: the eating of a banana and the slipping on its discarded peel. The sound effects—particularly the popping of corks—and the subsequent staggering provide humor. But it is muted humor, only slightly cutting the dark as the light does. In fact, in his directorial work with the play

Beckett has stripped away many of these routines. Krapp no longer wears a white face or painted nose, his clothes are old not garish, and he no longer fumbles with keys or envelope since the desk is unlocked. He still eats two bananas but throws both peels over his shoulder into the dark. Added gestures underline the spectre of death and age. Krapp carries the items he uses; each is heavier and wears him down as Clov is worn by his repeated carrying and fetching. Three times he also looks over his shoulder. When Martin Held, an actor playing Krapp, asked Beckett why, the director/writer replied, "Old Nick's there. Death is standing behind him and unconsciously he's looking for it."[20]

*Krapp's Last Tape* is a transitional play, moving from the stage action of *Godot* and *Endgame* to the stasis of *Happy Days* and *Play*. It also paves the way for the monologues of the late period by offering a richness of vocal color, all words spoken by one individual. That Krapp often forgets that the words of the tape are his is a testimony to the variety of voice, but is also a reminder of the dislocations the individual suffers in time, that make him a stranger to himself, one who uses words that must be looked up in dictionaries, who commemorates events that have long since faded from his memory.

## *Happy Days*

In *Endgame* Nell, the only female in the play, goads Clov to "go away, into the desert," her last reported words. *Happy Days,* written five years later, is set in that desert, the grey light of *Endgame* replaced by unremitting "blazing light": "hellish light," Winnie says, inverting the "Holy Light" of Milton's *Paradise Lost. How It Is,* Beckett's novel written the year before, described a hellscape which the character traversed, looking for a fictive surrogate to hold. *Happy Days* offers a static picture of the same terrain. Winnie is buried to her waist in act 1, only able to use her hands and crane her neck, and buried to her neck in act 2, only able to move her mouth, eyes, and face. A woman slowly sinking into the earth—that "old extinguisher"—is among Beckett's most powerful images, made even more so because the audience is privy to the process, remembering the "old times" of act 1 in the diminution of act 2. Unlike *Endgame* that was reduced from two to one act, *Happy Days* in drafts expanded, the better to illustrate the gradual process of deterioration, the "something" strange that is happening.

The play presents yet another Beckett couple, this time husband and wife, both with similar names—Winnie and Willie—and, as usual, with equal letters. Winnie is stage front encased in her mound; Willie is behind her until his appearance at the end of the play, seen in brief glimpses as he reads his newspaper, doffs his boater, covers his head, and holds up his fingers. Although he says only fifty-two words in act 1—many mere ejaculations—and only one—"Win"—in act 2, he is there, company. "Ah yes, if only I could bear to be alone, I mean prattle away with not a soul to hear," Winnie says. But she cannot. She needs to think that "Something of this is being heard, I am not merely talking to myself, that is in the wilderness, a thing I could never bear to do—for any length of time." Willie is audience and link with the past, "the old days," the "old style," a verification that they were not always as they are.

A party to the conditions of the present, Willie is also cast in a familiar role: stereotypic husband, hiding behind his daily paper, grunting when spoken to, responding only when prodded. "Oh I know you were never one to talk, I worship you Winnie be mine and then nothing from that day forth only tidbits from *Reynolds' News,"* Winnie chides at the end of the play. Not only unresponsive husband, Willie is also child to Winnie's mother. "That's the good man," she tells him as he makes his way back to his hole. Most of Willie's activities are those of the infant: rubbing cream on his bare bottom, navigating on all fours, relishing his excretions. Whether Willie is morose and diffident or has been made so by Winnie is never clear. It is Willie who, at the end of act 1, provides the information that a hog is "a castrated pig raised for slaughter."

When Willie "curls up" on her, "there is of course the bag," another stay against the horror of her situation. In Beckett's first fiction *Dream of Fair to Middling Women,* the Alba, the hero's love, sat with him in the shadow of a rock "beautifying his fingers" with implements taken from "her fathomless bag." Other Beckett personae in their travels are also aided by a bag carrying their needs. Winnie's items—comb, brush, toothpaste, toothbrush, mirror, medicine, glasses, hat, music box, gun—are not only possessions, they are means of filling time. "There is so little one *can* do . . . One does it all." They provide solace between the bell that wakes her and the bell that calls her to sleep. However, Beckett specifies in the stage directions that they are for the most part ineffectual. Parasol and toothbrush have elongated handles and small shafts, toothpaste is finished, medicine about to be used up. Her handling of the items is also beyond her control. Thrown away, they appear again the next day in the bag; raised—like the parasol—they cannot be dropped until, as Winnie says, "something must happen, in the world."

The items themselves are those befitting her role: fifty-year-old matron, "blond for preference," with pearl necklet. They circumscribe the rituals of her day. She begins in act 1 with prayer, followed by brushing teeth—modestly spitting behind her—combing her hair or hairs, looking in her mirror, putting on her hat, and in lieu of ambulatory pursuits, reading her toothbrush, the only writing available. When these items no longer occupy her, there are still other activities: remembering "a part" of her classics, telling her story, and, when all else fails, singing her song. Winnie resembles the child of her Mildred story, forty-five years later (the same time span of tapings in *Krapp's Last Tape).* Brought up, presumably, in a small town, Borough Green, she is in her own words a "good girl" given to cheery phrases, "Another heavenly day," and sentimental memories, "My first ball. . . . My second ball!" Yet to see Winnie as mere caricature, a programmed toy, is to diminish the play and the character. While her habitual activities are all too familiar and real, they take place in a setting of surreal horror, a horror Winnie fully recognizes. This tension between the banal and the horrific gives the play and the persona their power.

Daily rituals, bag, and husband can never fully blot out the horror of her situation. Several times in the play she lowers her head and pauses before continuing her cheery prattle. "Sadness keeps breaking in." Like other Beckett characters she must not only activate herself with words—"Begin, Winnie. Begin your day, Winnie"—but must periodically prod her spirit to continue. "Gently" and "On" are repeated several times. As her condition worsens, her spirits flag; act 2 offers a more desperate Winnie, one whose resourcefulness is running out. "I used to" is now qualified by the addition "I say I used to. . . ." Time is her enemy, slowly wearing her down as the earth sucks her up. "To have been always what I am—and so changed from what I was," she says. Her difficulty is in remembering what she was. In act 1 she says, "And should one day the earth cover my breasts, then I shall never have seen my breasts." In act 2 breasts and memories of them rapidly fade. So do Winnie's "classics" which become more garbled and less "classic" as the play progresses. Milton's *Paradise Lost,* source for "Hail, holy light" and "Oh fleeting joys . . .," and Shakespeare's *Hamlet* and *Romeo and Juliet,* sources for "Woe, woe is me . . ." and "Ensign crimson . . . Pale flag," give way in act 2 to a quotation from Charles Wolfe—"Go forget me . . ."—that is the least "classic" and ironically the longest quote in the play.[21]

Though words run out, Winnie continues to speak until the end of the play; the monologue goes on while head and mouth remain above ground. What makes the play so riveting, despite its one constant voice, is Beckett's ability to divide the voice into voices, each with slightly different nuances. For example, in the following excerpt, there are at least six tones that Winnie offers.

> What now? (Pause.) Words fail, there are times when even they fail. (Turning a little towards Willie.) Is that not so, Willie? (Pause. Turning a little further.) Is not that so, Willie, that even words fail, at times? (Pause. Back front.) What is one to do then, until they come again? Brush and comb the hair, if it has not been done, or if there is some doubt, trim the nails if they are in need of trimming, these things tide one over. (Pause.) That is what I mean. (Pause.) That is all I mean.

Like a musical score, the sentences are variations on motifs repeated with slight variations. First Winnie questions herself, then offers a generalized statement, in slightly different pitch. Next she turns to Willie, her questioning of him not quite the same as of herself. When he fails to answer, she does the only "moving" possible in her condition, she alters syntax, from "Is that not so" to "Is not that so," said to underline the repetition. Against the silence, she once more turns front and delivers lines incorporating Willie's silence and her frustration. Her enumeration of her routine bears still a slightly different melody of annoyance and boredom, as do the repeated lines that she speaks with more finality the second time.

To accompany the voice or voices Beckett offers carefully controlled actions. There is a precision in Winnie's movements that, like her voices, underlines habitual routine and despair. For example, she always cranes toward Willie on the right, holds her parasol with right hand, picks the items from her bag on the right. In Beckett's direction of Billie Whitelaw in the 1980 London production, he also had her reach into her bag with the same unnatural, birdlike motion each time, emphasizing the birdlike nature of the encased woman. In act 2 hand gestures are no longer possible, so the eyes, mouth, and face provide the only possible variations of motion, and these too are carefully described by Beckett in his directions within the script, and further refined in his directorial notes.

More than the voices or the gestures, what makes *Happy Days* arresting is the stark visual image that it offers, an image that need not—and should not—be reduced to a simple definition. Beckett offers this warning and this impossibility of reduction within the play, when he has Winnie repeat her Cooker/Shower story. The man's question, "What's it meant to mean?" is answered by his companion with yet another question, "And you, she says, what's the idea of you, she says, what are you meant to mean?" Neither question is answered. Moving couple and stationary couple are not explained, they simply are; the first, like Pozzo and Lucky, walk the earth; the second, like Vladimir and Estragon, wait and sink.

The same refusal or inability to reduce to expected answers shapes the end of the play as well. Just as *Endgame* plays on traditional dramatic expectations of resolutions in the final curtain, *Happy Days* ends in uncertainty. Why does Willie come over to Winnie's side of the mound? What does he "win?" Will he touch her or kill her? Or himself? As the strains of the "Merry Widow Waltz" fade, the couple is frozen staring at each other, the questions unanswered.

## *Chapter Seven*

# Animated Hieroglyphics

Winnie in *Happy Days* is the last Beckett character until the men in *Ohio Impromptu,* written twenty-two years later, to have "someone to hear me," a visible character. Beginning with *Play,* written in 1962, Beckett's stage world is almost always filled with isolated figures, speaking to themselves or to spectres from their pasts, speaking in one or several voices, but always alone. While in the first period only two women appeared—Nell and Winnie—in the following plays for theater there are twenty-two characters, of which eight are men, ten are women, and four are of indeterminate sex. Another change in these plays is the increasing brevity. *Play* runs about forty minutes with repetitions; *Rockaby* about fourteen. *Play* also begins the practice of two- and three-word phrases—"Yes, strange, darkness best, and the darker the worse, till all dark, then all well . . ." *Rockaby* is built entirely on clipped three- and four-word lines, more poetry than prose—"all blinds down / never one up / hers alone up." Earlier works often were balanced on a dichotomy between memories of the past and the figures in the present. After *Play* the balance perceptibly shifts. Characters are still there in body, but progressively they return to the dark hole of the past, "that time," to relive its pleasures and its pains. Yet, while giving voice to other times, the figures create vivid images of their own present condition. The central characteristic of the following works is their attention to the visual image denoting presence over the aural evocation of past. These figures that pace, walk, smile, rock, and stand become the "animated hieroglyphics" Artaud described, images whose presence bespeaks meanings beyond words.

## *Play*

In most of Beckett's plays the personae feel themselves observed. "At me too someone is looking," Vladimir says in the closing moment of *Godot.* More skeptical, in harmony with the tone of his play, Hamm in *Endgame* speculates about "a rational being" who might "get ideas into his head if he observed us long enough." Winnie in *Happy Days* has a "Strange feeling that someone is looking at me. I am clear, then dim, then gone, then dim again, then clear again, and so on, back and forth, in and out of someone's eye." In *Play* that eye is an indifferent spotlight, randomly fixing on each of the three interred figures. Beckett in a note to George Devine, the first English director of *Play,* called the light "the inquirer," itself "no less a victim of his inquiry than they and as needing to be free."[1] Like the goad in *Act Without Words II,* that darted across the stage prodding the inhabitants of the two sacks, the light activates speech and silences it as it moves swiftly from one figure to another. In darkness they are silent, in light voluble. Like Winnie at the instigation of the bell in *Happy Days,* they "begin" when it calls them to action.

There are two women and a man, each woman desiring sole possession of the male, he desiring both of them. From their first words the three are further differentiated. W1, the first unnamed woman, seems the most forceful of the group, given to superlatives: "darkness best." She and the man repeat "all" four times. He uses a formal, less direct language, employing the pronoun "one" and slightly unusual syntax: "yes, peace, one assumed." W2 is more hesitant. Her opening lines are laced with indefinite words: "perhaps," "suppose," "some," "might," "doubt," "not really." Instead of four "alls" she has four "shades."

The story of the three can be pieced together in the first part of the play. When questioned by W1, M denies seeing W2. W1 remains unconvinced, smelling her rival on him, seeks out W2, threatens her, and demands that M give her up. W2 likewise demands that she not be harassed by W1 and says to M, in less emphatic words, that he give up her rival. At first M lies to both, continuing the affair, but finally he confesses to W1 and temporarily stops seeing W2, only to return again. At last, saying he cannot go on, he leaves. W1 assumes he has fled with her rival and goes to her house, finding it empty. "On the way home she . . ." The sentence is incomplete, and the implication is that she, like the other two, dies separately. The scene of her accident is the corner of Ash and Snodland, names that indicate the ash to come and perhaps the hope that death will at least "put in order"—the meaning of *snod*—the messy affair.

This is the plot, typical fare of soap operas, complete with requisite detective paid by W1, paid off by M, and butler named Erskine, co-opted from *Watt,* who lets people in and out. Yet set against this banal tale—like the all-too-familiar relations of Winnie and Willie in *Happy Days*—is the horrific nature, of the setting. The three characters, thinking themselves alone, are each housed in three-foot urns reaching to their necks, their immobile faces "so lost to age and aspect as to seem almost part of urns." The voices are toneless, as they are "provoked" to speech by the single spotlight, a "unique inquisitor." Further moving the story away from realism and stage convention, Beckett has the three stories begin as a chorus, spoken in unison, and after the three tell their fractured tale of betrayal, they lower their voices as the light lowers, indicating their present situation in some ongoing purgatory from which they cannot escape. The words of their previous lives become fused with their hellish present, the three partially reacting as they have in part 1. "Get off me," W1 forcefully demands; W2 laughs, and M removes himself by foisting two extended fantasies: of the women meeting and mutually mourning him over tea, and of the three in a "little dingy." However, while only W2 showed hesitancy in life, in death both W1 and M also repeat "perhaps." W1 and M also both use the word *play,* when referring to the light. She asks when it will be "weary of playing with me," he "when will all this have been . . . just play." Yet it is W2 who issues the most anguished cry: "Are you listening to me? Is anyone listening to me? Is anyone looking at me? Is anyone bothering about me at all?" She also offers the most striking image of their condition: "like dragging a great roller, on a scorching day. The strain . . . to get it moving, momentum coming—" At this point the spot goes off but immediately returns—the only time it focuses on the same person twice—so that she may complete her image, "Kill it and strain again."

After the second section of the play that interlaces past and present, the stage directions say, "repeat," and the play begins again, ending finally with the section that follows the chorus, thus creating the sense of endless repetition. Under his own direction, and in the radio version of the play, however, Beckett varied the order of the same words, indicating that while repetition is the mark of torture, so too is permutation, endlessly repeating with slight variation. Beckett, in his letter to the director George Devine, offered another change: lessening the light and the sound of the voices to create "the impression of falling off." Hell thus is turned into purgatory, with the possibility of some far distant cessation, both of light and speech. In any given cycle of the play, however, the torture *seems* unending, interminable like that other twentieth-century hellscape, *No Exit.* But whereas in Sartre's play hell is other people, in Beckett's world hell is oneself condemned to relive the past in a seemingly unchanging present.

## *Come and Go*

In 121 words, in the Grove Press edition, *Come and Go* sketches a basic human experience, growing old, and a basic human need, connection.[2] Three women of indeterminate age named Flo, Vi, and Ru sit stage center on an unseen log dressed in full-length coats, buttoned high, in dull shades of violet, red, and yellow, with nondescript brimmed hats shading their faces. The action is likewise divided into three sections: an invocation, ritual enactment, and conclusion. Vi begins by calling their names, rousing them to answer a question: "When did we three last meet?" Avoiding the question, Ru responds, "Let us not speak." The trio lapses into silence marking the end of Part 1. Part 2 is itself divided into a tripartite ritual of comings and goings. Each woman in turn leaves her place and moves into darkness at right, while the remaining pair talk of her, one asking about her appearance, the other responding with "I see little change," "She seems much the same," or "One sees little in this light." The first then whispers something unheard by the audience to which the receiver responds with the identical ejaculation in all three permutations, "Oh," and questions: "Does she not realize?" "Has she not been told?" or "Does she not know?" The answer to each contains the word God: "God grant not," "God forbid," or "Please God not." Each sequence concludes with a running thread from the past. Pieced together, the lines sketch their shared youth "in the playground at Miss Wade's" and their maidenhood "dreaming of . . . love," concluding after the third exit and reentry with three questions: "May we not speak of the old days?" (Silence) "Of what came after?" (Silence) "Shall we hold hands in the old way?" The three, now sitting with Vi still the center but Flo and Ru on opposite sides, take hands, Vi holding the outer hands of her friends, Ru and Flo connecting their inner hands. The last line is spoken by Flo: "I can feel the rings." The stage directions indicate the women's hands are bare.

Beckett's trio resembles other female trios. Their opening lines echo those of the three weird sisters in Shakespeare's *Macbeth,* except that this group dwells on the past, the witches on the future: "When shall we three meet again?" They also call to mind the "Three Little Maids from School" in Gilbert and Sullivan's *The Mikado,* except that they are no longer young—"Pert as school girls"—and "Life is a joke," ending not "just begun." Not weird or young, the women act as witnesses to the gradual erosion of time enacted on each. They sit as they sat "on the log," the same yet different. Rather than fill the interstices with the details of the changes, Beckett creates a visual device that marks the passage of time. He has the women come and go, from the light into the dark and back, a visual shortcut of their progress from one log to the next.

Against the comings and goings, Beckett offers the bonding of hands. The intertwined hands form a double helix, a sign for the basic component of life. Yet it is life that leads inevitably to death and decay, signaled by the rings the women feel. The word *ring* has several connotations that tie the piece, and the women, together. It may recall school, similar to Emily Dickinson's "recess in the ring": the ring of a bell, the ring formed in play. It may also represent marriage, maidenhood's desire; and finally it may mark deterioration that is displayed like rings on a tree, an inevitable sign of age, the cyclical process of life, and shared human vulnerability in this inescapable decline.

## *Breath*

It is difficult to imagine the cycle of life compressed any further than Beckett offers in *Come and Go;* yet the next year he once more created an image of "birth astride of a grave," this time denuded of any words at all. *Breath,* written "before it was sent to New York, in 1969, in response to Kenneth Tynan's request for a contribution to his review *Oh! Calcutta!*"[3] is a sound-and-light show signifying the same nullity. The piece begins with minimum light illuminating "miscellaneous rubbish" horizontal on the stage. After five seconds there is a "faint brief cry" activating the increase of light and commensurate inspiration reaching a simultaneous maximum in ten seconds, held in silence for five seconds. The last part is expiration and slow decrease of light until in ten seconds the initial condition is reached in a repetition of the "recorded vagitus." Thirty-five seconds trace birth, development, and cessation, with the implication, as in *Play,* that the process, after an interval, will begin again. Beckett indicates that the parameters are not to be total dark or light: on a scale from 0 to 10, the field is to be from 3 to 6. The speaker in *Company* says, "No such thing as no light," and presumably in these later plays no such thing as "blazing light." As in *Play,* even light seems enervated, desiring surcease too.

## *Not I*

Unintelligible words emanate from behind a curtain as house lights dim to black. For ten seconds the audience sits in darkness straining to hear, and then the curtain rises revealing a gaping mouth, also surrounded by black, suspended eight feet above the playing stage. For the next twelve minutes the audience listens and watches: listens as a stream of words pour out of the orifice, spoken as if without a pause for breath; watches as the mouth, at first recognizable, contorts and takes on a life of its own, some new species complete in itself "whole body like gone." *Not I* is Beckett's consummate, animated hieroglyphic, an icon for the entire oeuvre: a mouth unable to understand the words it speaks, driven to say in order to stop saying. In the play Beckett has the audience viscerally share the experience, as they strain to catch the torrent pouring out of the almost inaudible Mouth.

The speaker is a woman who begins by tracing a birth, in clipped phrases of three or four words, punctuated by ellipses and questions: ". . . out . . . into this world . . . this world . . . tiny little thing. . . ." With neither father nor mother—"So no love . . . spared that"—she moves immediately from birth to "sixty when— . . . what? seventy" when the central event she narrates occurs. She suddenly finds herself one early April morning "in the dark" able to hear only "buzzes" in her head, and to see only "a ray of light," first stationary, then in motion. Initially she interprets the event as punishment for past sins; however, she denies her suffering and even thinks she should feign torment, if that is what is wanted. Given all her life to silence, she is amazed when the new condition is accompanied by words, "a voice she did not recognize," a "steady stream." It recalls events of her past: silently shopping, awaiting sentence in court, crying while sitting on "a little mound in Crokers Acres," or her biyearly outpourings "always winter." She wonders if there is something she has to tell or think, but, while rejecting both possibilities, she describes "something in her begging . . . begging it all to stop." The play concludes with Mouth for the third time returning to the beginning, running through the events one more time—in fewer words and images—searching both for explanation and cessation.

Through the monologue Mouth responds to an unheard voice that halts her flow twenty times, correcting her, or editing her account: "What? . . . girl? . . . yes . . . tiny little girl." Five times Mouth responds with ". . . what? . . . who? . . . no! . . . she!" The fifth time, the last "she" is repeated with added vehemence. After each renunciation Mouth clasps shut like a vice, and then pants, lips hanging open. The voice seems to be the inner "me"—the "twin" Fox refers to in *Radio II,* the speaker with no means of egress to the outer world in "Fizzle 4." Condemned to silence, the inner self deters the "I" from claiming sole dominance of the personal pronoun. This refusal to say "I" because of a "me" that cannot be covered by the pronoun and cannot be articulated lies at the heart of *Not I.* Mouth's five refusals are less rejections of self than the inability of the speaker ever to merge the inner and outer voices of the ego.

In the original stage version, and still included in the printed text, a figure labeled Auditor, dressed in black djellaba with hood, remains silent raising hands in a "gesture of helpless compassion" four times as Mouth recovers "from vehement refusal to relinquish third person." When Beckett directed the play in Paris in 1975, he omitted the Auditor. He allowed another shift by permitting the play to be produced, as a television play in 1978, starring Billie Whitelaw, who played the part in the London production. Heinz Hollinger has also written an opera based on *Not I,* employing electronic amplification, duplication, and multimedia effects.

## *That Time*

Mouth expands to an entire disembodied head in *That Time,* written in 1975. An "old white face, long flaring white hair," is suspended off center ten feet above stage, another of Beckett's portraits. This time the mouth remains silent, and instead three voices of self, labeled in the text, A, B, and C, broadcast memories of "that time," A describing his attempted return to the scene of his childhood solitude, B a time of youthful summer love and its demise, and C a winter wandering in and out of public places. The piece, like *Come and Go* and *Not I,* is divided into three sections, of twelve paragraphs, with each voice speaking four times per section. While not in sequence, Beckett does present them in a specific formula: the first three of each section are in identical order, the fourth a variation with first and second reversed. The following section is predicated on a reversal of the second and third speakers from the preceding paragraph. For example, in section 1 A, C, B is repeated three times, and it ends in C, A, B; it is followed by C, B, A in the next section, also repeated three times.

The stage directions indicate that the three voices, while spoken by the same man, are to be played "without solution of continuity." Within the text this disjunction is apparent. The voices offer no consistent chronology. A is presumably the oldest—"white hair pouring out down from under the hat"—though it is he who tries to recapture childhood. B is the only voice that remembers scenes of companionship but is outflanked by A who begins and C who ends. It is B who repeats "that time" most often, trying to conjure up memories of a past; yet it is also B who indicates that the evocation of the past cannot counteract "a great shroud billowing in all over you." The shroud in B becomes the dust in C, a dust that covers the picture of youth, in art as in life.

Each voice has its own fractured memories and verbal signs. A repeats the dichotomy up/down. He goes up to the refuge of the past, down to the village, having found nothing left of what he remembered.

For C the pull is between in and out; the man going "in off the street out of the cold." It is he who has the last words, the realization that what the "it"—which all three refer to—imparts is the recognition of "come and gone come and gone no one come and gone in no time gone in no time"—the sentence ending without a period. The words are a summary of the wisdom of the three aspects of self; "That time" gives way to no time.

As the face listens to the three voices, he reacts by opening and closing his eyes. At the beginning of each section the eyes open for seven seconds in silence while the breath is audible. After the voice begins its reveries, the eyes close and remain so until the section concludes. Only at the end, after section 3, does the ritual vary. The stage directions say, "After 3 seconds eyes open. After 5 seconds smile, toothless for preference. Hold 5 seconds till fade out and curtain." Coming as it does at the end of an almost static portrayal, the smile has the impact that great physical activity on stage might otherwise have. It is unexpected, it is disorienting, it is shocking. It is also ambiguous. Is the listener smiling with happiness, with resignation, or with relief? The audience is not sure. But it is a smile that Beckett will repeat. In *A Piece of Monologue* he calls it "That nevoid smile" implying perhaps the smile nullifying the void, albeit temporarily. He also has the figure at the end of the television play *Ghost Trio* smile in the same ambiguous way, after living through a play of disappointment and frustrated expectations (although the act is not in the printed text).

## *Footfalls*

*Footfalls,* like *That Time,* was written in 1975 and first performed during the seventieth birthday celebration for Beckett at the Royal Court Theatre in London. Yet another image is created on the stage, this time the figure of a woman pacing back and forth over the length of a nine-step, one-meter section of stage, lit by a gradually dimming light, most intense at foot level and fading to head. Like the women in *Come and Go* she is ambulatory, but her terrain is shorter than theirs. *Footfalls,* however, is divided into four sections, demarcated by a single chime, progressively diminished in intensity. In Part 1 May—"the child's given name"—is in her forties and speaks to her mother aged ninety, represented by an offstage voice, a voice seemingly in the mind of the daughter. Twice May calls her mother, and twice is called. Images of a deathbed emerge from May's questions. "Would you like me to inject you again?" she asks. "Straighten your pillows? (Pause.) Change your drawsheet?" Three times she repeats "again," and the mother three times responds "Yes, but it is too soon." The exchanges create verbal chimes, like the reverberating "deep/sleep" from which Voice comes and to which she invites her daughter: "Will you not try to snatch a little sleep?" The section concludes with Mother calling daughter twice, a reverse of the opening, entreating her, "Will you never have done . . . revolving it all?" The unnamed "it" is never specified in

*Footfalls,* just as it went undefined in *That Time.* The image of the pacing May becomes a visualization of the "it all" of life.

Part 2—indicated by a fade-out on strip, darkness, silence, long pause, and then chime—begins with a now inert May facing right front, listening to the voice of her mother alive in her head. The voice offers a monologue melding herself to the silent spectre on stage: "I walk here now. (Pause.) Rather I come and stand. . . . She fancies she is alone." May in the section is described as an object, "she," identified with the "I" and by the "I," explained from a vantage point outside herself. A few facts are provided. The place is "the old home" where "It all began." Differentiated from the present scene is the specific time that "this"—presumably the walking—began. Having described the two beginnings of "it" and "this," the voice moves into a dialogue, taking the parts of May and her mother as she relates May's request to remove the carpet so that the child might "hear the feet, however faint they fall." Part 2 closes with the voice returning to questions and answers: "Does she still sleep?" and "Still speak?" Both are answered with "Yes." The "it all" that concludes the section repeats the double ending of the preceding part and is foreshadowing of the same conclusion at the end of Part 3.

In the third section May again appears right front, but this time it is her voice, not her absent mother's, that speaks. She begins with the word "Sequel," repeated twice. The word has several implications for the play. First, in feudal law the word indicates "offspring" as well as "follower." May is both: her mother's progeny and follower in the same "footfalls," pacing toward ninety, illness, and death. Beckett purposely blurs the distinctions between the two women, both referred to as "she." For example, when May says, "A little later, when she was quite forgotten, she began to . . ." it is not clear to whom the pronoun refers. The word *sequel* also has literary allusions that Beckett uses in the play. Meaning a story that follows a former tale, the word marks the double voices and double narrative devices in *Footfalls:* the story of Mother and May, and the two embedded stories, at the end of Parts 2 and 3, the former told by voice in the guise of mother and daughter, the latter by May, taking on the roles of fictive surrogates Amy—an anagram for May—and her mother, named Mrs. Winter. While the former story indicates the beginnings of May's obsession with walking, the latter tells of its desired end: absence. For as in the tale of Amy, May wishes to be "not there."

It is a wish she achieves in Part 4. When the chime signals the opening of this final section, the light comes up on a bare stage, May like her fictional creation "not there."[4]

May traces the repetitive pattern of travel in Beckett's plays, here reduced to a nine-step world, and diminished even further during the course of the play. The figure in her "faint tangle of pale grey tatters" becomes a concentrated hieroglyphic of "come and go" with the addendum "gone." May both walks away her life and walks toward her mother, a linear equivalent to the cyclical patterns sketched in other Beckett plays.

## *A Piece of Monologue*

*A Piece of Monologue* written for the actor David Warrilow, and first presented by him at La Mama in New York in December 1979, once more attempts to do on the stage what Beckett has done in fiction: allow the two parts of the self to exist simultaneously. The central figure is an old man with "white hair, white nightgown, white socks," the rest of the body attached to the face that appeared in *That Time.* He has survived "two and a half billion seconds" and "thirty thousand nights" that works out to be seventy-nine years of seconds and eighty-two years of nights, a typical Beckett calibration which doesn't quite work—similar to Watt's mathematical calculations. The setting is a room with a window facing west, a bare wall once covered with pictures on the east, and the white foot of a pallet just visible extreme right. It is much like the room in the later television play *Ghost Trio* without the mirror. One additional object has been added, however, and it becomes the focal point of the work: a standard lamp the same height as the actor, with a skull-sized white globe. The central physical action described involves the lighting of the oil lamp at nightfall, a routine that takes on the ritualistic nature of May's walking in *Footfalls.*

Despite the description of action, however, there is no indication of any movement in the play, for the speaker is not the "I," the macrocosmic figure facing the world and claiming the use of the first-person pronoun, but rather the inner "me," that objective self that watches and reports but has no means of independent articulation or being. Unlike *That Time,* where the figure at least opened and closed his eyes and smiled while the voices of self talked, or unlike *Footfalls,* where May moved as Voice spoke her thoughts, here the figure remains impassive—like the figure in the Fizzle "Still"—while the voice within describes the man without.

The play is perhaps closest to *Not I,* where Mouth used the third-person pronoun, refusing the acknowledgement of "I." However, in that play Beckett made clear that the two voices of self existed simultaneously, albeit unheard. The constant interruptions, the questions, the reminders came from the inner voice. In *A Piece of Monologue,* although the speaker uses "he," the pronoun is questioned only twice, and the speaker seems at ease with his role as inner voice of the external, silent figure.

Part of the reason for the absence of tension between the two parts of self comes from the departure in the play: here the focus is less on a replaying of the past "it all" than on the experience of the present and the future; the central concern in the play is not the acknowledged blackness within but the blackness without. The emphasis on the outer void rather than the inner is expressed by Beckett in a 1974 poem entitled "Something There": "something there / where / out there / out where / outside / what / the head what else / something there somewhere outside / the head."[5] The carefully crafted verbal balance in the poem echoes the two voices of self conducting a familiar Beckettian dialogue. Their desire is not to plumb the nature of the world within but rather the nature of the "something" without, which the poem concludes is "something / not life / necessarily."

*Monologue* is concerned with the same attempt. Though brief (the printed script runs to only four pages), the play is an intricately woven text, as finely balanced as the poem that preceded it. On the stage, the struggle to pierce the blackness is indicated by images of light and dark. The stage directions indicate that the play takes place in faint light, and that thirty seconds before the play ends the lamplight begins to fail. The stage is not left in blackness but in barely visible diffuse light, for there are two kinds of light in the play: light that the central lamp makes and that man controls, and light that comes, the speaker says repeatedly, "Whence unknown." When he wakes, habitually at nightfall, and gropes to light his lamp, there is already "Faint light in room." This other light is always there: "Light dying. Soon none left to die. No. No such thing as no light. Starless moonless heaven. Dies on to dawn and never dies."

The parameters of the play are set between the two blacknesses, in shadows made by the lamplight and the light "Whence unknown." The place between the two impenetrable states is set off in *Monologue* by the dual images of birth and death. In the very first lines of the play Beckett creates this primary binary opposition: "Birth was the death of him." And a few lines down he continues, "Born dead of night." The connection between "born" and "dead" within a cliché is a familiar device for Beckett, who often describes man's entrapment in the life cycle as a corollary of man's entrapment in language. The tensions between birth and death are continued in the following image, "Sun long sunk behind the larches. New needles turning green." The death of the day is balanced by the birth of the year.

As Beckett has done in previous works, he connects birth and life with man's need to find words to talk about his living; words and speech become synonymous with living. The words in the opening speech of the play trace human growth through complementary speech development: the velar stops *g* and *c,* followed by the more sophisticated fricative *f,* finally give way to rhyme and more complex language structures and transpositions: "From mammy to nanny and back."

This initial mention of birth and the few shards of personal biography are part of an ongoing ritual. The speaker first wakes, gropes for the lamp, lights it, and then talks—and always about birth. Each reference to biography becomes more rapid and increasingly more nebulous, the inchoate origins of speech more discernible. For instance, the time between the first and second reference to the word "birth" is approximately two pages of the four-page text: the next two references are separated by less than half a page, thus indicating the accelerating of time with the parallel growing difficulty of emitting the word with each attempt. The opening lines of the play which relate to the ritual of speaking about birth are short and clipped, somewhat in the style of the Voice in *Not I.* However, by the second cycle of speech more emphasis is on the preparation for speech which precedes the word "birth," as if Beckett were pushing the speaker back to some preverbal area from which he must struggle to reach even the point of beginning. "Stares beyond into dark. Waits for first word always the same. It gathers in his mouth. Parts lips and thrusts tongue forward. Birth." In the last two attempts to evoke birth the speaker is not even able to emit the word and can only describe the struggle toward speech: "Mouth agape. Closed with hiss of breath. Lips joined. Feel soft touch of lip on lip. Lip lipping lip."

Although the speaker has said that the image of birth "Parts the dark," death is another image which, when evoked, "Dark parts," the contrary force indicated linguistically by the very transposition of the two words "parts" and "dark." The one scene repeated three times in the play is a scene of funerals. Each time the image becomes more menacing, more directly associated with the approaching death of the speaker, and more powerful in the pull between birth and death.

As the speaker finds himself unable to utter the word "birth" he finds himself more and more drawn to the image of death represented by the funeral scene. Just as the first mention of birth is the most detailed, with each becoming progressively vaguer until the word remains unuttered, in Beckett's skillful balance in the work, the first mention of funerals is general, with each subsequent reference more detailed until it virtually subsumes the opposing images of birth. On page 1 of the text the word "birth" appears twice, on page 3 three times, but on the final page not at all. In contrast, on page 1 the word "funeral" appears once, on page 3 twice, but on page 4 it becomes the sole image. The speaker can no longer summon the beginnings of life but only the now-dominating image of death. "Ghost light. Ghost nights. Ghost rooms. Ghost graves. Ghost . . . he all but said ghost loved ones. Waiting on the rip word." The mention of "the rip word" is at first curious, having connections with the tearing of the blackness, the attempt which has been described in the play. The word *ripping* appears twice in the text. But there is also the pun of R.I.P. *requiescat in pace,* which carries the image of death as the final way of ripping the dark, of piercing that "other blackness." The outer darkness, Beckett seems to indicate, may be *ripped* by death, but as long as man lives, he may only temporarily part the dark. Faint light will continue.

What is new about *Monologue* is the "unremitting" quality of the awareness of death, countered feebly by the attempt to utter the word "birth," an attempt that fails before the play concludes. Yet even more than the insistence on death, *Monologue* is startling because of its form. In it Beckett creates a work that is totally static with not even the opening and closing of eyes that activated *That Time.* Obviously great risks are involved with a presentation that defies the basic tenet of drama—action. However, as in plays that immediately precede it—*Not I, That Time,* and *Footfalls*—Beckett has been able to take a state of being, the schism of self, and make it active through the imagery of his play. No misunderstanding is possible here; the voice that speaks and the figure that listens are one, the "me" and the "I" of the self, starkly depicted in the white, silent figure that stands listening to himself.

## *Ohio Impromptu*

*Ohio Impromptu* was written between *A Piece of Monologue* and *Rockaby,* two works that place a virtually silent, inert figure on stage listening to a recorded voice emanating from an unseen source. Here silent Listener, labeled L, and speaker, labeled R for Reader, are together, mirror images of each other, two aspects of a single self, indicated by the shared hat that lies on the table between them. Both are dressed in long black coats, with flowing white hair. Both lean on right hands that cover their faces, the left hand of R turning the pages he reads, the left hand of L knocking twelve times during the reading of the text to force R to return to the preceding sentence—sometimes a few words, sometimes several lines—to reread it before proceeding with the "sad tale."

The reading is divided into three parts, all told in the past tense, the first two marked by the repetition of "Little is left to tell," the last preceded by "Nothing is left to tell." The three phrases are the only words in the present. In the first part R outlines a brief story about a "he" who, seeking "relief" has moved from "where they had been so long together" to a room alone "on the far bank" from whose single window he can see "the downstream extremity of the Isle of Swans." The "unfamiliar" room, however, provides no "relief" nor do his daily walks on the islet, back and forth. Unlike the eddies he sees that "conflowed and flowed united on," he turns alone, dressed in his long black coat and Latin Quarter hat. His dreams warn him against this change, the "dear face" delivering "the unspoken words." He wonders if he could return to "where they were alone together," renounces the possibility—"Nothing he had ever done alone could ever be undone"—and suffers anew from the old terror of night.

In Part 2 the Reader introduces a man who comes from the "dear name" carrying "a worn volume" which he reads, returning periodically to repeat "the sad tale through again." In silence, the two "grew to be as one" until the day the man indicates that "the dear one" says he is not to come again. After he delivers his message and reads the tale through once more, "they sat on as though turned to stone," oblivious to the world outside, sunk in "profounds of mind."

R then moves to the third part: his avowal "Nothing is left to tell," said while he "makes to close book." L's knock causes him to repeat the line as the book shuts. The two now raise their heads from behind their right hands and stare without expression, thus fulfilling the story within the story; they are "as though turned to stone."

*Ohio Impromptu* is an unusual work in the Beckett canon. Although he has written pieces for certain actors—*Krapp's Last Tape* for Patrick Magee, *A Piece of Monologue* for David Warrilow, *Footfalls* for Billy Whitelaw—Beckett has only written four times for a specific occasion: *Rockaby* for the Beckett Festival at the State Univeristy of New York at Buffalo, *Catastrophe* for the Avignon Festival, *What Where* for Graz Festival, and *Ohio Impromptu* for the Samuel Beckett Symposium at Ohio State University in Colombus, Ohio. Only the latter, however, carries its origin in its title, along with its form, an impromptu. Originally designated as a musical composition, an impromptu is a work that is written as if improvisatory, but in fact is carefully planned. Dramatic impromptus—Moliere's *Impromptu de Versailles,* Giraudoux's *Impromptu de Paris* or the recent Ionesco *L'Impromptu de l'Alma* (also called *Improvisation or The Shepherd's Chameleon* in English)—have the added characteristic of embodying in a play within a play the dramatist's artistic theories and a parody of the critical responses they elicit. Both the words *Ohio* and *Impromptu* are significant in understanding this work written for Ohio and written as impromptu. Beckett plays upon both words in shaping his text.

"What is high in the middle and round at the ends or high in the middle and nothing at the ends," an American children's riddle goes. The answer to both versions is "Ohio," a name that uncannily mirrors the central configuration in Beckett's plays: two voids or "nothings"—birth and death—and between the "high" of life, the double inhalation and expiration of breath that sandwich life. While the coincidence of place name and theme are fortuitous, even more so is the specific city of venue: Columbus. The name gives rise to the image of discovery, of new worlds to explore. In the play, however, the modern avatar of the famed explorer discovers nothing; rather his travels are reduced to short meanderings back and forth over the Isle of Swans, that end in turning inland. A discoverer manqué, the figure in the play is also a poet manqúe. The Isle of Swans ironically titles him. Not like Homer, "the Swan of Meander," Virgil, "the Swan of Mantua," or Shakespeare, "the Swan of Avon," this bard is condemned to write nothing but only listen and read the words of another.

If the word *Ohio* and the implied *Columbus,* call up images of diminished travel, exploration, and creation, the second word of the title—*Impromptu*—is ironic and double-edged. There is nothing impromptu about the piece. The two characters only act after the fact and in accordance with the text, a text written in the past tense. To further underline their lack of volition, neither figure is the instigator of the story. It comes from or under the aegis of "the dear one." The two figures may only read and listen, occasionally repeating but not altering. Once R is taken aback by certain wording, he checks it, but does not change it. To alter the text or to stop reading is beyond either's power.

In the novel *How It Is* the narrator repeats the refrain: "I say it as I hear it." In *Ohio Impromptu* R must say it as someone else writes it. This idea has often been explored in Beckett's writings: the sense of the self as fragmented, therefore not the prime source that creates but merely one of a series of intermediaries who stretch back to some unnamed "deviser." If this is the condition of the artist, Beckett's artist, then it is also the condition of Beckett's critics—like those gathered in Columbus—sharing with him the same "profounds of mind" as they puzzle a text not their own, prey to the same limitations and the same lack of volition, ciphering vague words and ideas that emanate from outside themselves. While Beckett, thus, uses his impromptu to make a comment on his art, he is not parodying his critics, as other playwrights have done; instead he is empathizing with them. Both he and they struggle toward clarity and sense; both, Beckett has long recognized, are doomed to fail since the texts—like Ohio—start with zero and end with zero.

## *Rockaby*

In the Museum of Modern Art in New York City there is a painting by the sculptor Giacometti entitled *The Artist's Mother* (1950). It shows in faint outlines the figure of a seated woman in what may be a rocking chair. All around her are shadows, and she seems about to fade into them. The drawing, "a faint tangle of pale grey tatters," immediately brings to mind Beckett's *Rockaby,* the animated depiction on the stage of Giacometti's image. A lyrical poem of 251 lines, taking under fifteen minutes to perform, *Rockaby* offers one of Beckett's most arresting portrayals: that of an old woman, dressed in her "best black" dotted with jet beads and hat set askew, sitting, immovable in a rocking chair as it rocks her off to death.[6] Like all Beckett's plays, it begins with a tableau held for several seconds, the light beginning on the woman's face and then moving to capture the chair, that slowly begins to rock, seemingly of its own volition, without the control of the figure seated in it, as she says her opening word "More." The word is repeated four times, marking the four sections of the play. Each "more" is softer as the woman's strength ebbs until the last one—as uttered by Billie Whitelaw in the American première production—is merely a sound and a gesture: the mouth opening in what could just as well be a cry and a last definite struggle against death. Besides these four words, the woman only speaks to echo the words of her recorded thoughts that conclude each section, a total of fifteen words during the play. For the rest she sits and listens, eyes opening and closing, almost totally shut near the end, while the voice sketches the course that has led her to this chair and this night.

The words are among Beckett's most melodious, appearing in the printed text as lines of poetry, three- and four-word passages, punctuated by vocal pauses. They are hypnotically repetitive as is the rocking: only ninety-six lines repeated in different order and couplings. Ironically, as the woman tires, the variety increases. There are nineteen new lines out of fifty-one voice speaks in Part 1, fifteen out of fifty-six in Part 2, nineteen out of fifty-seven in Part 3, and forty-three out of eighty-three in Part 4—the longest section. These sections are punctuated by the woman's four utterances of the word "more."

Parts 1 and 3 are connected by their shared opening line "till in the end," and Parts 2 and 4 by the variation "so in the end." In all sections the woman repeats "time she stopped," usually followed by the echoing live refrain; however, as the end approaches the phrase diminishes. Said seven times in Part 1, four each in 2 and 3, it is uttered only once in Part 4, as the moment of death nears. The desire for "more" battles the inevitable stoppage of rocker, words, and life. As long as she can utter, the woman postpones silence and stasis.

The uttering takes the form of a bare outline of a life, first a "going to and fro," given visual counterpoint by the rocking that keeps time with the words. Next the image becomes stationary "time she went and sat / at her window," "window" the dominant word in the section, repeated as she sits "facing other windows." The voice then expresses the desire for human contact "for a blind up / one blind up," the play on words apparent as she "blindly" scans the windows for "another creature there/somewhere there / behind the pane," another play on words. Unable to fulfill her desire, "to see /be seen," she slips finally from "blind up" to window "down," the echoing word now, as she leaves her window seat and makes her way "down the steep stair / let down the blind and down / right down / into the old rocker," the rocker in which she sits as she listens to the voice. It is her mother's rocker, where her mother—dressed in the same black—rocked herself to death. The woman follows her mother, the cycle of the ages compressed to successive rockings, the daughter now the mother, like the bonded pair of women in *Footfalls* or the father/son commingling in *Company* and *Endgame*. Death in life and life in death seem to balance on the moment, as daughter sinks down into rocker, down into mother, down into death. The voice that has spoken to itself in the past sections, repeating the refrain "saying to herself / whom else"—emphasized by Whitelaw with muted irony—now renounces this inner directedness, turning instead to mother and rocker, to the outer world and the death that wait: "saying to herself / no / done with that / the rocker / those arms at last / saying to the rocker." The last six lines almost imperceptibly propel the woman off. Since five of the lines are three-word spondees, the two-word line "fuck life" both shocks because of the word choice and the break in rhythm. It becomes one last protest before the end, when "more" cannot be summoned but acceptance is not given.

This brief description does not take into account the richness that comes from the spoken voice, particularly that of Billie Whitelaw, who creates a music as she gives a particular lilt to "a little like," almost a playfulness; a suppressed anger to her three "nos" and "whom else"; who becomes her mother as she describes the way the woman was dismissed with "off her head they said / gone off her head"; and a monotony and desire to continue as she repeats "rock her off." Whitelaw herself, in the film of the preparation and presentation of *Rockaby,* tells director Schneider, "I'm not playing the right music," as they begin rehearsals, and later comments just before the opening night that "Beckett blows the notes," and that they must "come out of me."[7] Her own hands in rehearsal seem to be leading an inner musical score, fluttering, rising, and sinking as her voice follows. It is a music that plays against the mechanical metronome motion of the chair and its occupant which marks off the moments of life, while the light fades and the words die.

As the head slowly sinks onto the chest, fulfilling once more a description embedded in a play—the image of the dead mother now the dead daughter—a peace and a return to childhood are created. *Rocker* may denote both the person rocking and the object; here they become one as do the old woman, the child she once was, and the mother she has become. The "rockaby" of the title becomes a child's song of sleep and an old woman's song of death. The old mother "off her rocker" and the daughter now in it fuse in the closing tableau, in death returning to the childhood of them both. This conclusion is one of Beckett's most charged moments. The unsaid "more" is palpable in the silence. Form and content, human and mechanical object, life and death, fuse in the image that slowly fades before the eyes, sinking into the darkness that engulfs in reverse order the chair and then the face, now a death mask.

## *Catastrophe*

Samuel Beckett is usually perceived as an apolitical writer, this despite his underground activities in Paris in World War II that won him the croix de guerre and Médaille de la Résistance and despite his creation of one of the most powerful images of human subjugation: Lucky with his running sore in *Waiting for Godot.* In 1982 Beckett clearly dispelled the image of noninvolvement by answering the call from the Artists Defending other Artists (Artistes en defense d'autres artistes) to write a play honoring the imprisoned Czech playwright Vaclav Havel. Beckett's contribution to the evening presented at the Avignon Festival on 21 July 1982 was *Catastrophe,* a play that takes the suppression of the artist and translates it into an image of all types of tyranny.

The play appeared on a triple bill in its New York opening, along with *What Where* and *Ohio Impromptu.* It is closer to the form of a dramatic impromptu than the play that bears that title since it presents a play within a play, a play concerned with the mounting of the play the audience is to see. It also follows the impromptu by commenting on the action of the play within the play and on the responses of the fictive audience and the real audience who view it. The central figure is the Protagonist. He is the catastrophe of the director's play, an image of the way art can be co-opted to turn life into artifice at the dictator's will, thereby threatening to denude it of its horror, making of it an occasion for spectacle that can deny its humanity. He is also the image of Havel, and of all suppressed people who fight against their own dehumanization.

The play presents three other characters: a director, his female assistant, and an unseen figure named Luke who is in charge of the lighting. The director controls the action: he asks questions the assistant must answer, barks the commands she must fulfill. He is engaged in presenting the spectacle of the Protagonist, and the assistant aids him in his task. He is also presented as a political leader, who goes to a "caucus." Reminiscent of Pozzo in *Godot,* he controls the world on "the board." While treating the Protagonist as an object to be manipulated as he wills, he also shows his total disdain for the woman who helps him. In the stage directions she is referred to as "his female assistant," and her only words are in response to his orders. She lights his cigar when it goes out, repeats the action, as she prepares the Protagonist for exhibition. While showing some sympathy for the suffering man she positions—"he's shivering" she repeats—she does the director's bidding, although it is clear she abhors him. When he leaves to view his handiwork from the audience, she sits in his abandoned chair only after wiping it. Beckett draws a parallel between the director's handling of her and his abuse of the silent Protagonist. Both are victims. Beckett implies that sexual harassment is at heart another form of political suppression.

Luke provides another kind of assistant: unseen, seemingly indifferent to the spectacle he is asked to light. When the director calls him twice, Luke announces "Luke around," but then seems to pay no further attention. In response to further orders, he asks "What?" Yet finally he too obeys.

After several experimental positionings and drapings, the director from his vantage point in the audience finally gets the results he has sought. "Terrific! He'll have them on their feet. I can hear it from here," he says, pleased with his creation. And in fact the last sound of the play within the play is the distant applause of the invisible audience, reacting as predicted. It is stopped, however, by an unexpected act: the Protagonist, up to this point malleable as a manikin, suddenly raises his head and "fixes the audience." The stage directions read, "The applause falters, dies." The figure remains impassive, head high, during a long pause, while the lights slowly fade, leaving only his face and silence.

The word *catastrophe* has several meanings. It can refer to a calamity or disaster; it can also describe a sudden turn or overturning. In drama it indicates change or reversal which produces the conclusion or final event of a dramatic piece, that is the denouement. The play Beckett presents embodies these several meanings of the word. Central is the image of the disaster that befalls the helpless victim, the Protagonist. It is he who is draped and manipulated in the play within the play, in preparation for his exhibition as an objet d'art on the "plinth," a column on which an art work is usually shown. Yet something goes wrong with the catastrophe; he refuses his role. Against the express instructions of the director and the compliance of the assistant and Luke, he raises his head at the end of his presentation, immediately causing the applause to subside in embarrassed silence. He thus causes a reversal, a catastrophe for the play as envisioned by the director, a different denouement than anticipated or desired. And yet since this is a play within a play, there is yet another ending, the ending of the play entitled *Catastrophe* which the live audience is viewing. It is they who may provide the possible "overturning or reversal" not only of the expected conclusion of art but of the condition being described: suppression.

By withholding applause for the spectacle they have witnessed and refusing to be taken in by the play of the director, the audience has the possibility of creating its own ending, one that denounces the suppression of Havel or any person. They are aided by the active defiance of the Protagonist who will not be cowed, but raises his head at the end. Unlike the subjected assistant or the indifferent Luke, they can rewrite the frame play by denying tacit acceptance to staged spectacles that are created for their consumption, and to mask tyranny. Becoming his own director, the Protagonist at the end of the embedded play becomes a model for human action in the face of almost overwhelming dehumanization, and for the audience who have the same power, if they choose to exercise it.

## *What Where*

In the early 1960s Beckett wrote two pieces for theater and two for radio that he called "Roughs." They are published under the heading "Odds" in the collection *Ends and Odds.* Two of them, *Radio II and Theatre II,* offer a bridge between the more recent plays *Catastrophe* and *What Where.* In *Radio II* an animator, early model of the director, and a stenographer who does his bidding, like the assistant, attempt to gain some secret from someone called Mr. Fox, a prisoner tortured by a silent character named Dick who strikes the victim with a bull's pizzle, perhaps a play on his own name. In *Theatre II* characters identified only as A and B pore over evidence concerning a C. Both sets of investigators seem intent on eliciting proof of an ego and on plumbing the creative act. In *Theatre II* they find the task impossible, confronted by C's "black future, and unpardonable past—so far as he can remember." In *Radio II* the best that Fox can offer is to speak of another, "my brother inside me, my old twin."

The acts of torture, described in these works, are approximated in *Catastrophe,* where they seem gratuitously on display, devised to elicit no response other than acquiescence. In *What Where* torture is again employed, but here the end is to extract some secret not specifically of self or art as in the two early "Roughs" but more generally of "what/where."

The four figures in the play are Bam, Bem, Bim, and Bom. The names harken back to earlier writings. Thomas "Bim" Clinch, a man of "overweening ability," and his twin brother Timothy "Bom" were nurses in the Magdalen Mental Mercyseat where Murphy worked. In *How It Is,* Beckett again used the names, this time Bom was the torturer, replacing the victim Pim, in the procession of selves that wended their way eastward. The narrator of that novel also employed the name Bem, indicating that any name ending in M and of one syllable would do. *How It Is* provides more than just names for *What Where;* it also provides the idea of a self that is both victim and victimizer in turns, that is Pim then Bom or Bem—or Bam or Bim.

*What Where* offers the self divided into these four identically dressed figures, in long grey robes and grey hair, visual spectres of an unseen Voice, that is itself marked by light. While the four figures move in and out of a rectangular playing area, stage right, the Voice, called V, has its own square of light "in the shape of a small megaphone at head level" stage left front, from which it directs the progression of figures and their torture. Beginning "First without words," it introduces the tableau of couples who enter with head "haught" or high. V stops the action by turning off the light on the area, and makes each reenter alone with head bowed, until only Bam appears with head "Haught," the others with heads "bowed." This concludes the first part of the work. In Part 2 a ritual is repeated three times, reminiscent of the formations of *Come and Go.* In each, one figure calls in another, asks him to report on the torture of yet a third. When the torturer indicates his failure to wrest the secret "it" later defined as "what" and "where," he is himself sent to be tortured by another character. All are "given the works," remain silent, or deny disclosure, and are tortured till they faint. Bam thus calls Bom, who in turn is taken out and tortured by Bim, who is similarly tortured by Bem. Between each substitution V offers a brief respite and indicates the passage of time from spring to winter. By the third repetition the process is reduced, V saying merely "so on" instead of enumerating the routine. Bem, the last figure, alters the words too by asking "What must I confess?" instead of "What must he confess?" Bem leaves along with Bam, who returns now with bowed head. While Bam stands mute, V ends the piece saying "I am alone. In the present as were I still. It is winter. Without journey. Time passes. That is all." His last lines are "Make sense who may. I switch off." With that the lights fade, first on the playing stage, then on the lighted area of V.

Appropriately *What Where* was presented last in the triple bill with *Ohio Impromptu* and *Catastrophe,* for it seems if not a conclusion, at least a return to the lines that ended the first play on the bill: "Nothing is left to tell." At the end of the trilogy of plays perhaps the same voice V repeats the same idea. Both stage time and human time have passed. Images of life have been created, tableaux fixed. Beyond that there is nothing that may be told with certainty; what and where still are unknown. The last words of Beckett's most recent play not only return to the starting point of one particular night, but to the words of his first-produced—and most famous—play, *Waiting for Godot.* Not certain for whom they wait or where, the two clowns, surrogates for modern society, can only be certain that "time passed." But as even they ruefully recognized, "It would have passed anyhow." They know at the outset of their wait that there is "nothing to be done." They are uncertain of themselves, time, their past, and salvation. They can only be sure that in any one moment they *are* and that they *will continue to be.* Beckett has been able, through his stagecraft, to capture that moment of *thereness,* animate the fear, suffering, and questioning, but not provide the answers to *what where,* or even the simple *who* of selfhood, torture as he or his personae may. In the modern world and the modern theater that reflects it, that is all that is possible, Beckett believes. "All I can manage, more than I could." And after thirty years of dramatic writing—fifty years of fiction—he is still presenting questioners, trying to get the answers that elude them, that even resist "the works."

# *Chapter Eight*
# Other Media

Samuel Beckett has consistently discouraged attempts to transfer his writings from one genre to another. Typical is his letter to his American publisher arguing against bringing *All That Fall* to the stage: "Whatever quality it may have . . . depends on the whole thing's *coming out of the dark,*" he stated.[1] To hear a Beckett radio play is to hear characters and ideas already introduced in his fiction and drama, but to hear them in the singular, aural world created by sound waves from which they spring. Any attempt to transfer plays so directly connected to their medium of origin distorts this fundamental relationship between form and theme. "If we can't keep our genres more or less distinct, or extricate them from the confusion that has them where they are, we might as well go home and lie down," Beckett continued in the same letter. Because of the basic connection between medium and content, I have broken with the otherwise chronological discussion of Beckett's writings in order to present as a unit those plays specifically created for radio, film, and television. In each work Beckett has grappled with familiar ideas in new contexts, and the context has shaped the central vision of each play.

## Radio

***All That Fall.*** Clas Zilliacus, in his book *Beckett and Broadcasting,* offers a detailed description of Beckett's introduction to radio drama in 1956 through the agency of the BBC Third Program, a program designed to present new works written specifically for the medium. At first, Beckett seemed doubtful about writing for radio; however, in a letter to his friend Nancy Cunard in July 1956 he wrote, "Never thought about Radio play technique but in the dead of t'other night got a nice gruesome idea full of cartwheels and dragging of feet and puffing and panting which may or may not lead to something."[2] Two months later the play was completed, and it was first aired on 13 January 1957.

The title comes from Psalm 145:14, the text upon which the Minister Hardy will speak: "The Lord upholdeth all that fall and raiseth up all those that be bowed down." In the context of the play the lines become ironic, worthy of the thirteen seconds of "wild laughter" they were given on the first broadcast. The world Maddy Rooney, née Dunne—ruined/done—encounters on her walk to and from the station is in a state of decay. People, objects, nature, even language have declined with no sign of resurrection. The child crushed under the wheels of the train is only one of all that fall.

The first indication of the spectre of death and decay comes at the beginning of the play. Before words come the faint strains of Shubert's "Death and the Maiden," a testimony to youth forestalled by death. The music draws forth an image in the opening lines: "Poor woman. All alone in that ruinous old house." This static woman and the moving woman, Maddy, become loci for the same conditon, as Maddy indicates on her journey: "It is suicide to be abroad. But what is it to be at home." Both ways bring the same "lingering dissolution."

Mrs. Rooney's encounters provide further examples of the same state of human decay and cyclical deterioration. She greets all passersby with inquiries about their loved ones and learns that Christy's wife is "no better," his daughter "no worse"; that Tyler's daughter has had "the whole . . . er . . . bag of tricks" removed leaving him "grandchildless"; that Mr. Slocum's mother is "out of pain"; that Mr. Barrell's father is dead. Tommy is an orphan; Jerry is alone. The inhabitants of Boghill seem literally "bogged down," impeded. They may live on a hill but for them and their children the direction is clearly downward. While Maddy mourns the loss of her own child Milly, she indicates that, had she lived, the girl would now be "fifty, girding up her lovely little loins, getting ready for the change," becoming her mother just as Mr. Barrell is now "in his father's shoes." Change means decay, the cyclical wearing down of life in time. Worn down physically, the characters are also worn by routine, that twin destroyer of life, that Beckett described in *Proust*. Dan bemoans his daily trips to his office but imagines the even more debilitating routines of home; "the dusting, sweeping, airing, scrubbing, waxing, waning, washing, mangling, drying."

Decline, however, is not limited to people. Things too fall apart; what moved no longer does. Each conveyance that approaches Maddy is more complex but equally flawed. Christy's hinny so anxious to continue suddenly stops short. Tyler's bicycle wheel recently pumped hard is now flat. Mr. Slocum's car dies. The train is late. A similar falling off is seen in nature as well. Asses become hybrid hinnies, a sunny day turns rainy and windy, a beautiful tree, the laburnum, has leaves that droop and fall. Language also weakens and alters. In Grimm's Law, as Dan points out, sounds move from voiced to voiceless; words also lose their meaning and become archaic, phrases are no longer remembered, or half remembered. "Sometimes one would think you were struggling with a dead language," Dan says to his wife, conceding that his own speech often sounds strange "when I happen to overhear what I am saying." Languages can also die; Gaelic, for example, Maddy notes. Other human sign systems don't fare much better. Counting—"one of the few satisfactions in life!"—for Dan leads him to faulty conclusions, as it does most of Beckett's counters, who can't count.

Against this picture of shuffling, treading, panting, and suffering Beckett places images of religion—the force that should uplift. It doesn't. Christy, whose name indicates a Christ figure, rides into town on a hinny, not an ass, and he dispenses dung, sty dung. Several images from Psalm 145 reverberate ironically through the play. "Tender mercies" shown to Mrs. Rooney are all regretted since the offerer receives no praise or recompense; the "singing of the righteous" becomes "Death and the Maiden," the "eyes of all who wait for thee" become the blind gropings of Dan Rooney, and instead of the prophecy "One generation shall laud thy works to another," one generation passes their maladies and human suffering to the next. In fact, the only prophecy that is fulfilled in the play is the one offered by the unnamed mother to her daughter Dolly, "one can be sucked under," an image fulfilled when Jerry describes the child's death "under the wheels."

Rather than being uplifted, Maddy and her husband are bent over, on a horizontal, much like their path across the landscape. The dichotomy between vertical and horizontal is represented by the late train. Due to arrive at twelve thirty, a time when the hands of the clock would be in a straight vertical line, it arrives, instead, at twelve forty-five, when the vertical is cut by the horizontal at a right angle. The clock becomes an icon for the world of Boghill: the plodding walk of the inhabitants at right angles to the desired "flying up" or salvation, and both predetermined by time. It is only in death, Maddy says, that one can drift "down gently into the higher life."

While many of these themes are familiar ones in Beckett's plays, what is new in *All That Fall* is the aural accompaniment. All the people and objects Mrs. Rooney encounters are first heard as faint noise that grows in intensity and diminishes into silence. The pattern reinforces the central patterns of life in Beckett's plays: from void to life to void ("birth astride of a grave"—from silence to speech to silence (cry, breath, cry). "Are you going in my direction?" Mr. Slocom asks Maddy, and she replies, "I am Mr. Slocum, we all are." The sound effects etch this direction in the mind's ear.

Yet Beckett does not stop with sound used for thematic reinforcement. Sounds also provide humor in the work, a particular type of humor designed for the medium. The dropping of pants and sleights of hand that leavened Beckett's earlier play are precluded; humor must come from the imaginative reaction to verbal suggestions. For the most part, sounds create a fecund, funny world controlled by the writer. A slap on the face introduces wasps, a groan a hit in the stomach, a squawk the death of a hen. Other images are more suggestive and depend on the imaginative resources of the listener. For example, Mr. Tyler balancing on his bicycle, unable to doff his hat, must be visualized in the mind; his position after Connelly's truck passes must be guessed. Maddy's "Ah there you are!" leaves the listener great room for creation. Conversely, the image of Maddy entering and exiting from Mr. Slocum's car—that hilarious aural vaudeville routine—must be suddenly altered when Tommy exclaims, "Mind your feather, ma'am" "What feather?" the listener must ask; but to ask "What feather?" is to open the way for the more disturbing question that is embedded in the center of the play: "What Maddy?" As her long story about the girl who was never born indicates—a story Beckett first heard when attending a lecture by Carl Jung in London in 1935—a haunting human sensation is that of nonbeing. "Never there," May says in *Footfalls,* the play that most closely approximates *All That Fall.* Miss Fitt expresses the same feeling. Radio, that offers only words and sound as proof of being, seems an ideal medium for re-creating the sense of invisibility. It also allows Beckett to explore characters' duality. Beckett suggests this schism of self by having Maddy talk to those she sees and talk to herself, the latter words heard only by the audience. The people she meets hear only one part of the self.

The tacit acceptance of artifice makes the radio listeners believe in a Maddy they cannot see. Beckett also explores the possibilities of complacency in the form itself by purposely exploding one convention that radio drama shares with theater: the desire to have things explained. Just as theater audiences want to know if Clov leaves, and if Willie kills or caresses Winnie, radio audiences, used to having the culprit revealed in the last minute, want to know if Dan killed the child. Beckett's refusal to have the mystery solved seems one more indication of fall, the fall of a form where all is neatly explained. Audiences, like Boghill inhabitants, are creatures of habit. By allowing those habits to fall, if only for a moment, Beckett may be indicating the possibility of a resurrected form, the radio form itself, in which "the suffering of being" that he describes in *Proust* may break through for the listener if not for the characters.

***Embers.*** Beckett's second radio play, *Embers,* was presented 24 June 1959, on the BBC Third Program, directed by Donald McWhinnie, and starring Jack MacGowran as Henry. A brief excerpt from the play also appeared on MacGowran's recording *MacGowran Speaking Beckett,* on the Claddagh label, produced in 1966. *All That Fall* was written soon after the play *Endgame* and shares with it descriptions of physical activity and daily routine. *Embers* immediately follows the one-man monologue *Krapp's Last Tape* and has affinities with it. Although the setting of *Krapp* is indoors and *Embers* takes place on a strand, the real landscape of both is the inner world of the skull, where both men relive and try to rekindle the embers of the past: Krapp by replaying his own voice recorded at an earlier age, Henry, by invoking spectres, sound effects, and stories "to be with me." The dominant figure for Henry is his father, presumably drowned in the bay near which Henry sits. Unlike the voluble ghosts of his wife Ada, his child Addie, and her retinue—music teacher and riding master—the father is silent, never answering the repeated calls that punctuate the text. Above all, Henry needs him, "someone who . . . knew me, in the old days, anyone, to be with me, imagine he hears me, what I am, now." Ada and Addie are precluded by the choice of the pronoun. While first called "he," the father later becomes "you." "You," however, also covers yet another validator of Henry's existence: the radio audience. It is to them that Henry in his exposition describes the setting. "That sound you hear is the sea," he explains. The audience becomes by the transference of pronouns part of the silent audience assembled to "be with me."

Listeners and father may be silent, but wife isn't. Conversation with her, Henry says "that's what hell will be like, small chat to the babbling of Lethe about the good old days . . . Price of margarine fifty years ago." The description seems a foreshadowing of the prattle of Winnie in *Happy Days* written two years later. Ada shares with Winnie a concern with propriety—"The least feather of smoke on the horizon and you adjusted your dress and became immersed in the *Manchester Guardian*"—and she is committed to perpetuating these values in her daughter. Music and riding she must learn, "she shall learn," Ada declares. Like Winnie, she is also cast as mother to her husband, her "don'ts"—don't sit, don't wet boots—a replacement for her fading "don't" that led to sexual submission. Beckett has carefully chosen the names of wife and child to indicate their roles. Ada comes from the Hebrew word meaning "to adorn with jewels." Addie, however, means "trapping" or "harness"—what both wife and child ultimately become, keeping Henry tied to place, or shore, and middle-class responsibilities. In this role he becomes a variation on the archetypal male held in check by time and the procreative process, represented by woman, yearning for freedom, company of males, escape to sea. "Perhaps I should have gone into the merchant navy," Henry muses, paralleling the actions of his father who sought escape from the world of women by sitting silently by the sea, or possibly escaping "to Argentine."

Memories of the past linked with the desire for respite from female intrusion is one part of *Embers;* it is balanced by a fictional creation that Henry conjures to keep himself company; the story of Bolton and Holloway. One of the advantages of radio drama is the possibility of fixing both memory and fiction equally in the present world of Henry's imagination without the necessity for the differentiation that a stage presentation would demand. Yet read as a play, *Embers,* because of this coalescence, is a difficult work to follow. Keeping the voices separate, the memories removed from the fiction, and both from the reality of the present is taxing, but a task that Beckett seems purposely to create in the play. What occurs in the past is no longer referentially proven; it becomes no more or less than a story recalled and retold, like the story of Bolton and Holloway, a story that cannot end since the life that recounts it continues. Thus, Bolton and Holloway fuse with images of Henry's father, all finally subsumed into "old men, great trouble," with Henry the latest to join the ranks.

The fiction of Bolton and Holloway is also a strain at the resources of the radio and the audience's imagination since it is drawn not in narrative sequence but as a series of images of light and dark. Bolton, dressed in a red dressing gown, stands before a dying fire in his home, on a cold, white, winter night, waiting for his friend, a doctor named Holloway, whom he has summoned for some reason that is never made clear. "An anaesthetic?" Holloway inquires, but is met with only Bolton's repeated "Please" and his final stare as the two remain in the dark room, lit only by a candle since the embers have long since gone out. Does Bolton beg for a shot, companionship, or death, the ultimate anesthetic? Using the embedded imagery of the text, does he wish the embers to rekindle or to fade? Beckett and Henry don't say. Rather the images present the balance between the two alternatives, much as Bolton, playing with the opening in the window hangings, causes the room to become first white and then black. The action is similar to that performed by Watt, when he first enters Mr. Knott's house. But instead of the comparative effect, "redden, greyen," the extremes of white and black are contrasted. The story that does not finish fictionally represents Henry's own ambiguity toward his wife, his father, and the life he has chosen to lead. These suggestive images in *Embers* are among Beckett's most powerful, made even more so because they exist in the disembodied world of sound. Like memories and stories, the words have no physical component, are only shadows.

Unable to complete his story, Henry turns at the end of the play to another book, a diary, and slowly reads his schedule for the week. "Nothing this evening," "nothing tomorrow" followed by "nothing on Sunday." Only on Saturday the "plumber" called for "the waste." Henry follows this with "Words," indicating that the plumber must unstop what words have blocked, dispose of the refuse, so that what is needed may flow again. The three days listed may also be a reference to the three days of fast in the Christian church referred to as Ember Days. At their conclusion, on the next Sunday, ordination is usually performed. In this play Sunday only promises "nothing," and "not a sound."

***Words and Music.*** Beckett's early dramatic pieces employ music. Vladimir sings a round about a dog, Estragon whistles; Winnie sings her "Merry Widow Waltz," Willie whistles it. In the printed version of the play *Krapp's Last Tape* Krapp sings "Now the day is over." Later Beckett plays abandon melodies as they themselves become progressively more lyrical, words creating musical motifs. One of Beckett's late plays is even titled by the musical label *Rockaby.* Two radio plays of the 1960s, *Words and Music* and *Cascando* (not to be confused with the 1936 poem of the same name), mark the transition from plays with music to plays as music, and appropriately both deal with the balance between the two.

*Words and Music,* the last of the radio plays written in English to be presented on the BBC, is a text by Beckett and music by his cousin John Beckett. In the play Words (Joe) and Music (Bob) work for a club-wielding man named Croak, who keeps them "cooped up here, in the dark." Music begins by tuning up, Words by running through a set speech on the theme of sloth. With the arrival of Croak, the presentation begins with Croak proffering the themes: love, age, and "the face." Using the set speech previously rehearsed, Words substitutes love for sloth and gives a perfunctory paragraph, greeted by Croak's groan, and thumps; Music, also fails to please. Words again tries to expostulate on age, but soon loses his advantage to Music who leads the way in the composition, Words attempting to keep up. The result is a fourteen-line lyric of decrepitude, about a man still desiring both love and the loved one's face before him. The image of "The face in the ashes" leads Croak to demand that the pair turn their talents to the face alone. Words more assertively attempts to create the image, ignoring the "warm suggestion" from Music who finally cannot contain his ardor and again leads in the completed ten-line lyric, at whose close a silent Croak, dropping his club, retreats. Left alone, Words willingly summons Music, calling him by his rightful name. The piece ends with a "deep sigh" issuing from the silent Words.

Clas Zilliacus in his study of the radio plays makes a strong case for *Words and Music* being a medieval work, Croak the master of the Gothic "tower," Words and Music his minstrels. Words's perfunctory speeches on love and sloth then become the expected arguments, borrowing their form from the familiar period discussions of the seven deadly sins. Yet as the themes replace each other, focusing at last on face, the image becomes one not of spirit or intellection but of body: the image of the woman and man in postcoital separation. This shift from spirit to body is a repetition of that struggle embodied in *Krapp's Last Tape,* where the repeated image of the moment in the punt overwhelms all words and actions, sinking other concerns and goals in its powerful sway.

The same effect is achieved here, with Croak no longer able to listen to the composition that has moved beyond his control. It is Words, in his final sigh, who seems to acknowledge the power of Music, and transcendency of it over the formulaic cold language that has preceded. If Croak is a writer, then he must now deal with the results of Music leading and suffusing Words, something that at least at the end of *Words and Music* he seems not yet able to do. Or perhaps his absence is his abdication, allowing the two to function independently of his thud and control, letting them imaginatively mix without predetermined direction from himself, who can alone only croak, without sound. The word *croak,* after all, is also slang for *death.* Beckett may be marking the death of the separation of the two forms, clearly delineated in the plays that precede *Words and Music,* becoming one in those that follow.

***Cascando.*** With *Cascando* Beckett shifts back to French. The name comes from the musical term that marks the diminishing of volume. The play was originally presented by the ORTF (French television) at the end of 1961, with musical score supplied by the Rumanian composer Marcel Mihalovici, who also wrote the opera version of *Krapp's Last Tape.* At first glance, the play seems to resemble *Words and Music,* the sounds this time designated as Voice and Music, with an Opener replacing the master, Croak. At the end of both pieces, Voice and Music embrace "As though they had linked arms" and Opener, while not absenting himself like Croak, is only able to affirm "Good" as he listens to their collaboration.

Voice sounds strikingly like the protagonists in the trilogy, his own panting to "finish this one" story, reminiscent of Malone and the Unnamable's desire to finish their stories and themselves in the process. "If I could speak and yet say nothing, really nothing?" the Unnamable asked. But since he existed in a novel and novels—despite the music in *Watt*—are made of words, he could find no way out of the impasse of language. Not so with radio plays, however. Since they employ both Words and Music, as well as pure sound, they offer possibilities not viable for fictive characters. Beckett seems to be playing with the possibilities of nonrepresentational prose, combined with music, in an attempt to find a less rigid form that embodies human experience. Opener may be writer or rational mind attempting to exert control over the material of Voice's story, starting and stopping the flow of Voice and Music at will, denying that the material exists in Voice's head, affirming his own power to control. Yet as the story progresses, the feverish attempts to follow the trail of the fictive Woburn with Voice and Music in consort, seem to make Opener extraneous, an impediment done away with at the end. Opener's last full speech may indicate the reason for his capitulation. Not only is he extraneous to Voice and Music, he also takes the composition in the wrong direction. His refrain is "So, at will," implying that it is his force that wills the story to continue. His last complete speech begins, "There was a time I asked myself, What is It." By the end of the same speech he says, "But I don't answer any more. I open." If only to open, the critical, rational mind is not needed. Voice and Music can do just as well without it and its unanswerable questions and its will. Opener, with his repeated "I," may actually be tainting Voice and Music, the "observer infecting the observed" as Beckett said in *Proust.* If Voice and Woburn merge, then Opener is only a third party who makes coalescence of storyteller and story harder to achieve, himself as changeable as the fictive creation. Music, on the other hand, can be mediative, allowing the self to pursue its elusive core without—as Malone recognized—the corruption of the smallest words that bring with them an avalanche of meaning.

The play ends with Voice and Music issuing the prod to "Come on" that Opener had spoken earlier, seemingly no longer in need of his control or his prodding.

***Radio I and II.*** Not included in Zilliacus's fine study are *Radio I* and *II,* published only in 1975 under the general heading "Roughs" in the collection *Ends and Odds,* the two radio plays and *Theatre I and II* being the "odds." Ruby Cohn in a note in her book *Just Play,* indicates that the order of the radio plays, all written in 1961 and 1962 is probably *Words and Music, Radio I, Cascando,* and *Radio II,* although *Radio II* may predate *Radio I.*[3] The first three deal with similar subjects: the connection between language and music in the creative process, and relationship between the artist and his works. In *Radio I* an unnamed woman listens to words and music, uncapitalized this time, that seem to emanate from what appears to be a radio. Turning the dials to "the right" she finds that both go on "without cease," that the music is "more than one," the words "alone," and that neither can hear the other though they are now "one." The man explains that to listen to them is "a need," something the woman does not seem to understand or share. When she departs, the man makes a telephone call, presumably to a doctor, demands that his call be returned, hangs up, and repeats the procedure. The telephone rings twice, paralleling his two calls, the first time to gather more information about "what the trouble is," the second to inform the man in broken phrases about "a confinement?" "two confinements?" a "breech?" ending with "tomorrow noon?" The questions are uncertain since only the man is heard. The man returns to the receiver and whispers, after the words and the music once more feebly whisper, "Tomorrow . . . noon."

While Croak and Opener resented the joint efforts of Voice and Music, the unnamed man in *Radio I* needs their comfort, is lost without them, fears the moment when they will fade. It is ironic that the person he seeks is away tending to a birth, while he is tending to a death. The other irony is that while he is unable to share his fear with the woman who appears, he attempts to convey his dilemma to a disembodied Voice on the other end of a telephone, perhaps to the same woman.

By having sounds come over a radio, in a play written for radio, Beckett is creating a meta-level comment on radio writing, possibly on the writer Beckett writing himself out, and the ensuing death of the creative impulse that sustained earlier radio pieces. Again, as in the Bolton/Holloway story in *Embers,* it is to a doctor that the protagonist turns, and again the desired fix, life or death, is not indicated.

*Radio II* is a far more developed piece and differs from the preceding three by joining two themes that have appeared in earlier Beckett works: the schismatic self and the creative relationship of the writer to his craft. In the piece an animator and a stenographer torture one Fox (Martin Esslin suggests the name is linked to the French *voix,* or voice) into making certain disclosures. They are aided by a mute character referred to as Dick, who strikes with a bull's pizzle when Fox lapses into silence. What the group wish Fox to disclose is never stated. It may be a sign of an ego or self. If so, Fox disappoints them. The best he can do is to speak of "my brother inside me, my old twin." Fox may also be tortured into disclosing the impetus for his creativity. Here Beckett plays directly with his own critics, just as he has in *Cascando,* when he has Opener talk about a "they" who claim that "it's in his head." In *Radio II* Beckett offers references to the linguistic philosopher Mauthner, to Dante, and to Laurence Sterne, all suggested by critics as inspirations for Beckett's own writing. Of Mauthner he says, "The least word let fall in solitude and thereby in danger, as Mauthner has shown, of being no longer needed, *may be it'*—three words underlined." This reference, which reduces Mauthner's notion of language to virtual philosophical double-talk may be Beckett's personal joke, directed at those scholars who might fix on Mauthner—or Dante or Sterne—as a key to Beckett's writing, as *it—three words underlined.* Beckett, like Fox, may feel tortured by those who wish him to make disclosures, when like Fox all he can acknowledge is the sense of duality. In the face of Fox's silence the animator resorts to creating his own scenario, putting words in Fox's mouth, as critics may in desperation do. *Radio II* thus combines questions of self with questions of creative impetus. To both, the voice of Fox can only ramble on, not saying what will allow his captors to free him and not saying what will allow his captors to be free of him or he of the schism within himself.

## Film

Beckett's one film is entitled, appropriately, *Film* because it does not tell a story as much as it displays the nature of the medium. His radio plays were aural exchanges emanating from the dark; his film, and subsequent television plays, are ocular exchanges between object and camera, with the audiences a duplicating force, seeing as the camera sees, just as before they were a validating presence for the speaking self, hearing him be. It is important to note that Beckett does not do on film what he does on the stage, that other visual medium. On film he seems less concerned with making animated hieroglyphics than with probing the movements of his characters, through the intermediary position of the intruding eye of the camera. In the theater the audience may view at will; in film and television the audience is subject to the absolute control of the vision of the mechanical object, seeing only what the camera sees. Therefore, the effect created by film and television plays is quite different; angle becomes statement, close-up, an imposition both on the object being viewed and on the spectators who must follow without volition in the direction they are being led.

Beckett makes this camera control the theme of *Film.* Using as its motto the phrase from the philosopher Berkeley, *Esse est percipi* (To be is to be perceived), the work presents two angles of vision, represented by two cameras. The first and dominant angle is called E for Eye. It is the perceiver, the pursuer. Beckett's general introductory notes make clear that until the end of the film the audience is not to know who or what the "pursuing perceiver is." Established from the beginning, however, is the horror that E causes those who come under its gaze. Beckett's early notes for the project indicate, "Those who look at Eye {on} street stairs turn horrified away."[4] What they see is themselves as objects. It is the second camera, designated O for Object, that represents the perceived, the pursued. To differentiate between these two angles of vision is important. Since the central object O is a man with one eye, his vision is blurred. Therefore, in the first two sections of the film—on the street and in the vestibule—O's vision is introduced, so that when E and O are alone in the room in the third section, it will be apparent who is perceiving the objects within the room. Such distinctions are technically difficult, and Beckett recognized the constraints under which he was working. "We're trying to find," he told the production crew, "a . . . cinematic equivalent for visual appetite and visual distaste . . . a reluctant . . . a disgusted vision {O's} and a ferociously . . . voracious one {E's}."[5]

The technical interplay between the two "visions" becomes the central dilemma for the filmmakers, compounded because the film is silent except for a "sssh!" which serves to underline its nonverbal state. Beckett, in his production notes, accompanying the printed script, indicates that his original model for the work was the silent slapstick films of the 1920s. "Climate of film comic and unreal. O should invite laughter throughout by his way of moving," Beckett writes. Thus described, the film is a variation on the old Keystone Kops chase, except that pursuer is the one eye—I—that won't be eluded.

In part because of its conceptual genesis, Beckett chose for O a famous actor from the Keystone days, the deadpan comic Buster Keaton, when it became impossible for him to get his first choice, Jack MacGowran. He is the object E follows through the three parts of the film: down a street, into a vestibule, and up to a room. The printed script calls for the street scene to include people, all in couples, walking to work in a "small factory district." However, in filming this scene proved too difficult to do, and instead the film opens with a close-up of Keaton's hawklike eye, peering directly into the camera, a kind of icon for the ocular chase to follow. The substituted introduction reflects the original title of the work, *The Eye.*

Although it is summer, O is dressed in a long overcoat, collar pulled up, and Keaton's trademark, a porkpie hat. Contrary in dress, O is contrary in direction to those on the street, bumping into an elderly couple in his frantic attempt to escape E. As long as E stands at an angle not exceeding 45° behind O, O does not experience "anguish of perceivedness," as Beckett says in his notes. Exceeding this angle, as E does on the street, in the stairwell, and in the room—O cringes, hides his face, and attempts to elude his pursuer. Whetting the audience's curiosity and preparing for what Beckett labels the "investment"—the final confrontation between E and O—Beckett has E momentarily focus on the couple with whom O collides and an old flower seller descending the stairs in the vestibule. Each exhibits the same facial reaction: mouth open, eyes wide in horror. These early confrontations become preface to the climactic one in the room.

In section three, the longest part of the film, O goes through a ritual of ridding the sanctum of all possible eyes. Windows, doors, parrot cage, and fish bowl are covered; dog and cat—after a long vaudeville-inspired routine—are ejected; a print of "the face of God the Father" on the wall is torn into four pieces. Even a manila envelope, whose circles seem to resemble eyes, is turned to dispel the illusion. E observes O in his pursuits, while O in turn observes through his blurred vision each of the threatening objects. Having satisfied himself in his scouring, O sits in a rocking chair, whose covered back resembles yet other peering eyes, and opens the briefcase he has been carrying. Within are seven photographs, which he takes out one at a time and places on his lap, as E observes them from a vantage point over his left shoulder. The pictures depict his life in chronological order, from infancy to "30 years. Looking over 40." In the first six, eyes scan O's face. One of the pictures—a mother peering down at her kneeling four-year-old—is autobiographical of Beckett's own life, and already received mention in *How It Is*. Starting with the last, that resembles the dour face of O in the present, he tears each in four, as he did the print. Having finished, O lapses into sleep, as the rocking chair comes to rest. It is then that E moves, circling the room confronting O twice, once retreating, and then, rousing him from sleep, in Beckett's words "investing him with self perception." O's look of recognition repeats that of the couple and flower seller: open mouth, eye wide. Now the gaze finally reveals the pursuer. O is shown staring in horror into the face of the perceiving self, himself, whose look is "impossible to describe, neither severity nor benignity, but rather acute intentness." Next to the head of E, a big nail is visible. At the sight O raises his hands, covers his eyes, and after glimpsing E once more, slowly drops his head, as the rocking motion of the chair subsides again.

In Beckett's focus on the eye of the perceiver he creates a film about film, depicting the unique property of the form. The audience is not, as in conventional films, lulled into forgetting the manipulation of the controlling camera eye; here audiences become allied with camera since they must see, at this severely restricted angle, what E sees, while all the time in doubt about who or what E is. The final investment, thus becomes a shared one: O unable to avoid self-recognition, the audience unable to avoid the imposition of the camera. Predictably such a film experience was not greeted with great enthusiasm. When first shown, at a Buster Keaton retrospective, it was loudly booed. Beckett's desired comedic effect was ironically produced by the irate audience desiring to see the familiar, deadpan face, and forced by the all-controlling camera to view it only from the rear.

*Film* was originally directed by the late Alan Schneider, who had directed all the American productions of Beckett's plays—except *A Piece of Monologue*—but had never directed a film before—or after. Schneider's essay, appended to the Grove Press edition of *Film,* details the experience. Beckett's involvement with the filming is a hallmark in itself, since it marks the one and only time he came to America—to New York City in the summer of 1964 to observe the production. A second version of *Film* was made in 1979 by David Clark for the British Film Institute. Filmed in color, with sound effects and an elaborate opening scene, it is a busy film far different from the black-and-white version of the original.

## Television

***Eh Joe.*** Two years after *Film* Beckett wrote another play that employed the camera but this time the television camera. *Eh Joe* was written for the English actor Jack MacGowran, and produced by BBC television on 4 July 1966. In the play the camera is singular, and has nine demarcated positions, moving four inches closer to the lone figure, Joe, at intervals between speeches, until it stands peering into his eyes. Joe's movements at the beginning resemble those of the furtive O in *Film,* checking and securing window, door, cupboard, and bed, all outsized and clearly not realistic. Convinced he is undetected, Joe sits on the edge of the bed as the television dolly slowly moves in for the first shot, stopping as a voice begins. It is not the voice of Joe, however, but of an unseen woman, whose speech appears to emanate from within Joe, as he sits intently listening. "You're all right now, Eh?" she asks; "The best is yet to come, you said," she taunts. She describes voices Joe has heard before in "that penny farthing hell you call your mind"; voices of father and mother, dispelled by Joe. "Mental thuggee you called it"—a description of the divestment of the spectres that haunted him.

The central tale she comes to tell, however, is not of herself or of his parents, but of a lost love that has committed suicide over Joe: "The green one. . . . The narrow one" with "the pale eyes." "The way they opened after," she reminds Joe, in a few brief phrases that sketch a familiar Beckett image: eyes of love that either keep the loved one out or, in the past, have let him in. Refusing to "cut a long story short," the voice gives the graphic details of the girl's death, concluding with the picture of the inert body lying "in the stones." "There's love for you," she says, placing the girl in opposition to other spectres of past love easily vanquished from mind. It is the girl's death, made even more powerful by the intermediary presence of the other woman, that now haunts Joe, the lost love that the loveless Joe has killed, but cannot vanquish from his mind, a fact his tortured face at the end reveals.

Unlike the motion picture screen, the television screen is small, compact, and therefore the face of Joe fills it, making his suffering more acute and intimate. As the camera hovers only a few inches from Joe's eyes, the features become a mask of sorrow, moving in their enlarged details. For example, in the German version with Deryk Mendel that Beckett directed, the furrow over the bridge of the actor's nose mesmerizes the viewer, becoming an eloquent counterpoint to the sordid story the head contains. *Eh Joe* tells a banal story, but the camera work allows the image to transcend the tale, all without the protagonist uttering a word. Unlike his radio counterpart, Henry in *Embers,* and the unnamed man in *Radio I* who fears silence and struggles to retain the sounds of the past, Joe has himself throttled love and its voice, leaving only a secondhand account of guilt to taunt him. As the speaker indicates, when her voice starts to fade, Joe, like the others, will soon be alone "in his stinking old wrapper hearing himself" with only one voice left to torture him—"your Lord." "Wait till He starts talking to you," the woman warns. Joe looks on in silence.

***Ghost Trio.*** Ten years separate *Eh Joe* from the 1976 television plays *Ghost Trio* and . . . *but the Clouds* . . . , the latter works a fulfillment of the state described in the former: "That's the worst . . . Isn't it, Joe? . . . The odd Word . . . Straining to hear . . ." However, while Joe was haunted by the voices alive in his head, desiring their end, the unnamed men in the following plays seek desperately for the presence or at least the image of the loved one.

In *Ghost Trio,* the most effective of the three, a white-haired figure dressed in a long greatcoat is seated in a room, "the familiar chamber," a female voice says. The voice labeled V is not that of a loved one; rather it is the depersonalized voice of a narrator, directed to the television audience, describing room, objects, and figure in the same flat tones. "Good evening. Mine is a faint voice, kindly tune accordingly," she says twice. She calls the viewer's attention to the room, first in general terms, "Look," then in more detail, "Now look closer." Each item is isolated, a segment of it representing the whole. Floor, wall, door, window, pallet are described in that order, and then flashed on the screen in reverse order, after which the voice says "look again." Only then is the inert figure at right mentioned in a sentence that places him last: "Sole sign of life a seated figure" called F. All of the objects in the room are displayed from angle A, the furthest remove of the camera, and then from close up while the figure is approached from three angles of the camera, A, B, and C, and finally, in a close-up. Only at B does music sound—the Largo from Beethoven's Fifth Piano Trio (*The Ghost*)—emanating from a small hand-held tape recorder F's fingers clutch, left hand in a clawlike position, right hand with four fingers straight, the thumb hidden. The segment ends with the camera returning to a general view of the room.

The play is divided into three parts, designated 1: Pre-action, 2: Action, and 3: Re-action, each consisting of numbers indicating camera angles and shots: 1—35 shots, 2—38, and 3—41. Part 2, shot entirely from A, except for the last twelve items, places F in motion.[6] Twice the voice indicates "He will now think he hears her." With each anticipation F's left hand is abruptly raised, the head turned toward the door. After the second motion, F stands, goes to the door, listens, and then slowly opens it, bending down almost in half to peer outside, then returning to the upright position as the door slowly closes and the third "No one" is spoken by V. From the door he moves to the window and repeats the whole movement. V repeats, "No one," and then he moves to the pallet and mirror. Peering into the mirror, V records his surprise, with an "Ah!" rising in intensity. The circuit brings F again to his stool, where he takes up the recorder, begins to listen, and once more thinks "he hears her." After the second return the music becomes audible at A. The section ends with V commanding "Stop" and "Repeat."

Part 3 is a repetition, or nearly, of Part 2, except that this time there are two angles of camera—reminiscent of the dual angles in *Film*—one from the camera observing at a remove of C, and the other from the vantage point of F, indicating for the first time what F sees as he peers out door, window, and in mirror. The only other added views are those of the recorder on the stool and a mirror presented from neither perspective. As F opens door the first time, the rectangular shape of the hallway against the walls is visible; as he looks out the window he sees a steady downpour of rain, and as he looks into the mirror he sees himself, long, white, mangled hair, harried eyes. Finally when he rises a second time to open the door, he responds not to his imagination but to actual footsteps and an actual knock. In the hall is a small boy, come out of the rain, wearing a rubber hat and coat. The child says nothing, but closes his eyes and shakes his head from center to left, and repeats the slight action before turning and moving slowly down the hall into darkness, his feet echoing as he moves. Returning once more to his position on the stool, F begins the music once again, and it plays on till the end. This time, however, the hands that have remained in the same position since Part 1 shift: both hands now clasp the recorder with clawlike ferocity and continue until the end, when the head slowly raises and a look, not indicated in the text—almost a smile—graces the face. At that, the camera retreats to A and the figure remains inert; the hands, however, are now crossed, with fingers straight in a visual indication of finality, no longer anticipatory or clutching.

This brief description omits the central power of *Ghost Trio,* and that is the use Beckett makes of the camera. As much as the play is about the anticipation of a loved one, it is also about the expectation of seeing. V in Part 1 trains the viewer's attention on parts of the room, signaling the recurrent rectangles, the dominant form in *Ghost Trio.* Each rectangular form is seen against a still larger form: the window against the wall, the door against the wall, the pallet against the floor, even the tape recorder against the stool. The horizontal rectangle of floor that opens the first section is balanced by the horizontal rectangle of the pallet that closes the visual tour. All these rectangles, of course, are subsumed in the framing rectangle of the television screen, possibly being viewed in the rectangle of "the familiar room" of the viewer: world within world ever expanding—or receding.

Once V has taught the viewer how to see, she teaches the viewer how to perceive movement around these rectangular shapes. In highly stylized, nonrealistic, balletic fashion F glides, ghostlike, to the strains of the *Ghost Trio,* touching the now-familiar objects, viewing them in search of the illusive loved one. Having gone through the ritual once, a trial run, under the directorial instructions of V, F moves silently again, and the audience is shown the now doubly familiar room from yet a third perspective: that of F, both object in it and subject.

Yet even at this point Beckett still indicates that there may be another angle of vision possible: that of another looking at both F and the room. To indicate this other angle, Beckett introduces two shots not subsumed under either of the established angles: a shot of the tape recorder shown while F looks away from it, and a shot of the mirror reflecting no one. The two shots may be Beckett's way of once more exploding a carefully constructed world, as he did in his narratives by always leaving in doubt who the final narrator was behind the revealed narrators. In *Ghost Trio* the final viewer remains in doubt. The viewer must "react" to the imposition of another view and of the force of the music which must be integrated within the frame of the screen world, causing the viewer to "re-see" the scene yet again.

***. . . but the Clouds . . .*** Rectangles dominate *Ghost Trio;* the circle dominates and shapes *. . . but the clouds . . .* The playing area is a luminous circle, brightest at the center. Into it a bent, slowly moving man dressed in a long coat and hat appears from the west, designated in the text as "the road," crosses east to "closet," where he changes into nightgown and cap, and from there progresses to north, his "sanctum" into which he disappears at night and reappears at morn when the process is reversed. Each entrance is marked by five steps which bring the figure, designated M, to the center where he pauses before moving either across or up—both directions out of the light, into the dark that surrounds the circle. Only south is not his territory, since it is from this angle that the stationary television camera, at some remove, records his movements. This view is broken by repeated views in close-up of M, from behind, in his sanctum, head on hands. In the BBC version the image is impossible to decipher, a nonrepresentational mass of shadows and folds, unlike the more recognizable form in the German version that Beckett directed. The other image is that of a woman's face that appears, momentarily lingers, or stays and moves lips silently to accompany the voice of the man, designated V, who recites the last lines of William Butler Yeats's poem "The Tower."

Unlike *Ghost Trio* or *Eh Joe,* the speaker in this play is the figure presented and he describes in the first person his repeated entrances, exists, and attempts to call up the loved one's face. The opening shot of the play is of him in his sanctum, presumably the place from which he spins the scenario his moving image will follow. Editing as he goes, he indicates his pleasure with the words and actions by uttering "right" six times during the play. After each verbal description, there is a silent depiction, much like the explanation/enactment in Parts 2 and 3 of *Ghost Trio.* Dividing the ritual of entrance, disrobing, and exits to sanctum into constituent parts, the voice says, "Let us now make sure we have got it right," and the silent figure goes through the motions once again, ending the first part of the text. Part 2 describes the attempt in the sanctum to evoke the face of the beloved. Yet the lines are in the form of questions, not declarative statements. "For had she never once appeared, all that time, would I have, could I have, gone on begging, all that time?" The question is deferred by the logical mind of the speaker dividing it into the three "cases": her momentary appearance, lingering stay, and an unlabeled possibility, accompanying his recitation of ". . . but the clouds . . ." This section concludes like the first with a replay—"Let us run through it again"—the voice punctuating the images of the woman with "Look at me," in the second case, and "Speak to me," in the third. Neither action is forthcoming.

In Part 3 the speaker indicates a fourth possibility: "case nought, as I pleased to call it" which he admits is the "commonest": "say of nine hundred and ninety-nine to one, or nine hundred ninety-eight to two" that she does not appear at all, and that he is condemned to busy himself with something else "more . . . rewarding, such as . . . such as . . . cube roots, for example, or with nothing." Having revealed this case, the common one, the figure once more reemerges from his "dead of night," the same as before, but changed in the viewer's perception because he comes most likely not having seen his desired one, but having spent the night "with nothing." The same image thus takes on different meaning, as in *Ghost Trio,* because of the added information supplied. The audience sees it in a new way. The final shot of the play, after the figure has disappeared west to tread "the back roads," is of the face and the voice concluding the poem. The effect of the words seems melancholy, yet in the original Yeats poem the intention is somewhat different. After bemoaning old age—"decrepit age that has been tied to me / As to a dog's tail"—and indicating his still lively imagination, the speaker makes some peace with the situation, indicating in the final stanza that "the wreck of body / slow decay of blood" and "The death of friends, or death / Of every brilliant eye / That made a catch in the breath— / Seem but the clouds of the sky / When the horizon fades." Beckett's omission of *seem* is important, turning simile into statement of situation, not providing resolution as much as a continued longing in the face of either waning imagination or unheeded evocation. Both works, however, conclude with the final "deepening shades" closing in; in the television play, visually the circle of light on which the figure has trod becomes the only discernible stage left for his comings and goings, a small enclave of light.

***Nacht und Träume.*** *Nacht und Träume* takes its title from the Schubert lied of the same name, the lyrics by the German poet von Collin. The play begins in evening in a room, reminiscent of that in *Ghost Trio,* although only a sole window upper back is visible. The figure is seated left foreground, head bowed, hands resting on a table. The image created seems out of a medieval woodcut, entitled "A dark night of the soul," or "The scholar dozing at his books." As the dreamer, designated A, sleeps, there appears at right about four feet above floor level the image of B, his dreamt self, in the same position as the dreamer except seen from left in profile. From outside the small circle of light a disembodied left hand comes down and rests on B's head, which he slowly raises as the hand is withdrawn, and at the same time a right hand emerges offering first a cup which it brings to B's lips, then a cloth to wipe his brow. Raising his head further to "gaze up at invisible face," B raises right hand palm upward and is met with a right hand coming out of the dark to clutch it. On both B places his own left hand, and the directions say, "Together hands sink to table and on them B's head." At this point the left hand once more appears and is placed on B's bent head. This concludes the dream. The light focuses again on the waking A, the lied is heard, the light fades, and the pattern repeats, at the close of which both the dream and the dreamer fade.

"Schubert's music seems to me to be more nearly pure spirit than that of any other composer," Beckett told his cousin John Beckett when the two worked together on *Words and Music*.[7] In *Nacht und Träume* the music supplements the image, as the Beethoven trio did in *Ghost Trio*, and as Music did in *Words and Music* and *Cascando*. Rather than the dreamer dreaming of a loved one or a past event, the dreamer here dreams of himself dreaming, comforted in his dream by hands that do not exist or do not comfort him in his waking hours. The cycle of dream and waking is repeated as in the lyrics to the song, that describes the dreamer listening to the dream "with joy," and calling "return sweet night, sweet dreams return" (my translation).

***Quad I* and *II*.** *Quad* completes the geometric configurations that shape Beckett's recent television plays. This time the form is a square, with sides designated A, B, C, and D intersecting at E. "E supposed a danger zone," Beckett's notes indicate, and each of the four draped figures who move diagonally into the space from each corner turn abruptly to their left to avoid this point, forming in their movements a smaller square within the larger, a patterned mandala created by their scurrying movements to the beat of four types of percussions. Each figure is represented by an instrument and a color: white, blue, red, and yellow. In the printed text each was also to receive a light but the cameraman Jim Lewis explained that the effect was "too distracting" and had to be abandoned.[8] So too the plan to have each percussion visible. In the actual filming each player stands at designated entrances only slightly visible.

Each figure is given a sequence of entrances and exits. Number I begins from A "completes his course," and is joined by 3, then 4, and finally 2. They exit in reverse order, leaving 2 alone to start the second series. In numerical order each figure has one solo, and there are six duos (two twice) and four trios all given twice. Paralleling the movement, the percussions also combine in all possible combinations, taking their cues from the figures for which they are aural equivalents. Each player is further designated by a particular footstep sound. To catch the motion, the camera remains stationary "raised frontal." Although Beckett originally thought the piece would take approximately twenty-five minutes, his notes indicate "Overestimated." The actual playing time is slightly less than fifteen minutes.[9]

When the piece was first transmitted under Beckett's supervision by Süddeutscher Rundfunk in Germany in 1982, Beckett added a variation, entitled *Quad II.* In this brief, five-minute work there are no percussion accompaniments, and the only sound is that of the bare feet of the figures, who move at a slightly slower pace than in *Quad I.* The piece is in black and white, unlike *Quad* which is in color.

More performance piece than play, both works convey Beckett's preoccupations with precision and with continuous permutations in designated routes. All the figures are clad in the familiar long drape Beckett has used in the past. Their faces are hidden, and they are bent, much like the pacing May in *Footfalls.* Almost like rodents in a maze, they scurry without cease, fulfilling some plan that controls their entrances and exits, part of some will not their own. They begin in dark, move into light, fulfill their required course, and return once more to darkness. Sound and motion in the piece form a visualization of activities described in earlier plays: comings and goings, repetitions of activities, variations within a narrowly controlled grid. Most eloquently, their pacings mark off the dreaded E, the spot avoided at all costs.

The work calls to mind the repetitions and variations of choreographers such as Lucinda Childs and musicians such as John Cage and more recently Philip Glass, all of whom play with slight permutations of movement and sound, slight shifts in a formal schema, indicating the possible freedom accorded dancers or musicians within a circumscribed world of performance. So, too, on television, Beckett has redesigned the very shape of space—rectangular, circular, square—within the microspace rectangle of the small screen, itself a restricted form of the macrocosm it reflects. The play successfully breaks down the distinctions separating dance, theater, and performance pieces.

Beckett continues to work with television, a medium he says fascinates him because of its untapped potential. He calls television "peephole art" that allows the viewer to "see what was never meant to be seen."[10] His most recent writing (summer 1985) is a reworking of the theater play *What Where* for presentation on German television. The transference of a work from the medium in which it was originally written to another form is a shift away from Beckett's earlier refusal to alter the original medium of composition. Beckett has cut the original, ridding it of unnecessary elements. In a play that seems already as spare as it can be, the transposition and contraction are the most recent examples of the direction this book has traced: toward an ever retreating void which Beckett's art continually tries to give shape and voice.

# *Chapter Nine*
# Going On

In 1949 Francis Fergusson wrote *The Idea of a Theater,* a book that isolates those rare epochs when cohesive views emerge from a given society and a theater is able to reflect those concerns and shape them. The first such moment he cites is fifth-century B.C. Athens and the theater of Sophocles; the last is seventeenth-century London and the theater of Shakespeare. Embedded in *Oedipus Rex* and *Hamlet* lie "the complementary insights of the whole culture," Fergusson argues: the former a direct distillation of the communal, the latter a precarious balancing of a view that will soon sunder under the weight of the modern period before which it stands.[1]

In our own period Fergusson sees no commensurate centrality; rather he points to partial visions and fractured images: *ideas* not *the idea* of a theater. "Human nature seems to us a hopelessly elusive and uncandid entity, and our playwrights (like hunters with camera and flash-bulbs in the depths of the Belgian Congo) are lucky if they can fix it, at rare intervals, in one of its momentary postures, and in a single bright, exclusive angle of vision."[2] Were the modern world to produce a theater, its model, Fergusson suggests, would be not a play but an epic: Dante's *Divine Comedy:* not the "finality" of the *Paradiso*—somehow unfit for our period—but the more human, realistic world of the *Purgatorio,* that is set at "the outer edge of the human situation" where it is "close to the human-centered realm of Sophocles and Shakespeare, who imitate the tragic rhythm of human life in a world which, though mysterious, is felt to be real."[3]

Four years after Fergusson's book appeared Samuel Beckett's *Waiting for Godot* opened in Paris. Writing one month afterward, the novelist Alain Robbe-Grillet described it as a work, though new, that "From beginning to end the audience follows"; a work to which "experimental" could not apply but "simply theater, which everyone can see, from which everyone immediately derives his enjoyment."[4] What made the play so immediately apprehensible to Paris—and world—audiences was its clear connections with the reality of the modern world. Chaplin figures were recognizable everymen, their situations of boredom, routine, and endless waiting all too familiar; their failures all too predictable. The play offered fragments of life, but fragments that were not random shots at the jungle, but a cohesive picture of a life of chaos.

Fergusson quotes T. S. Eliot's assessment that the age of Shakespeare "moved toward chaos." If so, then the age of Beckett—and ourselves—resides only *in* chaos. In a rare interview in 1961 Beckett addressed himself to the centrality of chaos in modern life. "It is all around us and our only chance now is to let it in. The only chance of renovation is to open our eyes and see the mess. It is not a mess you can make sense of."[5] The statement is important in understanding Beckett's work: his goal is not to rationally explain chaos but to express it. Yet this incorporation of chaos in art is not the same as the sanction of a chaotic art. In fact, Beckett's writings are highly formal in their adherence to structure; structure often becomes a substitute for what in earlier works would have been explanation. "What I am saying does not mean that there will henceforth be no form in art," Beckett continued in the same interview. "It only means that there will be new form, and that this form will be of such a type that it admits the chaos and does not try to say the chaos is really something else. . . . To find a form that accommodates the mess, that is the task of the artist now."

If I am to assess the contribution of Samuel Beckett, I would have to say that beyond everything else he has been able to "find a form to accommodate the mess." In short stories, novels, and plays he has consistently struggled to find some discernible image or situation in which the diffuse elements of modern experience could cohere if only momentarily. A mirror held up to twentieth-century nature, Beckett's writings reflect the nature of the century: chaotic and contradictory. As Fergusson predicted, the works take their leave from Dante's *Purgatorio,* that study of daily life transferred to antehell, where endless—or seemingly endless—permutations of specified patterns frame the landscape; and where tortured and torturer stagger under the same "lingering dissolution." The entire body of Beckett's writing over his long career presents a seamless whole; a purgatorial world of "comings and goings" in which hapless, helpless humans hope for cessation, but never quite reach it. It is not a world of bleakness, however. For while Beckett has no *Paradiso* to meliorate against the sulfurous present, he has what comes closest in the modern world: laughter, jokes, wit, and—most important—courage.

It is his courage and humanity that have drawn younger writers and readers to him. That and his refusal to offer any quick fixes for the modern mess. For instance, the British playwright Harold Pinter, in a festschrift to honor Beckett's sixtieth birthday, writes: "The farther he goes the more good it does me. I don't want philosophies, tracts, dogmas, creeds, way outs, truths, answers, *nothing from the bargain basement*. He is the most courageous, remorseless writer going and the more he grinds my nose in the shit the more grateful I am to him."[6] The American director/actor Joseph Chaiken agrees: "Beckett goes to the boundary of things," Chaiken said in a recent television program of his own career, entitled *Going On,* an echo of the Unnamable's closing lines. Edward Albee also shares Chaiken's admiration. In his recent play *Finding the Sun* Albee pays tribute by actually having a character cite the same line: "It's hopeless, then. What did Beckett say? I can't go on; I'll go on?" The lines become the center of the play.

In the forming of his world, a reflection of our own, Beckett has also contributed to the idea of what theater and literature can be. Before Beckett few would have considered the dramatic possibilities of immobility and silence, of visual images divorced from words, or words from physical representation. Stories that shatter their own narratives would have been a contradiction in terms. Beckett has made the technique a mark of the only success he sees possible in a modern work, a fidelity to failure. Some of his most daring experiments have been with language. Beckett has placed language at the heart of his works, subsumed under it all knowledge, and then systematically denied its basic efficacy. By using language to indict itself, Beckett—like modern philosophers of language—has resurrected language for possible use in a modern world. He has also called attention to the connections between languages, by not simply translating his works, but by re-creating them in the process of translation. Not enough study has been done on Beckett as self-translator. His works offer unprecedented opportunities for study of the creative process and its grounding in particular languages.

Beckett has placed upon himself some of the most stringent restrictions under which any artist has worked. In writing after writing he has contracted his field, eliminating words, situations, characters, constantly skirting the very limits of creation. For Beckett the challenge has been to see how close he can come to creation out of nothing in order to define that void he sees at the center of human experience. The reader who has followed Beckett's writings through this study must marvel at the progressive stripping away of play and fiction and at the ever increasing daring that flirts with total cessation, but somehow still finds words and images—and courage—to go on.

# *Notes and References*

*Preface*

1. The only major Beckett works omitted from this study are *Rough for Theatre I* and *II* and *The Old Tune,* an English adaptation of a radio play by Robert Pinget. These works are included in *Collected Shorter Plays of Samuel Beckett* (New York, 1984).

2. "Dante . . . Bruno.Vico . . Joyce," in *Our Exagmination Round His Factification for Incamination of Work in Progress* (Paris, 1929); reprinted in *Disjecta,* ed. Ruby Cohn (London, 1983), 19–33.

*Chapter One*

1. As quoted in Israel Shenker, "A Moody Man of Letters," *New York Times,* 5 May 1956 (Sec. 2):1, 3; reprinted in *Samuel Beckett; The Critical Heritage,* ed. Lawrence Graver and Raymond Federman (London: Routledge & Kegan Paul, 1979), 148.

2. Samuel Beckett, *Dream of Fair to Middling Women,* 6. A photocopy of the original corrected manuscript is on file in the Beckett Archives, University of Reading, MS 1227/7/16/9. Quotations in this book come from that copy.

3. "Three Dialogues," *Transition* 49, no. 5 (1949); reprinted in *Samuel Beckett: A Collection of Critical Essays,* ed. Martin Esslin (New York; Prentice Hall, 1965), 16–22; also reprinted in Ruby Cohn, *Disjecta* (New York, 1984), 138–45.

4. As quoted in Tom Driver, "Beckett by the Madelaine," *Columbia University Forum,* Summer 1961, 21–5; reprinted in Graver and Federman, *Critical Heritage,* 220.

5. Lady Beatrice Glenavy, *Today We Will Only Gossip* (London: Constable, 1964).

6. Deirdre Bair, *Samuel Beckett* (New York, 1978), 14.

7. As quoted in Lawrence Harvey, *Samuel Beckett: Poet and Critic* (Princeton, 1970), 155.

8. This quotation is taken from correspondence from Mrs. Dorothy Dudgeon, a neighbor of the Beckett family in Foxcroft. It is on file in the Beckett archives, University of Reading.

9. As quoted in John Pilling, *Samuel Beckett* (London, 1976), 3.

10. Stuart Gilbert's phrase as quoted in Patricia Hutchins, *James Joyce's World* (London: Methuen and Co., 1957), 168. Maria Jolas, wife

of the editor of *transition,* described how Joyce had friends gather material, but she made clear that Beckett was never Joyce's secretary—a story that has circulated over the years. He was, in fact, only one of the many friends providing the same service to the nearly blind Joyce. See "Interview with Carola Giedion-Welker and Maria Jolas," *James Joyce Quarterly,* 11 (Winter, 1974), 106. Beckett also makes the same point in his interview with Israel Shenker.

11. As quoted in Ruby Cohn, *Back to Beckett* (Princeton, 1973), viii.

12. As quoted in Pilling, *Beckett,* 7.

13. As quoted in John Fletcher, *The Novels of Samuel Beckett* (London, 1964), 38.

14. As quoted in Cohn, *Back to Beckett,* ix.

15. As quoted in "Letters from Samuel Beckett to Alan Schneider," *Village Voice,* March 1956, 8, 15; reprinted in Cohn, *Disjecta,* 106–110.

16. Ruby Cohn, *Just Play* (Princeton, 1980), 295–305.

17. Bair, *Beckett,* 258.

18. Shenker; reprinted in Graver and Federman, *Critical Heritage,* 147.

19. As quoted in Fletcher, *Novels,* 59.

20. As quoted in Vivian Mercier, *Beckett/Beckett* (New York: Oxford University Press, 1977), 161.

21. Cohn, *Back to Beckett,* 57–60.

22. For a discussion of Beckett's career as a director see Cohn, *Just Play,* 230–299, and Martha Fehsenfeld and Dougald McMillan, *Beckett at Work* (London, in press).

*Chapter Two*

1. With the exception of *Proust,* all Beckett criticism discussed in this section can be found in Cohn, *Disjecta.*

2. Raymond Federman and John Fletcher, *Samuel Beckett: His Works and His Critics* (Berkeley, 1970), 4.

3. Bair, *Beckett,* 20.

4. Foreword to *Proust* (New York, 1957).

5. Articles about these painters, while not discussed here, can be found reprinted in Cohn, *Disjecta,* 115–52.

*Chapter Three*

1. Sylvain Zegel, "At the Théâtre de Babylone: *Waiting for Godot*"; reprinted in *Casebook on Waiting for Godot,* ed. and trans. Ruby Cohn (New York, 1967), 11.

2. "Assumption," *transition* 16–17 (June 1929):268–71; reprinted in *Transition Workshop,* ed. Eugene Jolas (New York: Vanguard Press, 1949), 41–44.

3. "Sedendo et Quiesciendo," *transition,* 21 (March 1932):13–20; "Text," the prose piece (not the poem of the same name) reprinted in *New Review* 2, no. 5 (April 1932):57. It can also be found in Harvey, *Samuel Beckett: Poet and Critic,* 329–30; other selections from *Dream* have recently been published in Cohn, *Disjecta,* 43–50.

4. Dante's *Paradiso,* 2:50–55, trans. John Sinclair (New York: Oxford University Press, 1972), 35.

5. "A Case in a Thousand," *Bookman* 86 (August 1934):241–42.

6. For a discussion of the Johnson project, see Bair, *Beckett,* 253–57, and Cohn, *Just Play,* 143–62; *Human Wishes* appears in Cohn, *Just Play,* 295–305; reprinted in Cohn, *Disjecta,* 155–66. My thanks to Ruby Cohn, who made the three Beckett notebooks of Johnson material available to me, and Samuel Beckett who allowed me to quote from them.

7. From Mrs. Thrale's *Anecdotes,* in *Johnson's Miscellanies* ed. G. Birbeck Hill (Oxford, 1897), quoted in Notebook 1.

8. Ibid.

9. Quoted in Bair, *Beckett,* 256.

10. Ibid., 253. W. Jackson Bate documents a sixteen year stay.

11. Quoted in Cohn, *Just Play,* 154.

12. W. Jackson Bate, *Samuel Johnson* (New York: Harcourt Brace Jovanovich, 1977), p. 502.

13. For the most complete source of Beckett's poems in English see Samuel Beckett, *Collected Poems in English and French* (New York: Grove Press, 1977). Poems discussed in this section come from this text.

*Chapter Four*

1. For discussions of other errors in *Watt* and the addenda, see John Mood, "The Personal System—Samuel Beckett's *Watt,*" *PMLA* 86 (1971):255–65; and Rubin Rabinovitz, "The Addenda to Samuel Beckett's *Watt,*" in *Samuel Beckett: The Art of Rhetoric,* ed. Eduoard Morot-Sir, et al. (Chapel Hill: University of North Carolina Press, 1976), 211–23.

2. For a discussion on Beckett and Mauthner, see Linda Ben-Zvi, "Samuel Beckett, Fritz Mauthner, and the Limits of Language," *PMLA* 95 (1980):183–200.

3. See Ruby Cohn, "Outward Bound Soliloquies," *Journal of Modern Literature* 7, no. 1 (1977):7–38.

4. *No's Knife: Collected Shorter Prose 1945–66* (London, 1967). All Beckett quotations in chapters 4 and 5 with the exception of those from "First Love," *Lessness,* and *The Lost Ones* come from this text. "First Love" can be found in *First Love and Other Shorts* (New York, 1974); *Lessness* (London, 1969); and *The Lost Ones* (London, 1971).

5. Cited in Fletcher, *Novels,* 102.

*Chapter 5*

1. Cohn, *Back to Beckett,* 220–69.
2. Quoted in Fletcher, *Novels,* 194.
3. *All Strange Away* can be found in *Rockaby and Other Short Pieces* (New York, 1981).
4. Richard Admussen, *The Samuel Beckett Manuscripts* (Boston, 1976), 39.
5. Martin Esslin, "Introduction to *Lessness,*" on BBC Radio 3, 25 February 1971, generously provided to me by Mr. Esslin, whom I thank.
6. There has been much critical debate about the sex of the narrator. See Peter Murphy, "That Nature and Art of Love in 'Enough,' " *Journal of Beckett Studies* 4 (Spring 1979):14–34. Actress Billie Whitelaw read the story on the same program as *Rockaby* having no doubt about the narrator's sex.
7. Fritz Mauthner, *Beiträge zu einer Kritik der Sprache (Critique of Language),* 3d ed., 3 vols. (Leipzig, 1923; reprinted Hildesheim: Georg Olms, 1967), 1:248.
8. Ibid., 1:420.
9. "Sounds," and "Still 3," *Essays in Criticism* 28, no. 2 (April 1978):155–57.

*Chapter Six*

1. For a discussion of *Eleuthéria* see Cohn, *Just Play,* 163–172.
2. As quoted in Colin Duckworth, Introduction to *En attendant Godot* (London, Harap 1966), xlv.
3. Antonin Artaud, *The Theatre and Its Double,* trans. Mary Caroline Richards (New York: Grove Press, 1958), 57.
4. As quoted in Alan Schneider, "Waiting for Beckett," in *Beckett at 60* (London: Calder and Boyars, 1967), 38.
5. As quoted in Duckworth, Introduction, xcvii.
6. As quoted in Walter Asmus, "Beckett Directs *Godot,*" trans. Ria Julian, *Theatre Quarterly* 19 (1975):21.
7. Ibid.
8. As quoted in Schneider, "Waiting for Beckett," 34.
9. See Asmus, "Beckett Directs *Godot.*"
10. As quoted in Duckworth, Introduction, lxiii.
11. As quoted in Asmus, "Beckett Directs *Godot,*" 22.
12. Johan Huizinga, *Homo Ludens: A Study of the Play Element in Culture* (Boston: Beacon Press, 1950), 10.
13. For religious imagery in *Endgame,* see Ruby Cohn, *The Comic Gamut* (New Brunswick, N.J., 1962), 242.
14. For Beckett's comments on *Endgame* see "Letters to Alan Schneider," reprinted in Cohn, *Disjecta,* 106–10.

15. As quoted in Clas Zilliacus, *Beckett and Broadcasting* (Âbo, 1976), frontispiece.
16. Artaud, *The Theatre and Its Double,* 58.
17. Mauthner, *Critique,* 1:432.
18. Ibid., 653–54.
19. James Knowlson, *Light and Darkness in the Theatre of Samuel Beckett* (London: Turret Books, 1972), 22. Also see Knowlson, "*Krapp's Last Tape:* The Evolution of a Play, 1958–75," *Journal of Beckett Studies,* no. 1 (Winter 1976), 50–65.
20. As quoted in Knowlson, *Journal of Beckett Studies,* 54–55.
21. For other allusions in *Happy Days,* see James Knowlson, *Happy Days/Oh Les Beaux Jours* (London: Faber and Faber, 1978).

*Chapter Seven*

1. As quoted in Cohn, *Disjecta,* 112.
2. The most complete text of the play is published in *Modern Drama,* 19 (September 1956), 257–60. The texts of *Come* and *Go* and the following plays are taken from *The Collected Shorter Plays of Samuel Beckett* (New York, 1984).
3. *Collected Plays,* 210.
4. Billie Whitelaw, for whom *Footfalls* was written, says that the one time she asked Beckett for a comment on his works was when she wanted to know what happened to May, whether she, as May, disappears at the end of the play. Whitelaw says that Beckett replied, "Let's say you're not quite there." Interview with Billie Whitelaw, April 1985.
5. "Something There," in *Collected Poems,* 63.
6. The play as published in *Rockaby and Other Short Pieces* (New York, 1981) contains 251 lines. In the Grove Press and Faber editions of *Collected Shorter Plays, Rockaby* has only 249 lines. In these editions the lines "one other living soul," after line 35 of part one, and "down the steep stair" after line 66 in part three, are omitted. Line 11 of part 4 reads in these editions "where mother rocked" rather than "where mother sat."
7. *Rockaby,* film by D. A. Pennebaker and Chris Hegedus, produced by Daniel LaBeille.

*Chapter Eight*

1. Zilliacus, *Beckett and Broadcasting,* frontispiece.
2. Letter from Samuel Beckett to Nancy Cunard, 4 July 1956, in Humanities Research Center, University of Texas at Austin; reprinted in *No Symbols Where None Intended* (Austin: Humanities Research Center, 1984), 93.
3. Cohn, *Just Play,* 283.

4. As quoted in S. E. Gontarski, "Film and Formal Integrity," in *Samuel Beckett: Humanistic Perspectives,* ed. Morris Beja et al. (Columbus: Ohio State University Press, 1983), 130.

5. Ibid., 135.

6. In *Ends and Odds,* Grove Press and Faber texts of *Ghost Trio* have different numbers of camera shots and different wording. References in this section come from *Collected Shorter Plays,* 246–54.

7. Zilliacus, *Beckett and Broadcasting,* 38.

8. As quoted in Martha Fehsenfeld, "Beckett's Late Works: An Appraisal," *Modern Drama,* no. 3 (Summer 1982):360.

9. Ibid., 365.

10. Conversation with Samuel Beckett, July 1985.

*Chapter Nine*

1. Francis Fergusson, *The Idea of a Theater* (Princeton: Princeton University Press, 1949), 2.

2. Ibid., 1.

3. Ibid., 5.

4. As quoted in Cohn, *Casebook on Godot,* 15–21.

5. Interview with Tom Driver, reprinted in Graver and Federman, *Critical Heritage,* 218–19.

6. Harold Pinter, "Beckett," in *Beckett at 60,* 86.

# *Selected Bibliography*

## PRIMARY SOURCES


The central bibliography for Beckett's writing and for criticism of his works to 1966 is Raymond Federman and John Fletcher's *Samuel Beckett: His Works and His Critics* (Berkeley: University of California Press, 1970). For bibliographical information on works in English and French from 1967 to 1976, see Robin J. Davis, *Samuel Beckett: Checklist and Index of His Published Works 1967–1976* (Stirling, Scotland: University of Stirling Library, 1979). For bibliographical information from 1976 to 1982, see Breon Mitchell, "A Beckett Bibliography: New Works 1976–1982," *Modern Fiction Studies* 29, no. 1 (Spring 1983):131–52.

1. Criticism

Most of Beckett's critical writings are collected in *Disjecta,* edited by Ruby Cohn (New York: Grove Press, 1984). The other important critical work is *Proust* (London: Chatto & Windus, 1931; reprint, New York: Grove Press, 1957).

2. Narrative Prose

*More Pricks Than Kicks.* London: Chatto & Windus, 1934. Reprint. London: Calder & Boyars, 1966.

*Murphy.* London: Routledge, 1938. Reprint. New York: Grove Press, 1957. French translation. Paris: Bordas, 1947. Reprint. Paris: Éditions de Minuit, 1965.

*Molloy.* Paris: Éditions de Minuit, 1951. Reprint. 1965. English translation by Patrick Bowles and Samuel Beckett. Paris: Olympia Press; New York: Grove Press, 1955. Reprinted in *Three Novels,* 7–176. New York: Grove Press, 1965.

*Malone meurt.* Paris: Éditions de Minuit, 1951. Reprint. 1963. English translation. *Malone Dies.* New York: Grove Press, 1956. Reprinted in *Three Novels,* 179–288.

*L'Innommable.* Paris: Éditions de Minuit, 1953. Reprint. 1969. English translation. *The Unnamable.* New York: Grove Press, 1958. Reprinted in *Three Novels,* 291–414.

*Watt.* Paris: Olympia Press, 1953. 3d ed. New York: Grove Press, 1959. French translation by Ludovic and Agnès Janvier and Samuel Beckett. Paris: Éditions de Minuit, 1968.

*Nouvelles et Textes pour rien.* Paris: Éditions de Minuit, 1955, third edition, 1965. English translation by Richard Seaver, Anthony Bonner, and Samuel Beckett. *Stories and Texts for Nothing.* New York: Grove Press, 1967.

"From an Abandoned Work." *Trinity News* 3, 4, 1956. Reprinted in *No's Knife: Collected Shorter Prose 1945–1966,* 139–49. London: Calder & Boyars, 1967. French translation by Ludovic and Agnès Janvier and Samuel Beckett. "D'un ouvrage abandonné." Paris: Éditions de Minuit, 1967. Reprinted in *Têtes-mortes,* 7–30. Paris: Éditions de Minuit, 1967.

*Comment c'est.* Paris: Éditions de Minuit, 1961. Reprint. 1969. English translation. *How It Is.* New York: Grove Press, 1964.

*Imagination morte imaginez.* Paris: Éditions de Minuit, 1965. Reprinted in *Têtes-mortes,* 51–57. English translation. *Imagination Dead Imagine.* London: Calder & Boyars, 1965. Reprinted in *No's Knife,* 161–64.

"Assez." Paris: Éditions de Minuit, 1966. Reprinted in *Têtes-mortes,* 33–47. English translation. "Enough." In *No's Knife,* 153–59.

"Bing." Paris: Éditions de Minuit, 1966. Reprinted in *Têtes-mortes,* 61–66. English translation. "Ping." In *No's Knife,* 165–68.

*Sans.* Paris: Éditions de Minuit, 1969. English translation. *Lessness.* London: Calder & Boyars, 1970.

*Mercier et Camier.* Paris: Éditions de Minuit, 1970. English translation. New York: Grove Press, 1974.

"Premier amour." Paris: Éditions de Minuit, 1970. English translation. "First Love." In *First Love and Other Stories,* 11–36. New York: Grove Press, 1974.

*Le Dépeupleur.* Paris: Éditions de Minuit, 1970. English translation. *The Lost Ones.* New York: Grove Press, 1972.

*More Pricks Than Kicks.* New York: Grove Press, 1972.

*All Strange Away.* New York: Gotham Book Mart, 1976. Reprinted in *Rockaby and Other Short Pieces.* New York: Grove Press, 1981.

*Pour finir encore et autre foirades.* Paris: Éditions de Minuit, 1976. English translation. *Fizzles.* New York: Grove Press, 1976.

"Sounds" and "Still 3." In *Essays in Criticism* 28, ii (April 1978):155–57.

*Company.* New York: Grove Press, 1980. French translation. *Compagnie.* Paris: Éditions de Minuit, 1980.

*Mal vu mal dit.* Paris: Éditions de Minuit, 1981. English translation. *Ill Seen Ill Said.* In *The New Yorker,* 5 October 1981, 48–58. Reprint. New York: Grove Press, 1981.

*Worstward Ho.* London: John Calder, 1983.

3. Plays

All Beckett's plays, with the exception of *Waiting for Godot, Endgame,* and *Happy Days,* can be found in the following texts: *Collected Shorter Plays of Samuel Beckett* (London: Faber & Faber, 1984) and *Collected Shorter Plays of Samuel Beckett* (New York: Grove Press, 1984). For other editions of plays see the following citations.

*En attendant Godot.* Paris: Éditions de Minuit, 1952. Reprint. 1963. English translation. *Waiting for Godot.* New York: Grove Press, 1954.

*Fin de partie, suivi de Acte sans paroles.* Paris: Éditions de Minuit, 1957. Reprint. 1965. English translation. *Endgame, Followed by Act Without Words.* New York: Grove Press, 1958.

*All That Fall.* New York: Grove Press, 1957. Reprinted in *Krapp's Last Tape and Other Dramatic Pieces,* 31–91. New York: Grove Press, 1960. French translation by Robert Pinget and Samuel Beckett. *Tous ceux qui tombent.* Paris: Éditions de Minuit, 1957. Reprint. 1968.

*Krapp's Last Tape.* In *Evergeen Review* 2 (1958):13–24. Reprinted in *Krapp's Last Tape and Other Dramatic Pieces,* 9–28. French translation by Pierre Leyris and Samuel Beckett. *La Dernière bande.* In *Lettres Nouvelles* 1 (1959):5–13. Reprinted in *La Dernière bande, suivi de Cendres,* 5–33. Paris: Éditions de Minuit, 1960. Reprint. 1968.

*Embers.* In *Evergreen Review* 3 (1959):28–41. Reprinted in *Krapp's Last Tape and Other Dramatic Pieces,* 93–121. French translation by Robert Pinget and Samuel Beckett. *Cendres.* In *Lettres Nouvelles* 36 (1959):3–14. Reprinted in *La Dernière bande, suivi de Cendres,* 35–72.

*Happy Days.* New York: Grove Press, 1961. French translation. *Oh les beaux jours.* Paris: Éditions de Minuit, 1963. Reprint. 1969.

*Words and Music.* In *Evergreen Review* 6 (1962):34–43. Reprinted in *Cascando and Other Short Dramatic Pieces,* 23–32. New York: Grove Press, 1967. French translation. *Paroles et musique.* In *Comédie et actes divers,* 63–78. Paris: Éditions de Minuit, 1966. Reprint. 1969.

*Acte sans paroles II.* In *Dramatische Dichtungen 1,* 330–37. Frankfort: Suhrkamp Verlag, 1963. Reprinted in *Comédie et actes divers,* 1969, 95–99. English translation. *Act Without Words II.* In *Krapp's Last Tape and Other Dramatic Pieces,* 137–41.

*Cascando.* In *Dramatische Dictungen 1,* 338–61. Reprinted in *Comédie et actes divers,* 1966, 47–60. English translation. In *Cascando and Other Short Dramatic Pieces,* 9–19.

*Play.* London: Faber & Faber, 1964. Reprinted in *Cascando and Other Short Dramatic Pieces,* 45–63. French translation. *Comédie.* In *Comédie et actes divers,* 1969, 9–35.

*Eh Joe.* In *Eh Joe and Other Writings.* London: Faber and Faber, 1967. Reprinted in *Cascando and Other Short Dramatic Pieces,* 35–41. French translation. *Dis Joe.* In *Comédie et acts divers,* 81–91.

*Come and Go.* London: Calder & Boyars, 1967. Reprinted in *Cascando and Other Short Dramatic Pieces,* 67–71. French translation. *Va et vient.* In *Comédie et actes divers,* 1969, 39–44.

*Film*. In *Cascando and Other Short Dramatic Pieces*, 1967, 75–88. Reprinted in *Film*. New York: Grove Press, 1969.

*Breath*. In *Gambit* 4, no. 15 (1969):5–9. Reprinted in *First Love and Other Shorts*. New York: Grove Press, 1974.

*Not I*. London: Faber & Faber, 1973. Reprinted in *First Love and Other Shorts*, 75–87. French translation. *Pas moi*. Paris: Éditions de Minuit, 1975.

*Footfalls*. In *Ends and Odds*, 39–50. New York: Grove Press, 1976. French translation. *Pas*. Paris: Éditions de Minuit, 1977.

*That Time*. In *Ends and Odds*, 1976, 35–38. French translation. *Cette fois*. Paris: Éditions de Minuit, 1978.

*Radio I*. In *Ends and Odds*, 1976, 103–122.

*Radio II*. In *Ends and Odds*, 1976, 113–28. French translation. *Pochade Radiophonique*. In *Minuit* 16 (November 1975).

*Theatre I*. In *Ends and Odds*, 1976, 69–80. French translation. *Fragment de theatre*. In *Minuit* 8 (March 1974).

*Theatre II*. In *Ends and Odds*, 1976, 81–102.

*A Piece of Monologue*. In *Kenyon Review* I, ii (Summer 1979):1–4. Reprinted in *Rockaby and Other Short Pieces*, 67–79. New York: Grove Press, 1981.

*Ohio Impromptu*. In *Rockaby and Other Short Pieces*, 1981, 25–36. Reprinted in *Ohio Impromptu/Catastrophe/What Where/Three Plays by Samuel Beckett*, 11–19. New York: Grove Press, 1983. French translation. *Impromptu D'Ohio*. In *Berceuse suivi de impromptu d'ohio*. Paris: Éditions de Minuit, 1982.

*Rockaby*. In *Rockaby and Other Short Pieces*, 1981, 7–24. French translation. *Berceuse*. In *Berceuse suivi de impromptu d'ohio*, 1982.

*Catastrophe*. In *Solo suivi de catastrophe*. Paris: Éditions de Minuit, 1982. English translation. *Catastrophe*. In *New Yorker*, 10 January 1983, 26–27. Reprinted in *Three Plays by Samuel Beckett*, 1983.

*What Where*. In *Three Plays by Samuel Beckett*, 1983, 41–59.

## SECONDARY SOURCES

For references to Beckett criticism to 1966, see Federman and Fletcher, *Samuel Beckett: His Works and His Critics*. For more recent criticism check the yearly *PMLA* bibliographies, in which Beckett is listed under twentieth-century French authors. Also check yearly bibliography of criticism in *Modern Drama*, arranged by author. For reviews of Beckett's writings from 1931 to 1977, see *Samuel Beckett: The Critical Heritage*, edited by Lawrence Graver and Raymond Federman

(London: Routledge & Kegan Paul, 1979). A further source of Beckett criticism is the *Journal of Beckett Studies,* begun in winter 1976.

1. Criticism

Because of limited space, only books are listed below. For significant articles, check endnotes and above bibliographies.

**Abbott, H. Porter.** *The Fiction of Samuel Beckett: Form and Effect.* Berkeley: University of California Press, 1973. A study of the early fiction through *How It Is.*

**Admussen, Richard.** *The Samuel Beckett Manuscripts.* Boston: G. K. Hall, 1970. A detailed review of unpublished manuscripts and early drafts of published works.

**Bair, Deirdre.** *Samuel Beckett.* New York: Harcourt Brace, 1978. The only biography presently available on Beckett. It contains factual errors and therefore must be used cautiously.

**Coe, Richard.** *Samuel Beckett.* New York: Grove Press, 1964. Philosophical introduction to Beckett's writing.

**Cohn, Ruby.** *Samuel Beckett: The Comic Gamut.* New Brunswick, N.J.: Rutgers University Press, 1962. A seminal study of the comic and comedy in Beckett's writing.

———, ed. *Casebook on Waiting for Godot.* New York: Grove Press, 1967. Documents the impact of the play and offers thirteen essays on interpretations.

———. *Back to Beckett.* Princeton: Princeton University Press, 1973. A further study of Beckett's fiction and drama, including the most accurate chronology of Beckett's works.

———. *Just Play.* Princeton: Princeton University Press, 1980. Focuses on Beckett's plays and includes detailed discussion of Beckett as director and the first printing of *Human Wishes.*

———, ed. *Disjecta.* New York: Grove Press, 1984. A collection of Beckett's critical writings.

**Esslin, Martin.** *The Theatre of the Absurd.* New York: Anchor Books, 1969. Places Beckett in the context of modern "absurdist" writers such as Ionesco and Pinter.

**Federman, Raymond.** *Journey to Chaos: Samuel Beckett's Early Fiction.* Berkeley: University of California Press, 1965. A careful analysis of Beckett's fiction from *More Pricks than Kicks* through the *nouvelles.*

**Fehsenfeld, Martha,** and **Dougald McMillan.** *Beckett at Work.* London: John Calder, in press. Interviews with those involved in key productions of Beckett's plays.

**Fletcher, John.** *The Novels of Samuel Beckett.* London: Chatto & Windus, 1964. Emphasis on comparison of French and English versions of fiction.

**Harvey, Lawrence.** *Samuel Beckett: Poet and Critic.* Princeton: Princeton University Press, 1970. Most complete study of Beckett's poetry.

**Kenner, Hugh.** *Samuel Beckett: A Critical Study.* New York: Grove Press, 1961. New approaches to Beckett, focusing primarily on language.

**Knowlson, John,** and **John Pilling.** *Frescoes of the Skull: The Later Prose and Drama of Samuel Beckett.* New York: Grove Press, 1979. Collection of essays on fiction and drama.

**Moorjani, Angela.** *Abysmal Games in the Novels of Samuel Beckett.* Chapel Hill: University of North Carolina Press, 1982. A discussion of Beckett's narrative techniques using theories of textural linearity, myth, and deconstruction.

**Pilling, John.** *Samuel Beckett.* London: Routledge & Kegan Paul, 1976. Overview of Beckett's career, offers connections to literary and philosophical schools.

**Zilliacus, Clas.** *Beckett and Broadcasting.* Âbo: Acta Academiae Aboensis, Ser. A Humaniora, 1976. Most complete book on Beckett's radio dramas.

# Index

DATE DUE